"I just finished reading *Chicken Soup for the Christian Soul* and felt compelled to write and commend you on your book. Your books are the best I've ever read! Your book touched my heart and my soul in a way that nothing else has. God bless you, your family and staff."

John Deranger

"I have used your *Chicken Soup* books to help me through some rough times in my life. I lost my mother at the age of ten and the sections on death and dying helped me to understand the reason for her death. I now know she is in a better place. When my grandmother passed away on Christmas, 1998, I read a story out of *Chicken Soup for the Christian Soul* at her funeral. It touched our whole family greatly. I am thanking you on behalf of my whole family. Thank you very much for the support you have given us."

Lauren

"I began reading *Chicken Soup for the Christian Soul* aloud to my roommate. Often she would look up from her homework and see me crying. I was raised Christian, therefore, it was no surprise how deeply I was touched by this book. In fact, it has touched my entire family. The copy I have in my possession is the fourth copy; the first went to my sister who realized one of her friends was more in need of the book; the second copy went to a woman my mother met on an airplane who seemed to be struggling; the third went to my uncle after he suffered a heart attack. Finally, we are able to have our own copy, but I wouldn't take back any of them that we have given away. It is amazing how people can find comfort in other people's stories. I guess sometimes it helps to know that we are not alone in the tough times of life and that other people have gone through some of the same hardships. Thank you again for all of your books."

Alissa D. Hupp

"Thank you very much for your books. We have given them to the police chaplain so that he may give them to the people who need them the most. Thank you for your gift and your prayers. May God bless you all."

Terri Pennington
Oklahoma City Police Department—Records
(books sent after the Oklahoma City bombing)

"One night while chatting with my grandmother, she picked up a copy of *Chicken Soup for the Christian Soul.* Due to her weak eyesight, I began reading stories to her. What started out as one story ended up in almost two hours of reading stories. We laughed, we cried and were both touched very deeply. We shared a very memorable evening together that neither of us will ever forget. Thank you for the blessings you have sowed into my life, as well as many others."

Kelly Koolhoven

"I'm sixteen years old and for Christmas I bought my uncle *Chicken Soup for the Christian Soul.* He is a really macho guy. You know, a construction worker. He told me that everything he had read so far was very touching and he admitted that he had cried. It was a hard thing for him to admit that."

Sabrina

CHICKEN SOUP
FOR THE
CHRISTIAN
FAMILY SOUL

Stories to
Open the Heart and Rekindle
the Spirit

Jack Canfield
Mark Victor Hansen
Patty Aubery
Nancy Mitchell Autio

Health Communications, Inc.
Deerfield Beach, Florida

www.hci-online.com
www.chickensoup.com

We would like to acknowledge the following publishers and individuals for permission to reprint the following material. (Note: The stories that were penned anonymously, that are in the public domain, or, that were written by Jack Canfield, Mark Victor Hansen, Patty Aubery or Nancy Mitchell Autio are not included in this listing.)

Mom's Last Laugh. Reprinted by permission of Robin Lee Shope. ©1999 Robin Lee Shope.

The Tablecloth. Reprinted by permission of Richard Bauman. ©1995 Richard Bauman.

(Continued on page 402)

Library of Congress Cataloging-in-Publication Data

Chicken soup for the Christian family soul: stories to open the heart and rekindle the spirit / Jack Canfield . . . [et al.].
    p. cm.
    ISBN 1-55874-714-X (hardcover)   ISBN 1-55874-714-1 (trade paper)
    1. Christian life.   2. Family—Religious aspects—Christianity. I.
    Canfield, Jack
    BV4515.2.C445 2000
    242—dc21

                     97-057883

Publisher: Health Communications, Inc.
                3201 S.W. 15th Street
                Deerfield Beach, FL 33442-8190

Cover design by Andrea Perrine Brower
Typesetting by Dawn Grove

*With love, we dedicate this book
to our families and to all of
the Christian families around
the world.*

Contents

Acknowledgments

Chicken Soup for the Christian Family Soul has taken over two years to compile and edit. It has been a labor of love and faith for all of us, and without the love and support of our family, friends and publisher, this book would never have happened.

We would like to acknowledge all of you who continue to love us and support us and allow us the time and space to create such wonderful books.

Our families, who allow us the time and space we need to work on each and every book we do. Thank you for giving us the love and support we need to continue this work. You are all Chicken Soup for our souls.

Our publisher, Peter Vegso, who continues to support us and keeps the *Chicken Soup* factory cooking.

Heather McNamara, our editor and dear friend, who spent hours and hours and hours editing stories, searching for better stories, finding sources on the Internet and reading with us late into the night. We absolutely could not have done this project without you or your wonderful assistant D'ette Corona.

To Christine Belleris, Matthew Diener, Allison Janse and Lisa Drucker, our editors at Health Communications, for working so closely with Heather and D'ette to make this book the best it could be. We appreciate you so much.

To the marketing, sales and PR staff, who continue to spread the word about *Chicken Soup*.

Sharon Linnea Scott, our outside editor, who continually guides us through the process of each *Christian Soul* project. Thank you, Sharon. You are the best!

Patty Hansen, the director of our legal and licensing department, who continually takes more and more of the business side of our world out of our hands so we can focus more of our time on the creative work of completing such wonderful books.

Leslie Forbes Riskin, who has become a permissions expert. Thank you, Leslie, for taking charge of the *Christian Family Soul* permissions process so we could complete this project.

Veronica Romero and Joanie Andersen, for continuously taking care of Patty Aubery and the day-to-day operations so we could stay focused on writing and editing.

Ro Miller, Teresa Esparza, Robin Yerian, and Deborah Hatchell, who tended to all of our normal duties that had to be handled during the last days of the project. You guys are truly amazing!

Lisa Williams, for taking good care of Mark and his grueling schedule which allows him to travel the world to spread the word of *Chicken Soup for the Soul*.

Laurie Hartman, for overseeing our licensing department and taking good care of our *Chicken Soup* brand.

To all of our coauthors: thank you, thank you, thank you, for continuing to support us and for sending stories our way that were better suited for *Chicken Soup for the Christian Family Soul*.

To our initial readers—Linda Mitchell, Barbara Lomonaco, Kelly Zimmerman, D'ette Corona and Sondra Keeler—for reading through thousands and thousands of stories to help us find the perfect stories to create the best book possible, and who offered moral support whenever we needed it.

To all of the people who dedicated a few weeks of their busy lives to reading, evaluating and commenting upon the final selection of stories. Your feedback was priceless. The panel of readers included Mavis Allred, Brenda M. Anderson, Fred Angelis, Mara Bennett, Alison Bray, Paula B. Brazil, Tim Breithaupt, Lynne Cain, Pam Carlquist, Dave Carruthers, Robin R. Chapuis, Jennifer Collica, Linda Day, Cathy Deighan, Phyllis DeMarco, Tria Dickerson, Eldon Edwards, Melanie Elrod, Julie Garner, Kathy Gerrard, Terri Guerrero, Judy Haldeman, Tom Hill, Sondra Keeler, Patricia Lambert, Martha Lang, Janice Masse, Don Oglesby, Leslie Forbes Riskin, Veronica Romero, Mary Sanchez, Michele Sprout-Murray, Noah St. John, Carla Thurber, Hollie Vanderzee, Robin A. Worman and Heide Wolfe.

Thank you to our fellow publishers for their continued support in the permissions process—Anthony Pekarik at Simon & Schuster, Faith Barbato at HarperCollins, Patricia Flynn and Carol Christiansen at Random House and Taryn Phillips Quinn at *Woman's World* magazine. Thank you.

To all of the people we haven't mentioned but without whom we could not have completed this project, including all of the wonderful writers who submitted their work to be included in the book, and everyone at Health Communications, Inc. We are grateful for the many hands that made this book possible. Thank you all!

Introduction

Since the publication of *Chicken Soup for the Christian Soul* in 1997, we have received thousands of requests from Christian readers for a book that focused specifically on family values and the special experiences that are only possible within a family that is focused on living a God-centered life.

Once we decided to create such a book, readers from all over the world sent us more than five thousand stories to consider for inclusion. The stories that you now hold in your hands are the result of countless hours of reading and rereading. We were seeking the best of the best stories—ones that would not only touch, uplift or inspire you, but would also clearly express how other people have experienced the presence of the divine in their lives through practicing faith, hope, love, charity and forgiveness.

We believe these stories of people who chose hope over helplessness when facing a dark time, who extended a hand to someone in need, or who put their faith in God when the odds were against them, will buoy your spirits and nourish your soul. They will deepen your faith; inspire you to commit greater acts of kindness and compassion; encourage you to forgive others; remind you that you are never alone no matter how difficult your circumstances; and encourage you to see the divine love everywhere—within you and around you—every day. We are also confident that these stories will act as a blueprint in your mind, giving you models for how to more closely walk with God within the context of your immediate and extended families.

Stories have the potential to help us see greater possibilities of how we can more fully express our commitment to be more Christlike in our everyday activities and in our interactions with those whom we love most—our family members. We pray that these stories will remind you of what is most important in life and encourage you to act in accordance with those higher priorities. They certainly have for all of us who worked on this project.

Finally, we sincerely hope that you and your families experience the same joy reading and discussing these stories as we did collecting and editing them. And so, from our hearts to yours, we offer you *Chicken Soup for the Christian Family Soul.*

Jack Canfield, Mark Victor Hansen,
Patty Aubery and Nancy Mitchell Autio

Share with Us

We would love to hear your reactions to the stories in this book. Please let us know what your favorite stories were and how they affected you.

Also, please send us stories you would like to see published in future editions of *Chicken Soup for the Christian Family Soul*. You can send us stories you have written or ones you have read and liked.

Send your stories to:

Chicken Soup for the Christian Family Soul
P.O. Box 30880-XF
Santa Barbara, CA 93130
To e-mail or visit our Web site:
www.chickensoup.com

We hope you enjoy reading this book as much as we enjoyed compiling, writing and editing it.

1

ON LOVE

I never knew how to worship until I knew how to love.

Henry Ward Beecher

Mom's Last Laugh

Consumed by my loss, I didn't notice the hardness of the pew where I sat. I was at the funeral of my dearest friend—my mother. She finally had lost her long battle with cancer. The hurt was so intense; I found it hard to breathe at times.

Always supportive, Mother clapped loudest at my school plays, held a box of tissues while listening to my first heartbreak, comforted me when my father died, encouraged me in college, and prayed for me my entire life.

When Mother's illness was diagnosed, my sister had a new baby and my brother had recently married his childhood sweetheart, so it fell to me, the twenty-seven-year-old middle child without entanglements, to take care of her. I counted it as an honor.

"What now, Lord?" I asked, sitting in the church. My life stretched out before me as an empty abyss.

My brother sat stoically with his face toward the cross while clutching his wife's hand. My sister sat slumped against her husband's shoulder, his arms around her as she cradled their child. All so deeply grieving, they didn't seem to notice that I sat alone.

My place had been with our mother, preparing her meals, helping her walk, taking her to the doctor, seeing to her medication, reading the Bible together. Now she was with the Lord. My work was finished, and I was alone.

I heard a door open and slam shut at the back of the church. Quick footsteps hurried along the carpeted floor. An exasperated young man looked around briefly and then sat next to me. He folded his hands and placed them on his lap. His eyes were brimming with tears. He began to sniffle.

"I'm sorry I'm late," he explained, though no explanation was necessary.

After several eulogies, he leaned over and commented, "Why do they keep calling Mary by the name of 'Margaret'?"

"Because Margaret was her name. Never Mary. No one called her 'Mary,'" I whispered. I wondered why this person couldn't have sat on the other side of the church. He kept interrupting my grieving with his tears and fidgeting. Who was this stranger anyway?

"No, that isn't correct," he insisted, as several people glanced over at us whispering. "Her name is Mary, Mary Peters."

"That isn't whose funeral this is."

"Isn't this the Lutheran church?"

"No, the Lutheran church is across the street."

"Oh."

"I believe you're at the wrong funeral, sir."

The solemn nature of the occasion mixed with the realization of the man's mistake bubbled up inside me and erupted as laughter. I cupped my hands over my face, hoping the noise would be interpreted as sobs.

The creaking pew gave me away. Sharp looks from other mourners only made the situation seem more hilarious. I peeked at the bewildered, misguided man seated beside me. He was laughing, too, as he glanced around; deciding it was too late for an uneventful exit. I imagined Mother laughing.

At the final "Amen," we darted out a door and into the parking lot.

"I do believe we'll be the talk of the town," he smiled. He said his name was Rick and since he had missed his aunt's funeral, he asked me to join him for a cup of coffee.

That afternoon began a lifelong journey for me with this man, who attended the wrong funeral, but was in the right place. A year after our meeting, we were married at a country church where he was the assistant pastor. This time we both arrived at the same church, right on time.

In my time of sorrow, God gave me laughter. In place of loneliness, God gave me love. This past June we celebrated our twenty-second wedding anniversary.

Whenever anyone asks us how we met, Rick tells them, "Her mother and my Aunt Mary introduced us, and it's truly a match made in heaven."

Robin Lee Shope
Submitted by Jane Etz

The Tablecloth

A young minister had been called to serve at an old church that at one time had been a magnificent edifice in a wealthy part of town. Now the area was in a state of decline and the church was in bad shape. Nevertheless, the pastor and his wife were thrilled with the church and believed they could restore it to its former magnificence.

When the minister took charge of the church early in October 1948, he and his wife immediately went to work painting, repairing and attempting to restore it. Their goal was to have the old edifice looking its best for Christmas Eve services.

Just two days before Christmas, however, a storm swept through the area, dumping more than an inch of rain. The roof of the old church sprung a leak just behind the altar. The plaster soaked up the water as if it were a sponge and then crumbled, leaving a gaping hole in the wall.

Dejected, the pastor and his wife looked at the defaced wall. There was obviously no chance to repair the damage before Christmas. Nearly three months of hard work had been washed away. Yet the young couple accepted the damage as God's will and set about cleaning up the damp debris.

It was a depressed minister and his wife who attended a benefit auction for the church youth group that afternoon. One of the items put up for bid was an old gold-and-ivory-colored lace tablecloth, nearly fifteen feet long.

Seized with an inspiration, the pastor was the high bidder at $6.50. His idea was to hang the ornate cloth behind the altar to cover the ragged hole in the wall.

On the day before Christmas, snowflakes mingled with the howling wind. As the pastor unlocked the church doors, he noticed an older woman standing at the nearby bus stop. He knew the bus wouldn't be there for at least half an hour, so he invited her inside to keep warm.

She wasn't from the neighborhood, she explained. She had been in the area to be interviewed for a job as a governess to the children of a well-known wealthy family. She had been a war refugee, her English was poor and she didn't get the job.

Head bowed in prayer, she sat in a pew near the back of the church. She paid no attention to the pastor, who was hanging the tablecloth across the unsightly hole. When the woman looked up and saw the cloth, she rushed to the altar.

"It's mine!" she exclaimed. "It's my banquet cloth!"

Excitedly she told the surprised minister its history and even showed him her initials embroidered in one corner.

She and her husband had lived in Vienna, Austria, and had opposed the Nazis before the Second World War. They decided to flee to Switzerland, but her husband said they must go separately. She left first. Later she heard that he had died in a concentration camp.

Touched by her story, the minister insisted she take the cloth. She thought about it for a moment but said no, she didn't need it any longer, and it did look pretty hanging behind the altar. Then she said good-bye and left.

In the candlelight of the Christmas Eve services, the tablecloth looked even more magnificent. The white lace seemed dazzling in the flickering light of the candles, and the golden threads woven through it were like the brilliant rays of a new dawn.

As members of the congregation left the church, they complimented the pastor on the services and on how beautiful the church looked.

One older gentleman lingered, admiring the tablecloth, and as he was leaving he said to the minister:

"It's strange. Many years ago my wife—God rest her—and I owned such a tablecloth. She used it only on very special occasions. But we lived in Vienna then."

The night air was freezing, but the goosebumps on the pastor's skin weren't caused by the weather. As calmly as he could, he told the man about the woman who had been to the church that very afternoon.

"Can it be," gasped the old man, tears streaming down his cheeks, "that she is alive? How can I find her?"

The pastor remembered the name of the family who had interviewed the woman. With the trembling old man at his side, he telephoned the family and learned her name and address.

In the pastor's old car they drove to her home on the other side of town. Together they knocked on her apartment door. When she opened it, the pastor witnessed the tearful, joyful and thrilling reunion of husband and wife.

Some people would call it an extremely lucky chance happening, the result of a hole in the church wall, an old tablecloth, a pastor's ingenuity in solving a problem and so on. But the combination of events was far too complex for it to have been merely "coincidence."

If one link in the fragile chain of events had been broken, the husband and wife might never have found each other. If the rain hadn't come, if the church roof hadn't leaked, if the pastor had decided not to go to the auction, if the woman hadn't been looking for a job or standing on that corner at just the right time . . . . The list of ifs is virtually endless.

It was simply God's will. And, as it has been said many times, He works in mysterious ways.

Richard Bauman

With These Rings

I was a new pastor's wife when my husband took me to a small town in Oklahoma. We fought until we learned to love each other during the two years we spent there. I was the new girl in town. I knew no one and barely knew my husband, Brad. He was busy with his church, and there I was, stuck. No money, no job and no friends. I was uncomfortable in my new role and resented it when others referred to me as "the preacher's wife." I failed to see what an honor that was. The parishioners made attempts to befriend me, but I was too busy being lonely and angry, and was bound and determined to let Brad know it. I pouted and packed, whined and packed, and threw things at him and packed. "I'm leaving!" I would scream when he came home. With the fifty cents I had in my pocket and no gas money, I don't know where I thought I was going, but I was adamant.

"Don't do me any favors," he would reply, which only caused me to turn on my heels and shout, "I'm staying, and don't try and stop me!" Who did he think he was? I wasn't about to let him kick me out.

Somewhere between my daily suitcase-packing episodes,

I remembered that I had promised to love him for better or for worse. In desperation, I found ways to entertain myself. I spent hours picking from the six pecan trees in the front yard. I quickly realized that even though we had no money, the pecans made great Christmas gifts. I even found a job. Then my husband came home one day and announced that he had an interview at a church in Louisiana. I had just learned to live in Oklahoma!

True to form, I pouted and griped on the way to Louisiana. Then something stopped me in my tracks. We were on our way through Texas when we ran right into what looked like a giant crystal bowl. An ice storm had hit the area a few days earlier, and it was the most beautiful sight I had ever seen. And there I was, gnawing on my husband. Somewhere between Denton and Sulphur, I had taken off my wedding rings and tucked them into the folds of my skirt so that I could apply some hand cream. The ice we were skidding on distracted me just enough that I forgot to put my rings back on. Three hours later I looked down and realized that I had lost my rings out on the highway when I had stepped out of the car to take a picture of a horse and buggy driving by. But which highway? Everything looks the same in an ice storm, especially when you are in country unfamiliar.

"I'll buy you another ring," my husband said.

I knew he meant well, but the ring was a family heirloom. "That ring can't be replaced," I cried.

"Honey, we don't even know where to begin looking," he said. "No, we're NOT going back," he insisted as he turned the car around and headed back to look for the rings.

It was hours before we found a location that seemed familiar. Occasionally some well-meaning person would pull his car over to the side of the road, roll down his window and yell, "Hey, buddy, what'd ya' lose?" At one point there must have been ten cars stopped on the side of the road, all abandoned by the occupants who had joined in the search. But with the sun going down, it was obvious that our chances of finding the rings were slim. I was crushed.

"Face it, Honey, they're gone," Brad said. "I know you're upset. I promise to try and find a suitable replacement."

I knew he was right. The walk in the cold that day had given me time to think about the day's events. I played the scene over and over in my mind, and what I saw was not a pretty sight. I had ranted and raved, nagged and wailed, and acted like a spoiled brat. I took a good long look at my husband pacing back and forth in the freezing cold. He had driven three hours back to this desolate area in the middle of a treacherous ice storm without one thought for himself, attempting to find something that was important to me. The rings might be gone, but there could never be a suitable replacement for my husband. Suddenly, the rings seemed so unimportant. I resolved right then and there to stop thinking only of myself.

It was at that very moment that I opened the car door and began to step inside. Something on the floor caught my eye. My rings! I grabbed them and waved them in the air. Brad rushed to my side and put them back on my finger. "This is where these rings belong," he whispered. I looked into his eyes, and knew that I had found what I was looking for. It wasn't my rings that were lost that day—I was the one who had been missing.

Life in the pastorate hasn't changed. The only thing that has changed is me. We still move around more than I like. And I still have to start over again every time we do. But I've learned to appreciate when people call me "the preacher's wife," because etched into my mind is a frozen road in Texas, and a voice that whispers, "This is where these rings belong."

Sharon M. Palmer

Step, Step, Roar

A little boy walked down the aisle at a wedding. As he made his way to the front, he would take two steps, then stop and turn to the crowd, alternating between the bride's side and the groom's side. While facing the crowd, he would put his hands up like claws and roar. And so it went—step, step, ROAR, step, step, ROAR—all the way down the aisle.

As you can imagine, the crowd was near tears from laughing so hard by the time he reached the pulpit. The little boy, however, was getting more and more distressed from all the laughing, and he was near tears by the time he reached the pulpit.

When asked what he was doing, the child sniffed back his tears and said, "I was being the ring bear."

Richard Lederer

"Let's pretend I'm getting married and you guys sing 'Here Comes the Prize.'"

Reprinted with permission from Bil Keane.

My Miraculous Family

There are no hopeless situations; there are only people who have grown hopeless about them.

Source Unknown

I never considered myself unique, but people are constantly telling me I am a miracle. To me, I was just an ordinary guy with realistic goals and big dreams. I was a
nineteen-year-old student at the University of Texas and
well on my way toward fulfilling my dream of becoming
an orthopedic surgeon.

On the night of February 17, 1981, I was studying for an
organic chemistry test at the library with Sharon, my girl-
friend of three years. It was quite late, so Sharon had
asked me to drive her back to her dormitory. We got into
my car, not realizing at the time that just getting into a car
would never quite be the same for me again. I quickly
noticed that my gas gauge was on empty, so I pulled into
a nearby convenience store to buy two dollars' worth of
gas. "I'll be back in two minutes," I yelled to Sharon as I
closed the door. Instead, those two minutes changed my
life forever.

Entering the convenience store was like entering the twilight zone. Outside the store I was a healthy, athletic, pre-med student, but on the inside I became just another violent crime statistic. The store appeared to be empty as I entered, but suddenly I realized it was not empty at all. Three men were in the process of committing a robbery, and my entrance had caught them by surprise. One of the criminals shoved a .38-caliber handgun to my head, ordered me to the cooler, pushed me down on the floor and pumped a bullet—execution style—into the back of my head. He obviously thought I was dead because he did not shoot me again. The trio of thieves finished robbing the store and left calmly.

Meanwhile, Sharon wondered why I had not returned. After seeing the three men leave the store she really began to worry, since I was the last person she saw entering. She quickly went inside to look for me, but saw no one—only an open cash register containing one check and several pennies. Frantically she ran down each aisle shouting, "Mike, Mike!"

Just then the attendant appeared from the back of the store yelling, "Lady, get down on the floor! I've just been robbed and shot at!"

Sharon quickly dropped to the floor screaming, "Have you seen my boyfriend . . . auburn hair?" The man did not reply but went back to the cooler where he found me choking on my vomit. The attendant immediately called for the police and an ambulance.

Sharon was in shock. She was starting to understand that I was hurt, but she could not begin to comprehend or imagine the severity of my injury.

When the police arrived they called the homicide division as they did not think I would survive. The paramedic reported that she had never seen a person survive who was so severely wounded. At 1:30 A.M. my parents, who lived in Houston, were awakened by a telephone call from Brackenridge Hospital advising them to come to Austin as soon as possible. They feared I would not make it through the night.

Surprisingly, I did make it through the night, and early in the morning the neurosurgeon decided to operate. However, he informed my family and Sharon that my chances of surviving the surgery were only four out of ten. The neurosurgeon further shocked my family by telling them what life would be like for me if I beat the odds and survived. He said I probably would never walk, talk or be able to understand even simple commands.

My family was hoping and praying to hear even the slightest bit of encouragement from the doctor. Instead, his pessimistic words gave my family no reason to believe that I would ever again be a productive member of society. Once again I beat the odds and survived the three-and-a-half hours of surgery.

Even though my family breathed a huge sigh of relief that I was still alive, the doctor cautioned that it would still be several days before I would be out of danger. However, with each passing day I became stronger and stronger, and two weeks later I was well enough to be moved from the ICU to a private room.

Granted, I still could not talk, my entire right side was paralyzed and many people thought I could not understand them, but at least I was stable. After one week in a private room the doctors felt I had improved enough to be transferred by jet ambulance to Del Oro Rehabilitation Hospital in Houston.

My hallucinations, coupled with my physical problems, made my prognosis still very bleak. But as time passed my mind began to clear. Approximately six weeks later my right leg began to move ever so slightly. Within seven weeks my right arm slowly began to move, and at eight weeks I uttered my first few words.

My speech was extremely difficult and slow in the beginning, but at least it was a start. I was looking forward to each new day to see how far I would progress. But just as I thought my life was finally looking brighter I was tested by the hospital neuropsychologist. She explained that, judging from my test results, she believed that I should not return to college but should set more "realistic goals."

Upon hearing her evaluation I became furious. I thought, *Who is she to tell me what I can or cannot do? She does not even know me. I am a very determined and stubborn person!* I believe it was at that very moment that I decided I would somehow, someday return to college.

It took a long time and a lot of hard work, but I finally returned to the University of Texas in the fall of 1983—a year and a half after almost dying. The next few years in Austin were very difficult, but I truly believe that in order to see beauty in life you must experience some unpleasantness. I resolved to live each day to the fullest and did the very best I could.

Besides attending classes at the university I underwent therapy three to five days each week at Brackenridge Hospital. I also flew to Houston every other weekend to work with Tom Williams, a trainer and executive who had worked for many colleges and professional teams, helping injured athletes, such as Earl Campbell and Eric Dickerson. Through Tom I learned: "Nothing is impossible and never, never give up or quit."

He echoed the same words and sentiments of a prominent neurosurgeon from Houston, Dr. Alexander Gol, a close personal friend of my parents who drove to Austin with my family that traumatic February morning. I received many opinions from various therapists and doctors but it was Dr. Gol who told my family to take one day at a time, for no matter how bad the situation looked, no one knew for certain what the brain could do.

Early in my therapy, my father kept repeating to me one of his favorite sayings. It could have been written by Tom or Dr. Gol, and I have repeated it almost every day since being hurt: "Mile by mile it's a trial; yard by yard it's hard; but inch by inch it's a cinch."

I thought of those words, and of Dr. Gol, Tom, my family and Sharon who believed so strongly in me, as I climbed the steps to receive my diploma from the dean of liberal arts at the University of Texas on a sunny afternoon in June 1986. Excitement and pride filled my heart as I heard the dean announce that I had graduated with "highest honors," was elected to Phi Beta Kappa and had been chosen as one of twelve Dean's Distinguished Graduates out of sixteen hundred students in the College of Liberal Arts.

The overwhelming emotions and feelings that I experienced that day, when most of the audience gave me a standing ovation, would never again be matched in my life—not even when I graduated with a master's degree in social work and not even when I became employed full time at the Texas Pain and Stress Center. But I was wrong!

On May 24, 1987, I realized that nothing could ever match the joy I felt as Sharon and I were married. Sharon, my high school sweetheart of nine years, had always stood by me, through good times and bad.

To me, Sharon is my miracle, my diamond in a world filled with problems, hurt and pain. Sharon dropped out of school when I was hurt so that she could constantly be at my side. She never wavered or gave up on me.

Her faith and love pulled me through so many dark days. While other nineteen-year-old girls were going to parties and enjoying life, Sharon devoted her life to my recovery. That, to me, is the true definition of love.

After our beautiful wedding I continued working part-time at the Pain Center and completed my work for a master's degree while Sharon worked as a speech pathologist at a local hospital. We were extremely happy, but even more so when we learned Sharon was pregnant.

On July 11, 1990, at 12:15 A.M. Sharon woke me with the news: "We need to go to the hospital . . . my water just broke." I couldn't help but think how ironic it was that my life almost ended in a convenience store and now on the date "7-11" we were about to bring a new life into this world. This time it was my turn to help Sharon as she had helped me over those past years.

Sharon was having contractions about every two minutes, and each time she needed to have her lower back massaged. Since she was in labor for fifteen hours that meant 450 massages! It was well worth every bit of pain in my fingers because at 3:10 P.M. Sharon and I experienced the birth of our beautiful daughter, Shawn Elyse Segal!

Tears of joy and happiness came to my eyes as our healthy, alert, wonderful daughter entered this world. We anxiously counted her ten fingers and her ten toes and watched her wide eyes take in the world about her. It was truly a beautiful picture that will be etched in my mind forever as she lay in her mother's waiting arms, just minutes after her birth. At that moment I thanked God for blessing us with the greatest miracle of all.

Michael Jordan Segal

The Smell of Rain

A cold March wind danced around Dallas as the doctor walked into Diana Blessing's small hospital room. It was the dead of night and she was still groggy from surgery. Her husband, David, held her as they braced themselves for the latest news.

That rainy afternoon, March 10, 1991, complications had forced Diana, only twenty-four weeks pregnant, to undergo emergency surgery. At twelve inches long and weighing only one pound, nine ounces, Danae Lu arrived by cesarean delivery.

They already knew she was perilously premature. Still, the doctor's soft words dropped like bombs. "I don't think she's going to make it," he said as kindly as he could. "There's only a 10 percent chance she will live through the night. If by some slim chance she does make it, her future could be a very cruel one." Numb with disbelief, David and Diana listened as the doctor described the devastating problems Danae could face if she survived.

She would probably never walk, or talk, or see. She would be prone to other catastrophic conditions from cerebral palsy to complete mental retardation, and on and on. Through the dark hours of morning as Danae held onto life by the thinnest thread, Diana slipped in and out of drugged sleep. But she was determined that their daughter would live to be a happy, healthy young girl. David, fully awake, knew he must confront his wife with the inevitable.

David told Diana that they needed to talk about funeral arrangements. But Diana said, "No, that is not going to happen. No way! I don't care what the doctors say, Danae is not going to die. One day she will be just fine and she will be home with us."

As if willed to live by Diana's determination, Danae clung to life hour after hour. But as those first rainy days passed, a new agony set in for David and Diana. Because Danae's underdeveloped nervous system was essentially "raw," the least kiss or caress only intensified her discomfort, so they couldn't even cradle their tiny baby. All they could do, as Danae struggled beneath the ultraviolet light, was to pray that God would stay close to their precious little girl.

At last, when Danae was two months old, her parents were able to hold her for the first time. Two months later, she went home from the hospital just as her mother predicted, even though doctors grimly warned that her chances of leading a normal life were almost zero.

Today, five years later, Danae is a petite but feisty young girl with glittering gray eyes and an unquenchable zest for life. She shows no sign of any mental or physical impairment. But that happy ending is not the end of the story.

One blistering summer afternoon in 1996 in Irving, Texas, Danae was sitting in her mother's lap at the ball park where her brother's baseball team was practicing. As always, Danae was busy chattering when she suddenly fell silent. Hugging her arms across her chest, Danae asked her mom, "Do you smell that?"

Smelling the air and detecting a thunderstorm approaching, Diana replied, "Yes, it smells like rain."

Danae closed her eyes again and asked, "Do you smell that?"

Once again her mother replied, "Yes, I think we're about to get wet, it smells like rain."

Caught in the moment, Danae shook her head, patted her thin shoulder and loudly announced, "No, it smells like him. It smells like God when you lay your head on His chest."

Tears blurred Diana's eyes as Danae happily hopped down to play with the other children before the rain came. Her daughter's words confirmed what Diana and the rest of the Blessing family had known all along. During those long days and nights of the first two months of her life, when her nerves were too sensitive to be touched, God was holding Danae on his chest, and it is His scent that she remembers so well.

Nancy Miller

THE FAMILY CIRCUS   **By Bil Keane**

"If you listen real carefully when the breeze blows, you can hear God whispering."

Reprinted with permission from Bil Keane.

The Birthday Check

In the 1950s, local banks sent personalized checks to noncustomers to try to generate new business. I was eight years old, proud of my new writing and spelling ability, so I begged for these checks from my parents.

In our family, special occasions meant gifts from parents, siblings and friends, but from others it meant cards with money. Cards with crisp ones, fives, tens or twenties meant "I love you." So using these advertisements—gimmick checks—I did the same. My homemade cards, heavily colored and flowery with prose and poetry, with a bogus check inside, were made out to the honoree in the amount appropriate to the extent of my love. For my brothers, it was a dollar. For my parents, it was thousands. For my Uncle Howard, it was a million dollars.

In July of 1958, we held a Sunday dinner birthday celebration for my uncle. He opened the card I'd made, read the message inside and looked at the check enclosed for a long time. Smiling at me from across the dinner table, he thanked me for the card and check. Then he took his wallet out of his back pocket, folded and tucked the check away, saying, "I'll just keep this with me until I need it."

Thirty-five years later, I sat drinking coffee, early in the morning, at that same table, across from the same smile, hearing the same voice, sharing the same memories of those thirty-five years, with the same Uncle Howard— probably for the last time. My uncle was dying of cancer. Radiation and chemotherapy had been administered without success and ended so his crew cut was growing back. The nausea that had plagued him during treatments was no longer a problem. He was eating again and putting on the weight he had lost. Sitting there talking about the good old days, I fooled myself into thinking this was a pleasure visit and there would be others to come. But deep down, I knew that this visit was for good-bye.

Putting down his coffee mug, he reached for his hip pocket. Unfolding his wallet, he reached inside and handed me a pale blue slip of paper, folded in half, saying, "Remember this?" There was the birthday check for a million dollars. He had kept it, carrying it with him, shifting it from old wallet to new wallet for thirty-five years.

"You never tried to cash it," I joked.

"I never needed it," he said. "I'll just keep this with me a little longer in case I need it yet." He put it away once more.

I left him that afternoon with final hugs, kisses, and the final good-byes. Four days later, he was gone.

Shortly after the funeral, I returned home from work and found a package on the kitchen table mailed to me, the handwritten return address from my aunt. Inside was another small package with a short note in Uncle Howard's handwriting. "Since I don't need this anymore, I thought you might want it back. With love, Uncle Howard." Enclosed was the check for a million dollars, mounted inside a frame. Thanks, Uncle Howard, for a million-dollar love that lasts longer than a lifetime.

Kathleen Dixon

The Brownie Story

Financially deprived. Yes, that's the perfect way to describe how it all began. My parents were uneducated out of necessity. Both were raised during the Depression and had quit school to help support their families.

My father was one of eight children, at least until his baby brother Johnny was killed at three years of age, a great tragedy from which the family never fully recovered. My mother was the third child of five. Her father died when she was four years old. Her mother didn't remarry until all of her five children were raised. My grandmother was an extraordinary lady.

I am the firstborn child of my parents—hence the name Dawn. They always told me my name was symbolic of the beginning of a new life for them. One evening they went to sleep as a couple, and they awoke the next day as something more: a family. Even though the story is corny and sentimental, I have always liked it. My sister was born eighteen months after me, with my brother following her fifteen months later. My parents were determined to have a son, and after his birth they felt their family was complete.

Female was a confusing gender in my family. Were they

the breadwinners and heads of the family as in my mother's family? Or were they supposed to be modern-day Cinderellas: washing, cleaning, staying within womanly domains, learning skills that would eventually be of some value to a wife, like taking care of a household and children? That was the path my sister chose. Me, well, I *did* learn to dust.

Don't misunderstand me. My dad loved me and had hopes for me, as long as any dream I had stayed within the boundaries of those dreams deemed appropriate for poor white trash. My mom, on the other hand, was always telling me there was a star out there, and it was my job to hitch my wagon to it. I was her hope. She wanted me to go where she had been afraid to tread.

For two years, when I was six and seven, we had no indoor plumbing, except for the cold-water pipe in the kitchen. We boiled water on the stove in order to take baths in our number-three washtub. We did, however, have a rather plush outside facility, because my father was fair at carpentry, and he designed our special rest room with two holes instead of one, in order for the children to go outside together. He hoped that this togetherness would minimize our terror of going to the outhouse in the dark.

The first day of school, I realized that something was different about me. Up until then, I had learned to talk early, sing in harmony, entertain my family with not-too-humorous stand-up comedy and help my mother with the other children (sometimes without being threatened), and I had a basic proficiency at getting my sister and myself to the outside facility. First grade taught me many different things. Other girls my age had a different dress for each day of the week. Dick jumped, Jane skipped and both of them saw Spot run. I also couldn't help but notice that most of the other children had lunch pails with thermoses to match. Not only was I short on clothes, I had to take my bologna sandwich in a brown paper bag with no thermos. Drinking water from the school cooler was perfectly suited to the family budget.

By second grade, I was convinced that somewhere along the way my parents had forgotten to pick up a couple of checks. One, I was quite sure, was sitting somewhere, written for the explicit purpose of a pink lunch pail with matching thermos just for me. I had a desperate desire to fit in. I wanted to belong. Then, out of nowhere appeared the ultimate opportunity. A flyer was passed around for joining Brownies. In second grade, in a small town in Oklahoma, Brownies is the quintessential little-girl experience and quite necessary for success in future marriage or business. Needless to say, I was devastated, as was my mother, when she had to explain that I couldn't be a Brownie because we were not able to afford the uniform and dues. My chances for belonging, blending in and being accepted were dim.

I remember my father attempting to explain life to me when he couldn't stand to see me hurt. He told me that living in a dream world, or being overwhelmed by some sort of fantasy, would only lead to the need to understand three very simple rules of life. Number one, money marries money. (I thought that was interesting, because I had only heard of *people* getting married.) Number two, good things happen to those who can afford them, which I had some understanding of since "the big five," the wealthy girls in my class, seemed to always have good things happen to them. And last, but certainly not least, number three, life was something one must endure until it was over. If I could grasp and believe in those concepts, I could be a successful member of the official poor white trash community. If not, I was begging for disappointment for the rest of my days.

Even as a child, this did not make sense to me. How in the world was grasping these concepts going to help me avoid heartbreak and disappointment? My father had grasped the concepts, and it sure wasn't saving *him* heartbreak. It appeared that there was something missing from this all-encompassing philosophy, and I figured that if I was going to be miserable in life anyway, I might as well have money and good things happen once in a while. My mother taught me about miracles. She used at least two sources to back up her claim of their existence: the movie *Miracle on 34th Street* and stories of miracles God had performed in the Bible. I believed that between God and Santa Claus, anything could happen.

Of course, my dad even had a story about Santa. He said that when he was seven years old, he still believed in Santa Claus. One day, this big sleigh drawn by horses came down his street. He almost lost his breath with the excitement of seeing Santa in person for the first time. He told me that Santa was throwing candy out for the children, but he didn't want any. He just wanted to touch Santa's sleigh to make sure he wasn't dreaming. He ran as fast as he could, his heart beating out of his chest. Just as he got to the sleigh, he breathlessly reached out to touch it and pushed out a weak, "I love you, Santa." Crack! He felt a jolt of pain. Santa had cracked his metal bells across Dad's knuckles. "Don't touch the sleigh, kid!" was all he could remember Santa saying. My dad lost whatever faith he had left in childhood fantasies that day.

It made me cry when I heard the story. I wondered why he didn't know that it must not have been the real Santa.

I remember spending my recess time alone, praying that my dad wasn't right about Santa or life. I wanted to believe that worth wasn't just about money, and that even if you didn't have money, dreams could still come true. Otherwise, hitching my wagon to a star was going to be impossible. But if miracles did exist, I still had a chance with both my wagon and Brownies. I felt torn. I knew I should listen to my father. Fathers should be respected and taken seriously. But he seemed to not have all of the information. Miracles had been scarce for him, and I wondered if that was because he didn't know how to believe in them. I was convinced the secret was in the believing. And I was determined to believe enough for both of us.

My second-grade teacher, Mrs. JoAn Stone, saw me huddled alone outside at recess one day and came over to find out what the problem might be. I told her that there wasn't a problem, I was just having a talk with God about being a Brownie. She asked me, "Why the talk with God?"

"I might not get to be a Brownie," I replied. "My mom can't afford a uniform and the dues, so I was hoping that God could give me some ideas."

Several days later, as my seven-year-old faith was being pushed to its limit, Mrs. Stone asked if I could stay after school for a few minutes. After school that day, she took me into her office and locked the door. She was acting rather strange, and I thought she might be angry with me. I could not figure out what I might have done wrong. She noticed my concern, smiled, and told me that she had a surprise for me. I was greatly relieved to know she wasn't mad. She opened a box. I couldn't believe my eyes! A Brownie uniform! She kept apologizing that it wasn't new. She said her sister had a little girl one year older than I was, and that this was her old Brownie uniform. She thought it might fit me.

She asked if we could try it on. I was hesitant because my slip was very old and torn, and I didn't want her to see it, but I thought I could live through the embarrassment if the uniform would just fit. My sacrifice was rewarded when it did. It was wonderful and soft, and Mrs. Stone even had the funny little beanie hat that went with it. I knew God had answered my prayers. I knew Mrs. Stone was the kindest woman in the world, and I knew from that moment on that my father was wrong—not because he was bad, but because someone had obviously lied to him, and he had believed them. I only wished he had had Mrs. Stone as his second-grade teacher. She would never have lied to him.

When I put on my uniform, I knew I wasn't meant to be just poor white trash. I was meant to be something wonderful. . . . I was meant to be a Brownie.

In Brownies we had a project. We made plaster of Paris puppy dogs. Everyone but me painted their puppies brown or black. My mother had just spent our dinner money on balcony tickets to the picture show to see *101 Dalmatians*. I remember sitting up there so high, looking down on all the people. I felt wonderful and special, so I painted my plaster dog white with large black spots to remind me of that wonderful feeling.

The big event in Brownies was the Father-Daughter Dinner. Only fathers were allowed to attend with their daughters. I had never had an evening out alone with my dad. One day, my mom found an old pedal sewing machine in an alley. She asked the man who owned the building how much he wanted for it, and he told her she didn't want that old machine because the bobbin had to be wound by hand, and it didn't run very well. He told her it was more of a headache than anything else. She told him that was a matter of perspective. She had children who needed clothes and the old machine looked wonderful to her. He felt sorry for her and ended up selling it to her for five dollars. She hand-wound the bobbin, cleaned and oiled the machine, and bought some material at a garage sale for a nickel a yard. She made a beautiful dress for me to wear to the dinner.

I thought that my dad was the handsomest man there. At one point the fathers and daughters began to sing "Let Me Call You Sweetheart" to one another. My dad lifted me up and stood me on a chair, and we did one of the things he loved most: we sang in harmony. He had a glorious voice.

There were tears in both our eyes as we finished singing. He leaned over and whispered into my ear, "When I look at you, my little Brownie, I can believe in miracles."

I'll never forget that moment. I imagine that he hasn't forgotten either. For a moment we weren't poor white trash, nor wealthy and powerful either. For a moment, none of that mattered. We were a father and a daughter experiencing one of the richest moments of my life. In that moment miracles were as real as we were, and the hope created for me out of that experience has led me forth ever since.

Dawn L. Billings
Greatness and Children: Learn the Rules

THE FAMILY CIRCUS®   **By Bil Keane**

"You hafta listen to me with your eyes, Daddy. Not just your ears."

Reprinted with permission from Bil Keane.

A Special Breakfast

Until last year, the greatest sorrow of my life was that my wife Alice and I couldn't have any children. To make up for this in a small way, we always invited all the children on our street to our house each Christmas morning for breakfast.

We would decorate the house with snowflakes and angels in the windows, a nativity scene and a Christmas tree in the living room, and other ornaments that we hoped would appeal to the children. When our young guests arrived—there were usually ten or fifteen of them—we said grace and served them such delicacies as orange juice garnished with a candy cane. And after the meal we gave each of the youngsters a wrapped toy or game. We used to look forward to these breakfasts with the joyful impatience of children.

But last year, about six weeks before Christmas, Alice died. I could not concentrate at work. I could not force myself to cook anything but the simplest dishes. Sometimes I would sit for hours without moving, and then suddenly find myself crying for no apparent reason.

I decided not to invite the children over for the traditional Christmas breakfast. But Kathy and Peter, my next-door neighbors, asked me to join them and their three

children for dinner on Christmas Eve. As soon as I arrived
and had my coat off, Kathy asked me, "Do you have any
milk at your house?"

"Yes," I replied. "If you need some, I'll go right away."

"Oh, that's all right. Come and sit down. The kids have
been waiting for you. Just give Peter your keys."

So I sat down, prepared for a nice chat with eight-year-
old Beth and six-year-old Jimmy. (Their little sister was
upstairs sleeping.) But my words wouldn't come. What if
Beth and Jimmy should ask me about my Christmas
breakfast? How could I explain to them? Would they
think I was just selfish or self-pitying? I began to think
they would. Worse, I began to think they would be right.

But neither of them mentioned the breakfast. At first I
felt relieved, but then I started to wonder if they remembered it or cared about it. As they prattled on about their
toys, their friends and Christmas, I thought they would be
reminded of our breakfast tradition, and yet they said
nothing. This was strange, I thought, but the more we
talked, the more I became convinced that they remembered the breakfast but didn't want to embarrass
Grandpa Melowski (as they called me) by bringing it up.

Dinner was soon ready and afterward we all went to
late Mass. After Mass, the Zacks let me out of their car in
front of my house. I thanked them and wished them all
merry Christmas as I walked toward my front door. Only
then did I notice that Peter had left a light on when he
borrowed the milk—and that someone had decorated my
windows with snowflakes and angels!

When I opened the door, I saw that the whole house
had been transformed with a Christmas tree, a nativity
scene, candles and all the other decorations of the season.
On the dining-room table was Alice's green Christmas
tablecloth and her pinecone centerpiece. What a kind ges-
ture! At that moment, I wished that I could still put on the
breakfast, but I had made no preparations.

Early the next morning, a five-year-old with a package

of sweet rolls rang my bell. Before I could ask him what was going on, he was joined by two of his friends, one with a pound of bacon, the other with a pitcher of orange juice. Within fifteen minutes, my house was alive with all the children on my street, and I had all the food I needed for the usual festive breakfast. I was tremendously pleased, although in the back of my mind I still feared that I would disappoint my guests. I knew my spur-of-the-moment party was missing one important ingredient.

At about nine-thirty, though, I had another surprise. Kathy Zack came to my back door.

"How's the breakfast?" she asked.

"I'm having the time of my life," I answered.

"I brought something for you," she said, setting a shopping bag on the counter.

"More food?"

"No," she said. "Take a look."

Inside the bag were individually wrapped packages, each bearing the name of one of the children and signed, "Merry Christmas from Grandpa Melowski."

My happiness was complete. It was more than just knowing that the children would receive their customary gifts and wouldn't be disappointed; it was the feeling that everyone cared.

I like to think it's significant that I received a gift of love on the same day that the world received a sign of God's love two thousand years ago in Bethlehem. I never found out who to thank for my Christmas present. I said my "Thank you" in my prayers that night—and that spoke of my gratitude more than anything I could ever say to my neighbors.

Harold Melowski
As told to Alan Struthers Jr.

A Guy Named Bill

I'd rather see a sermon than hear one any day.

Edgar A. Guest

His name was Bill. He had wild hair, wore a T-shirt with holes in it, blue jeans and no shoes. In the entire time I knew him I never once saw Bill wear a pair of shoes. Rain, sleet or snow, Bill was barefoot. This was literally his wardrobe for his whole four years of college.

He was brilliant and looked like he was always pondering the esoteric. He became a Christian while attending college. Across the street from the campus was a church full of well-dressed, middle-class people. They wanted to develop a ministry to the college students, but they were not sure how to go about it.

One day, Bill decided to worship there. He walked into the church, complete with wild hair, T-shirt, blue jeans and bare feet. The church was completely packed, and the service had already begun. Bill started down the aisle to find a place to sit. By now the people were looking a bit uncomfortable, but no one said anything.

As Bill moved closer and closer to the pulpit, he realized there were no empty seats. So he squatted and sat down on the carpet right up front. (Although such behavior would have been perfectly acceptable at a college fellowship, this was a scenario this particular congregation had never witnessed before!) By now, the people seemed uptight, and the tension in the air was thickening.

Right about the time Bill took his "seat," a deacon began slowly making his way down the aisle from the back of the sanctuary. The deacon was in his eighties, had silver-gray hair, a three-piece suit and a pocket watch. He was a godly man—very elegant, dignified and courtly. He walked with a cane and, as he neared the boy, church members thought, *You can't blame him for what he's going to do. How can you expect a man of his age and background to understand some college kid on the floor?*

It took a long time for the man to reach the boy. The church was utterly silent except for the clicking of his cane. You couldn't even hear anyone breathing. All eyes were on the deacon.

But then they saw the elderly man drop his cane on the floor. With great difficulty, he sat down on the floor next to Bill and worshipped with him. Everyone in the congregation choked up with emotion. When the minister gained control, he told the people, "What I am about to preach, you will never remember. What you've just seen, you will never forget."

Rebecca Manley Pippert

2

DIVINE INTERVENTION

There are only two ways that you can live. One is as if nothing is a miracle. The other is as if everything is a miracle. I believe in the latter.

Albert Einstein

A Miracle of Mermaids

The footprints of an angel are love. And where there is love, miraculous things can happen.

Angels in the Outfield

Rhonda Gill froze as she heard her four-year-old daughter, Desiree, sobbing quietly in the family room that morning in October 1993. Rhonda tiptoed through the doorway. The tiny dark-haired child was hugging a photograph of her father, who had died nine months earlier. Rhonda, twenty-four, watched as Desiree gently ran her fingers around her father's face. "Daddy," she said softly, "why won't you come back?"

The petite brunette university student felt a surge of despair. It had been hard enough coping with her husband Ken's death, but her daughter's grief was more than she could bear. *If only I could tear the pain out of her,* Rhonda thought.

Ken Gill and Rhonda Hill had met when Rhonda was eighteen, and had married after a whirlwind courtship. Their daughter, Desiree, was born on January 9, 1989.

Although a muscular 190 centimeters tall, Ken was a gentle man whom everyone loved. His big passion was

Desiree. "She's a real Daddy's girl," Rhonda would often say as Ken's eyes twinkled with pride. Father and daughter went everywhere together: hiking, dune buggy riding, and fishing for bass and salmon.

Instead of adjusting to her father's death gradually, Desiree had refused to accept it. "Daddy will be home soon," she would tell her mother. "He's at work." When playing with her toy telephone, she pretended she was chatting with him. "I miss you, Daddy," she'd say. "When will you come back?"

Immediately after Ken's death, Rhonda moved from her flat to her mother's home nearby. Seven weeks after the funeral, Desiree was still inconsolable. "I just don't know what to do," Rhonda told her mother, Trish Moore, a forty-seven-year-old medical assistant.

One evening, the three of them sat outside, gazing at the stars. "See that one, Desiree?" her grandmother pointed at a bright speck near the horizon. "That's your daddy shining down from heaven."

Several nights later Rhonda woke to find Desiree on the doorstep in her pajamas, weeping as she looked for her daddy's star. Twice they took her to see a child psychiatrist, but nothing seemed to help.

As a last resort, Trish took Desiree to Ken's grave, hoping that it would help her come to terms with his death. The child laid her head against his gravestone and said, "Maybe if I listen hard enough I can hear Daddy talk to me."

Then one evening, as Rhonda tucked her child in, Desiree announced, "I want to die, Mummy, so I can be with Daddy." *God help me*, Rhonda prayed. *What more can I possibly do?*

November 8, 1993, would have been Ken's twenty-ninth birthday. "How will I send him a card?" Desiree asked her grandmother.

"How about if we tie a letter to a balloon," Trish said, "and send it up to heaven?" Desiree's eyes immediately lit up.

On their way to the cemetery, the back seat of the car full of flowers for their planned gravesite visit, the three stopped at a shop. "Help Mum pick out a balloon," Trish instructed.

At a rack where dozens of helium-filled silver balloons bobbed, Desiree made an instant decision: "That one!" HAPPY BIRTHDAY was emblazoned around a drawing of the Little Mermaid from the Disney film. Desiree and her father had often watched the video together.

The child's eyes shone as they arranged flowers on Ken's grave. It was a beautiful day, with a slight breeze rippling the eucalyptus trees. Then Desiree dictated a letter to her dad. "Tell him 'Happy Birthday. I love you and miss you,'" she rattled off. "'I hope you get this and can write me on my birthday in January.'"

Trish wrote the message and their address on a small piece of paper, then wrapped it in plastic and tied it to the end of the balloon's string. Finally Desiree released the balloon.

For almost an hour, they watched the shining spot of silver grow ever smaller. "Okay," Trish said at last. "Time to go home."

Rhonda and Trish were beginning to walk slowly from the grave when they heard Desiree shout excitedly, "Did you see that? I saw Daddy reach down and take it!"

The balloon, visible just moments earlier, had disappeared. "Now Dad's going to write me back," Desiree said as she walked past them towards the car.

On a cold, rainy morning on Prince Edward Island in eastern Canada, thirty-two-year-old Wade MacKinnon pulled on his waterproof duck-hunting gear. MacKinnon, a forest ranger, lived with his wife and three children in the rural community of Mermaid.

But instead of driving to the estuary where he usually

hunted, he suddenly decided to go to Mermaid Lake, three kilometers away. Leaving his sports utility vehicle, he hiked past dripping spruce and pine, and soon entered a cranberry bog surrounding the nine-hectare lake. In the bushes on the shoreline, something fluttered and caught his eye. Curious, he approached to find a silver balloon snagged in the branches of a thigh-high bush. Printed on one side was a picture of a mermaid. When he untangled the string, he found a soggy piece of paper at the end of it, wrapped in plastic.

At home, MacKinnon carefully removed the wet note and let it dry. When his wife, Donna, came home, he showed her the balloon and note. Intrigued, she read: "November 8, 1993. Happy Birthday, Daddy. . . ." It finished with an address in Live Oak, California.

"It's only November 12," Wade exclaimed. "This balloon traveled nearly 5,000 kilometers in four days!"

"And look," said Donna, turning the balloon over. "This is a Little Mermaid balloon, and it landed at Mermaid Lake."

"We have to write to Desiree," Wade said. "Maybe we were chosen to help this little girl." But he could see that his wife didn't feel the same way. With tears in her eyes, Donna stepped away from the balloon. "Such a young girl having to deal with death—it's awful," she said.

Wade let the matter rest. He placed the note in a drawer and tied the balloon, still buoyant, to the railing of the balcony overlooking the living room. But the sight of the balloon made Donna uncomfortable. A few days later, she stuffed it into a cupboard. As the weeks went by, however, Donna found herself thinking more and more about the balloon. It had flown over the Rocky Mountains and the Great Lakes. Just a few more kilometers and it would have landed in the ocean. Instead, it had stopped there, in Mermaid.

Our three children are so lucky, she thought. *They have two healthy parents.* She imagined how their daughter, Hailey, almost two years old, would feel if Wade were to die.

The next morning, Donna said to Wade: "You're right. We have this balloon for a reason. We have to try to help Desiree."

In a local bookshop, Donna bought an adaptation of *The Little Mermaid*. A few days later, just after Christmas, Wade brought home a birthday card that read, "For a Dear Daughter, Loving Birthday Wishes."

Donna sat down one morning to write a letter to Desiree. When she finished, she tucked it into the birthday card and wrapped it up with the book. Then, on January 3, 1994, she mailed the package.

Desiree's fifth birthday came and went quietly with a small party on January 9. Every day since they released the balloon, Desiree had asked Rhonda, "Do you think Daddy has my balloon yet?" After her party, she stopped asking.

Late on the afternoon of January 19, the MacKinnons' package arrived. Busy cooking dinner, Trish looked at the unfamiliar return address and assumed it was a birthday gift for her granddaughter from someone in Ken's family. Rhonda and Desiree had moved out, so Trish decided to deliver it to Rhonda the next day.

As Trish watched TV that evening, a thought nagged at her. *Why would someone send a parcel for Desiree to this address?* Tearing the parcel open, she found the card, "For a Dear Daughter. . . ." Her heart raced. *Dear God!* she thought, and reached for the telephone. It was after midnight, but she had to call Rhonda.

When Trish, eyes red from weeping, pulled into Rhonda's driveway the next morning at 6:45, her daughter and granddaughter were already up. Rhonda and Trish sat Desiree between them on the lounge. Trish said,

"Desiree, this is for you," and handed her the parcel. "It's from your daddy."

"I know," responded Desiree matter-of-factly. "Here, Grandma, read it to me."

"Happy birthday from your daddy," Trish began. "I guess you must be wondering who we are. Well, it all started in November when my husband, Wade, went duck hunting. Guess what we found? A mermaid balloon that you sent your daddy. . . ." Trish paused. A single tear began to trickle down Desiree's cheek. "There are no shops in heaven, so your daddy wanted someone to do his shopping for him. I think he picked us because we live in a town called Mermaid."

Trish continued reading: "I know your daddy would want you to be happy and not sad. I know he loves you very much and will always be watching over you. Lots of love, the MacKinnons."

When Trish finished reading, she looked at Desiree. "I knew Daddy would find a way not to forget me," the child said.

Wiping the tears from her eyes, Trish put her arm around Desiree and began to read the copy of *The Little Mermaid* that the MacKinnons had sent. The story was different from the one her father had so often read to the child. In that version, the Little Mermaid lives happily ever after with the handsome prince. But in the new one, she dies because a wicked witch has taken her tail. Three angels carry her away.

As Trish finished reading, she worried that the ending would upset her granddaughter. But Desiree put her hands on her cheeks with delight. "She goes to heaven!" she cried happily. "That is why Daddy sent me this book. Because the mermaid goes to heaven just like him!"

In mid-February, the MacKinnons received a letter

from Rhonda: "On January 19, my little girl's dream came true when your parcel arrived."

During the next few weeks, the MacKinnons and the Gills often telephoned each other. Then, in March, Rhonda, Trish and Desiree flew to Prince Edward Island to meet the MacKinnons. As the two families walked through the forest on snowshoes to see the spot beside the lake where Wade had found the balloon, Rhonda and Desiree fell silent. It seemed as though Ken was there with them.

Today whenever Desiree wants to talk about her dad, she still calls the MacKinnons. A few minutes on the telephone soothes her as nothing else can.

"People tell me, 'What a coincidence that your mermaid balloon landed so far away at a place called Mermaid Lake,'" says Rhonda. "But we know Ken picked the MacKinnons as a way to send his love to Desiree. She understands now that her father is with her always."

Margo Pfeiff

Family Circus

". . . And if you find a purple balloon up there, it's mine."

Reprinted with permission from Bil Keane.

A Perfect Mistake

Grandpa Nybakken loved life—especially when he could play a trick on somebody. At those times, his large Norwegian frame shook with laughter while he feigned innocent surprise, exclaiming, "Oh, forevermore!" But on a cold Saturday in downtown Chicago, Grandpa felt that God played a trick on him, and Grandpa wasn't laughing.

Mother's father worked as a carpenter. On this particular day, he was building some crates for the clothes his church was sending to an orphanage in China. On his way home, he reached into his shirt pocket to find his glasses, but they were gone. He remembered putting them there that morning, so he drove back to the church. His search proved fruitless.

When he mentally replayed his earlier actions, he realized what happened. The glasses had slipped out of his pocket unnoticed and fallen into one of the crates, which he had nailed shut. His brand new glasses were heading for China!

The Great Depression was at its height, and Grandpa had six children. He had spent twenty dollars for those glasses that very morning.

"It's not fair," he told God as he drove home in frustration. "I've been very faithful in giving of my time and money to your work, and now this."

Several months later, the director of the orphanage was on furlough in the United States. He wanted to visit all the churches that supported him in China, so he came to speak one Sunday night at my grandfather's small church in Chicago. Grandpa and his family sat in their customary seats among the sparse congregation.

The missionary began by thanking the people for their faithfulness in supporting the orphanage.

"But most of all," he said, "I must thank you for the glasses you sent last year. You see, the Communists had just swept through the orphanage, destroying everything, including my glasses. I was desperate.

"Even if I had the money, there was simply no way of replacing those glasses. Along with not being able to see well, I experienced headaches every day, so my coworkers and I were much in prayer about this. Then your crates arrived. When my staff removed the covers, they found a pair of glasses lying on top."

The missionary paused long enough to let his words sink in. Then, still gripped with the wonder of it all, he continued: "Folks, when I tried on the glasses, it was as though they had been custom-made just for me! I want to thank you for being a part of that."

The people listened, happy for the miraculous glasses. But the missionary surely must have confused their church with another, they thought. There were no glasses on their list of items to be sent overseas.

But sitting quietly in the back, with tears streaming down his face, an ordinary carpenter realized the Master Carpenter had used him in an extraordinary way.

Cheryl Walterman Stewart

The Dime

One day I visited a businessman's office, and while we talked, I noticed that he constantly twirled a small paperweight with a dime in it. Curious, I asked him about it.

He said, "When I was in college, my roommate and I were down to our last dime. He was on a scholarship, while I had earned my tuition by working in the cotton field and a grocery store. We were the first two members of our families to ever attend college, and our parents were extremely proud of us. Each month they sent us a small allowance to buy food, but that month our checks hadn't arrived. It was a Sunday, the fifth of the month, and between us we had one dime left.

"We used the solitary dime to place a collect call to my home five hundred miles away. My mother answered. I could tell from her voice that something was wrong. She said that my father had been ill and out of work, so there was simply no way they could send any money that month. I asked if my roommate's check was in the mail. She said that she had talked with his mother. They also couldn't raise the extra money that month either. They were sorry, but it looked like we'd have to come home. They had put off telling us, hoping for some solution."

"Were you disappointed?" I asked.

"Devastated. We both were. We had one month remaining to finish the year, then we could work all summer to earn our expenses. My grades were excellent, so I had been guaranteed a scholarship for the next term."

"What did you do?"

"When I hung up the telephone, we heard a noise and dimes started pouring out of the pay phone. We were laughing and holding out our hands to catch the money. Students walking down the hall thought we were crazy. We discussed taking the money and using it. Nobody would know what happened. But then we realized we couldn't do that. It wouldn't be honest. You understand?"

"Yes, but it would have been tough to return it."

"Well, we tried. I called the operator back and told her what had happened." He smiled, remembering. "She said that the money belonged to the telephone company, so to replace it in the machine. We did, over and over again, but the machine wouldn't accept the dimes.

"I finally told the operator that the dimes kept falling back out. She said that she didn't know what else to do, but she'd talk to her supervisor. When she returned she said that we'd have to keep the money, because the company wasn't going to send a man all the way out to the school just to collect a few dollars."

He looked over at me and chuckled, but there was emotion in his voice. "We laughed all the way back to our dorm room. After counting the money, we had $7.20. We decided to use the money to buy food from a nearby grocery store and we went job hunting after class."

"Did you find a job?"

"Yes, we told the manager of the grocery store what had happened as we paid for our purchases with our dimes. He offered us both jobs beginning next day. Our money bought enough supplies to last until our first paycheck."

"You were both able to finish college?"

"Yes, we worked for that man until we graduated. My friend went on to eventually become a lawyer." He looked around him and said, "I graduated in business, then went on to start this company which today is a multi-million-dollar corporation. My own children have attended college, as have my roommate's, but we were the first."

"Is that one of your original dimes?"

He shook his head. "No, we had to use those, but when I got my first paycheck I saved a dime, which I carried all the way through college. I've kept it to remind me where I came from. When I count my blessings, I remember that once in my life, a single thin dime stood between me and the poverty my parents faced every day of their lives."

"Did you ever meet the telephone operator or tell her how much that money meant to you?"

"No, but when we graduated, my roommate and I wrote a letter to the local telephone company and asked if they wanted their money back.

"The president of the company wrote us a letter of congratulations and told us that he'd never felt the company's money was better spent."

"Do you think this was a fluke or meant to be?"

"I've thought about it often over the years. I wondered if the operator might have heard the fear in my voice; perhaps she prevented the machine from accepting the coins. Or maybe . . . it was an act of God."

"You'll never know for sure, will you?"

He shook his head, touching the paperweight as if he drew strength from it. "No, but I'll always remember that moment and that dime. I have repaid that debt many times over the years. I hope that I have helped someone else as much as a dime helped me."

Patricia S. Laye

The Miracle Picture

The desire of a man is his kindness.

Proverbs 19:22

May 11, 1995 was day six of our first family trip in many years to Orlando. It was also my forty-fifth birthday, though I had decided years before that I was not celebrating birthdays after the age of thirty-nine. But my husband Greg, fifteen-year-old daughter Kristina ("Nina"), and twelve-year-old son Dan thought otherwise. I was to choose where I wanted to go that day because, "It's your day, Mom." We'd been to Disney World, Epcot Center and Sea World; therefore, since neither Nina nor Dan had seen the ocean, Daytona Beach was my choice.

On the beach we hunted seashells and attempted to take some pictures. At one point Nina handed Dan the camera, one of those cardboard use-one-time-only numbers, rested her head on my shoulder, put her arm around me, and said, "Take a picture of Mommy and me."

We then sat on the beach and harmonized (badly, on my part) to some tunes from *The Sound of Music* medley her school choir would be doing when she got back. Nina also told me that when she got home she wanted to restart the chapter of Students Against Drunk Drivers. I was proud of her initiative and involvement.

We finally began the journey back to our hotel. I slept in the car and as I drifted in and out of my twilight sleep, I heard Dan and Nina's voices from the back seat of the car, playfully teasing each other. Typical siblings, they had sparred a lot lately, but not this week. This week it was just the two of them, best buddies again. Dan was three years younger, yet a head taller than Nina, but he looked up to his "petite but powerful" older sister. She was like his second mother, always there for him.

In the back seat, they were playing a game they played as youngsters called, "I bet you can't make me laugh." In a matter of seconds Dan would make the goofy face that would send Nina into gales of laughter.

It soon became quiet. I turned around and saw that Dan was laying down trying to sleep. He looked up at Nina. She affectionately looked down at Dan, looked at me, and smiled her most dazzling smile. Nothing was said, but our eyes met. I smiled back at her and turned back to continue my nap. What happened from that point on is still a blur.

I vaguely remember the sound of crushing metal and breaking glass, as a blue Dodge crossed the center median and smashed into us; our car twirling around as if in a cyclone, and then silence. I looked at my husband next to me, saw a trickle of blood run down his face, and watched as his eyes rolled back into his head. I then looked over my shoulder and saw Nina lying there. In the horrific aftermath, I don't even remember getting out of the car. But I do remember laying my head on Nina's chest and eventually comprehending the horrible truth: My precious, vivacious, incredibly beautiful fifteen-year-old daughter with the heart of gold was dead.

I remember hearing screaming (which turned out to be my own) and seeing Dan sitting on the side of the road, the shock of what had just happened etched on his face. I clutched at his clothing and sobbed, "Nina is dead" to which Dan whispered back, "I know, Mom." We were taken to the hospital by ambulance. Greg had suffered a skull fracture and Dan a fractured right arm. Worst of all, we were sent on our way to face life without our Nina.

My mind raced during the agonizing flight back to Minnesota. I suddenly remembered the camera which I had thrown into the trunk of the car before we headed back from Daytona Beach. I became obsessed with wanting that camera, remembering that the last picture taken that day was the one Dan snapped of Nina and me. Everyone I asked said the trunk had been demolished and that it would have been obliterated in the crash. I remember crying, "I want that picture." I repeated that over and over again, out loud, while my friends and family helplessly shook their heads, knowing that my request was impossible.

Three weeks later, we received a phone call from Corporal Jennings, the Florida state trooper who was investigating the accident. He called to tell us what we had suspected, that the driver responsible for the accident was drunk. Before my husband hung up, he asked if there was any possibility that the camera had been found. The trooper said that debris was scattered for over a mile and a half of the freeway, and it would take nothing short of a miracle for that camera to have survived the crash. He assured Greg that he would check it out anyway and get back to us. I pessimistically anticipated that the state trooper, thinking it was hopeless, had no intention of searching for the impossible.

About a week later, an envelope with a Florida postmark arrived in the mail. My hands shook as I opened it.

Inside was a note that said, "I walked that entire stretch of freeway. When I was about to give up, I glanced down into a drainage ditch and saw the camera, covered in water, with a tractor tire mark across it! I brought the flattened camera to the film developing store, and they did their best to salvage what they could." It was signed Corporal Gordon Jennings.

I cautiously opened the envelope, and there was a picture of Nina with her Mickey Mouse hat and trademark smile. I carefully thumbed through the pictures hoping against hope that the picture of the two of us had survived. Nearing the last picture, I held my breath and closed my eyes. When I got the courage to open them, incredibly there it was! But the most amazing thing of all was the picture had yellow, red and blue watermarks that streaked toward our figures on the beach, but then remarkably separated and left unblemished the last portrait of mother and daughter together!

Thank God for angels on Earth like Corporal Jennings. I truly believe that somehow my lovely daughter in heaven, with the radiant grin that I am sure is lighting up the skies, heard her mother's pleas for that amazing picture. With some help from God Almighty, Nina sent me one last priceless gift and the reminder that she is still very much with us.

Cathy L. Seehuetter

Led by God

The car heater was running full blast, but it was still freezing cold inside the blue Oldsmobile as Monica steered onto the main road. It was a few minutes before midnight, December 31. All of the businesses were closed and every house was pitch dark. *Everyone is out celebrating,* Monica thought as yet another spasm of pain gripped her like a vise.

Across the nation millions of people were eagerly awaiting the arrival of a brand-new year. Monica, alone and terrified, had a different kind of arrival to contend with.

Twenty minutes before Monica had been warm and cozy, gabbing with friends and having a wonderful time. She and her friend Dawn were swapping pregnancy stories and trying to guess which of their babies would be the first to arrive. Both women were due in early February.

Monica, who was separated from her fiancé, was looking forward to the arrival of her second child. So was her seven-year-old daughter, Amanda. Amanda was with her grandparents now, on their way to the family's beach cottage. Monica had stopped off to spend a few minutes with friends before making the forty-five-minute drive to join them.

It was just past eleven and Monica was buttoning her coat to leave when suddenly she felt a tiny cramp in her abdomen. "Are you okay?" her friends asked, concerned.

"It was probably just a false labor pain," Monica said, refusing their offer to rush her to the hospital. "I'm not due for another five weeks yet."

But starting her car, Monica felt a second cramp, stronger than the first. *Amanda was early. Maybe this baby will be too,* she thought, and headed to her folks' house to find her sister, Terry.

A few blocks from home Monica cried out in alarm as her water broke. *Stay calm,* she told herself. *The pains are still far apart. There's plenty of time before the baby comes.*

But the house was dark. *Terry must have gone out with her boyfriend,* Monica guessed. She briefly considered running inside and calling 911, but the hospital was only twelve miles away. *I can make it easily,* she thought.

It wasn't long before Monica deeply regretted her decision to drive on. "I'm in labor!" she cried out as an intense contraction took hold and refused to let go. "I need help! I can't have this baby alone!"

Monica sped to the nearest pay phone. But the phone had been removed, and every business in sight was closed for the holiday. It was twelve o'clock midnight, and there wasn't another car on the road anywhere.

Frantic, Monica turned off the main road and steered down residential streets searching for even one house with its lights burning. *Please, God, let someone be home,* she prayed, turning into a cul-de-sac where she discovered several houses with lights and cars.

Monica pulled in front of one house, threw open the car door and struggled unsteadily to her feet. But at the last second something told her to head the other way, across the street to a different house.

The front lawn seemed as wide as a football field as

Monica stumbled to the porch. "Please, someone call an ambulance!" she cried out, pressing the bell with one hand while banging on the door with the other. "I'm having a baby—right now!"

Dianne Minter, thirty-five, was awakened from a sound sleep by the sudden commotion at her mom's front door. Dianne, her husband Clyde, and their three kids had traveled all the way from Lynchburg, Virginia, through falling snow to spend New Year's Day with her parents, George and Joyce Ware. Dianne was exhausted, but the instant her mom called her name she was on her feet and racing to the stairs, still dressed in a pair of red pajamas.

"Oh my!" Dianne exclaimed when she saw the very pregnant woman all but collapsed in her dad's arms. "Lay her down so I can examine her," she instructed.

"I need an ambulance!" Monica sobbed. "I can feel my baby coming!"

"I've already called 911," Dianne's mom calmly spoke. "You certainly picked the right house to come to. My daughter is a labor and delivery nurse."

Dianne's dad gathered up sheets and blankets while her brother-in-law, Dale, a former emergency medical technician, held Monica's hand and monitored her pulse.

"I can see something coming," Dianne said after yet another contraction, only she wasn't sure it was the baby's head. When Monica visited her obstetrician just two days ago the baby had been lying sideways in her womb. Five weeks was plenty of time for the baby to shift into the proper position, the doctor had assured Monica. *But that was only two days ago,* Dianne silently worried. For Dianne knew all too well that if the baby was still transverse there was a good chance Monica might deliver an arm or a foot first, or the cord could get caught and without an emergency C-section Monica's pre-term infant might even die.

"Please don't let anything bad happen to my baby!" Monica begged, sensing something was wrong.

"Try not to push," Dianne coaxed her, hoping to delay the baby's birth until Monica could be taken to the hospital.

When the paramedics arrived, Dianne helped load Monica onto the stretcher, but it was too late to move her. "The baby's crowning!" Dianne exclaimed, greatly relieved because finally she could see the baby's head.

A few more contractions and the baby was out. A few seconds later she heard the sweetest sound in the world—her baby's first cries.

Dianne bundled the baby snugly and handed him to his mom. "Hold him close and keep him as warm as you can," she gently instructed.

"Thank you," Monica sobbed as she was carried away on the stretcher.

At the hospital the admitting nurse was about to have Monica taken to a delivery room when she heard the tiny cries. Instead she rushed the baby to a warming bed in the neonatal intensive care unit, where doctors soon pronounced baby Jacob healthy and fit as a fiddle.

The next morning Monica was cuddling her four-pound, thirteen-ounce newborn son in her arms when Dianne and her family arrived with a gift-wrapped baby outfit and rattle. Monica burst into tears the moment she spotted Dianne in the doorway.

"Thank you," she sobbed. "I know God must have led me to your house last night."

"It certainly was a New Year's Eve I'll never forget," Dianne replied.

Bill Holton
Excerpted from Woman's World *magazine*

Angel in a Different Pew

On Sunday mornings in church, Mary Ryerson loves the moment when the choir begins to sing and her young children settle into the pew by her side. *I'm so blessed,* she thinks.

But once in a while, her eyes search out an empty pew in the back—as if to look for the stranger who once sat there, a stranger who saved her family from unthinkable grief. . . .

Mary and her husband Loren were overjoyed when she gave birth to little Michael in 1991. After two miscarriages, the couple finally had a little brother for their nine-year-old son Loren.

"He's perfect!" Mary smiled as she held him for the first time.

"Yep—even if he did get the Ryerson head," her husband said as they fit the blue stocking cap nurses gave them over Michael's head—which filled the cap completely.

"Just like you and Loren," Mary grinned. She'd always had trouble finding hats big enough for her husband.

Still, as Michael grew those first few weeks, his longish head nagged at her.

"He's doing great," her pediatrician said. Still, Mary noticed he spent extra time checking for the soft spot on Michael's head at his three-month checkup. "His head is big—I'd like you to take him in for X-rays to make sure it's developing normally," he frowned.

Her heart pounding, Mary raced to the hospital. But hours later, the radiologist told her, "Everything's fine."

"Thank God!" Mary cried, relief washing over her.

Her worries were forgotten a few weeks later as she drove to church, with four-month-old Michael gurgling in his car seat as big brother Loren dangled plastic keys to keep him amused.

When they entered the church, Mary headed for the spot she always sat in: on the right side in the second pew from the front. But she found herself pausing halfway, then noticing a seat in the back on the left-hand side.

"Why don't we sit back there?" she asked.

Loren looked surprised. It was the first time in years they'd sat anywhere other than their usual seats. But he just shrugged and followed his mom to the back.

As she settled the boys into the pew, Mary sensed someone staring at her. Looking up, she saw a man nearby looking intently at her. The congregation was small, but Mary had never seen him before. *I wonder who he is?* she thought, and smiled at him.

Then, at the "handshake of peace," when parishioners stand to shake hands with one another, the man reached right over others to shake her hand. "Peace be with you," he said softly, holding on to her hand longer than was normal. *He wants to say something,* Mary realized. But the man hesitated, then let go and sat back down.

When the service was over, Mary glanced at her watch— she was late for a youth league soccer meeting. She was hurrying out with the children when she heard a voice.

"Excuse me," a man called. "May I speak with you?"

Turning, Mary saw the man who'd been looking at her.

"I don't want to intrude," he began, reaching out and gently touching Michael's head. Usually Michael was fussy with strangers, but with this man, he just cooed.

"Have you taken your baby to a doctor?" the man asked quietly.

"Yes," Mary replied. "He's fine."

"No, he's not," the man said gently. "He has sagital cranial synostosis."

"What?" Mary gasped.

"It's a condition where the plates in the head prematurely fuse together," the man explained. "I suggest you consult a pediatric neurosurgeon immediately."

"But—but—," Mary stammered. "How do you know?"

"I'm a pediatric neurosurgeon visiting from Ohio," the man replied. "Your son needs help."

Mary's stomach fell. "The doctor will explain everything," the man was saying. "But you have to get there soon."

By now, churchgoers were streaming out the door and all around them. "Thank you," Mary managed to stammer before the man disappeared into the crowd.

Alarmed, she called her pediatrician, who gave her the name of a doctor in Denver. "But it's almost impossible to get an appointment with him—you may have to wait," the pediatrician warned.

But we can't! Mary thought, alarmed.

And incredibly, she didn't have to. "We just had a cancellation the call before you," the doctor's office told her when she phoned.

In Denver, a pediatric neurosurgeon confirmed the stranger's diagnosis. The four plates in Michael's head had already fused together. "There's no place for his brain to grow," the surgeon explained. Without surgery, Michael would become permanently brain-damaged.

"Luckily, he's young so his skull is still soft enough to operate on," the surgeon added. "You brought him in just in time."

Mary felt tingles go down her spine as she recalled the man in church. *He knew!* she realized, amazed. *Oh, how I wish I had asked him his name!*

A few weeks later, Mary and Loren watched as little Michael was prepped for surgery. A team of doctors would remove his skull, cut it into pieces and reassemble it with wires, giving his brain room to grow. It was a terrifying prospect—but it was her baby's only hope.

In the waiting room, the hours dragged on endlessly; Mary couldn't concentrate on the magazines; exhausted, she couldn't sleep. At last, eight and a half hours later: "It went beautifully!" the surgeon announced. "Michael's going to be just fine."

"Oh, thank you!" Mary gasped through tears of joy.

Four days later, Michael was released. Though he had to wear a helmet for a year to protect his head, he healed completely. And as he grew—chasing butterflies in the garden, pleading for a Popsicle at the sound of the ice cream truck—Mary could only watch in wonder. *He is perfect,* she thought.

Today, when Mary watches six-year-old Michael play street hockey or ride his bike with the neighborhood kids, she thinks about that fateful day in church when a stranger cared enough to stop.

"Who knows what Michael's life would be like if we had sat in our usual seats?" she smiles. "We might never have shaken hands with our guardian angel."

Eva Unga
Excerpted from Woman's World *magazine*

Alleluia in the Operating Room

In quietness and in confidence shall be your strength.

Isaiah 30:15

Dateline—Medunsa Hospital, South Africa, December 30–31, 1997—After nineteen hours of surgery, Dr. Ben Carson and his medical team were exhausted. They were in the middle of separating two Zambian twins, Joseph and Luka Banda, who were born joined at the head. Ben describes what happened next.

Collapsing into the chairs around the conference room table, I called in all the medical personnel who weren't needed in the operating room to discuss the status of the operation. Everyone looked defeated.

"Perhaps we should consider stopping the operation at this point," I said. I wondered aloud if we should simply close up the wounds and give the boys and our medical team a chance to regain the strength to go on.

But everyone agreed that we should go on. They honestly didn't think they could keep the boys alive and healthy in their current state of partial separation. As dangerous as it looked to proceed at this point, the feeling was that to do anything else would be, in effect, a death sentence.

We had no choice but to press on. *Whatever will happen will happen.* As we walked back down the hall to the operating room, however, I began praying desperately that God would take over and simply use me to accomplish what only He could do.

I recalled one of the Bible verses I had read just the night before. Jesus made a rather remarkable promise to his followers:

"I tell you the truth, anyone who has faith in me will do what I have been doing. He will do even greater things than these, because I am going to the Father. And I will do whatever you ask in my name, so that the Son may bring glory to the Father." (John 14:12–13)

When we reentered the OR and stood again over those little boys, I prayed in Jesus' name that God would simply take over the operation. Since the scriptures don't tell about Jesus ever separating Siamese twins, I thought this probably qualified as one of those "greater than these" he promised we could do.

I began work on the engorged vascular structure that still stared us in the face. At home I would have had my operating microscope, an array of micro-instruments to work with, and a special operating chair with adjustable platforms to support and brace my arms and hands. Here I had only a scalpel with which I began painstakingly cutting between the transparently thin walls of the blood vessels before ever so gingerly pulling them apart.

Despite the exhaustion that had almost paralyzed me, I now sensed a remarkable steadiness in my hands. I felt calm, with an almost detached awareness—as if I were merely watching my hands move and someone else had actually taken over the surgery.

I can't count the number of times during my surgical career when I've successfully completed some particularly difficult surgery, only to have a family member in the waiting room inform me that they, and everyone they knew, had been praying for me. I could honestly tell them that I had genuinely felt that support. I have repeatedly experienced the effects of prayer.

But I have never experienced anything quite like what happened in the Medunsa operating room that day. One after another, more than a hundred interconnected veins were isolated, separated, clipped off or reconnected. When I separated the very last vein connecting Joseph and Luka, the stereo system at that very moment began playing "Hallelujah Chorus" from Handel's *Messiah*. I suspect every single person in that OR felt goosebumps and knew that something remarkable had taken place. And it was not our doing.

Twenty-five hours of surgery had passed. But there was no time to celebrate yet. We immediately divided into two teams—one for each twin.

We still had a lot of work to do. But all of the neurosurgeons, despite our growing fatigue, were absolutely jubilant. Neither of the brains exhibited any serious swelling and there had been remarkably little blood loss. We had used less than four units of blood for the entire operation.

Even more encouraging was the fact that we could see no remaining engorgement of any of the blood vessels. Circulation in both brains had been successfully restored. There seemed to be every reason to believe Joseph and Luka had not only survived the surgery, but that both boys might actually wake up to live completely normal lives.

That was almost too exciting to think about as we closed the open wounds and patched the protective covering of the dura with bovine pericardium (the heart lining of a cow). Finally, our neurosurgical team retreated once more to the conference room where, even before the plastic surgeons closed the scalps, we fell fast asleep sitting in our chairs.

Once the plastic surgeons finished their work, we returned to the OR and were absolutely flabbergasted to find one of the twins with his eyes open and gripping his endotracheal tube with both hands—trying to pull it out. By the time the boys reached the intensive care unit, the other twin was doing the exact same thing. After twenty-eight hours of surgery this was astounding to me. But I suspected it was no surprise to the Great Physician who actually headed our team.

Ben Carson with Gregg Lewis

[EDITORS' NOTE: *The surgery's success brought commendations from around the world. Both boys were crawling a few weeks later and made a full recovery thanks to Ben's gifted hands and the prayers of many.*]

Ethel's Irish Angel

Ethel was driving home from her job at a department store late one night, thinking how nice it would be to rest her feet, when the traffic light turned green and she eased into the intersection. She didn't notice the car streaking toward her from the side, careening through the red light. But behind her, on his way to a prayer meeting, the thirty-year-old seminary student Brendan did. *No!* he winced as the car smashed into the passenger side of the Dodge in front of him.

The terrifying impact flung Ethel across the seat. Her head smashed into the window and, in a flash, her world went black.

Dear Lord! Brendan gasped as he ran toward the mangled car, which had been pushed across the road by the force of the crash.

Seconds later, a couple emerged unscathed from the other car, which was now stopped in the middle of the road. "I'll call for help!" someone screamed, as Brendan hurried to the crumpled Dodge.

Just then, Ethel opened her eyes. *Oh, no!* she panicked. She was pinned to the car floor, her right foot stuck under the brake, her left leg beneath the seat. Waves of pain coursed through her neck. She wanted to scream, but no words came as her mind clouded in pain.

Then, through the fog, Ethel heard a man's voice say, "I'm on my way!"

The voice sounded calm and warm—exactly like her beloved husband George, who'd been gone twenty years. *Am I dying?* she wondered.

Brendan struggled with the jammed driver's door then ran to the passenger door and pulled it open. Leaning into the car, he saw Ethel pinned on the floor, and he froze in fear. *I've got to get her out,* he thought. But suddenly, a paramedic friend's advice echoed in his head: *Never move an injured person.* The words came so forcefully that Brendan's arms flew back to his side. "I'm right beside you, don't be afraid," he said.

With no light in the car and unable to turn her head, Ethel couldn't make out the man's face, but she did hear something familiar—an Irish brogue! *Am I imagining it?* she wondered hazily.

But the pain exploding inside her neck was all too real. "My neck hurts," she groaned. "I have to move."

"No!" Brendan said firmly. *What if her neck is broken?* he worried, sliding his hand under her head for support.

"Okay," Ethel sighed. But Brendan knew, by the slow rise and fall of her chest, that he was losing her. And he heard his friend's advice again: Never let an injured person lose consciousness. Closing his eyes, Brendan prayed, *Please, God, grant me the strength to help her.*

"What's your name?" he asked.

"Ethel," she breathed quietly.

He noticed it too, that unmistakable lilt. "Where were you born?" he asked.

"Belfast," Ethel managed. "In Ireland."

"I'm from the Old Sod myself!" Brendan replied, hoping to cheer her.

"Where?" she asked, comforted by his accent.

"Dublin," Brendan replied. *He's an angel sent to help me,* she thought as he asked more questions. But as minutes ticked by, her voice began to trail off.

I can't let her fade away! Brendan reminded himself. "Do you have a family?" he stammered.

"Yes," Ethel replied proudly, snapping back at the thought of them. "Four sons and a daughter. Two of my boys are policemen."

"How nice," Brendan smiled. "I'm here to study for the priesthood."

They were so deep in conversation that it startled Brendan when a police officer tapped him on the shoulder. "Her neck might be broken," he warned as the paramedics took over.

As they freed Ethel and light flooded her face, she saw Brendan for the first time. *Such kind eyes!* she noticed, as he squeezed her hand one final time.

At the hospital, doctors found that Ethel did have a broken neck. "It's a miracle," they told her. "If you'd moved even a tiny bit, you'd be paralyzed—or dead."

Ethel gasped. And when her sons Ian and Glenn arrived, she told them about the kind young man from Ireland who'd helped her. The brothers exchanged glances. *A rescuer?* they wondered. No one was mentioned on the police report.

The next day, Brendan couldn't get Ethel off his mind, and he finally headed to the hospital to check on her. When he stepped into her room, Ethel's eyes grew wide. "That's him!" she cried. "That's my Irish angel!"

"So, *you're* the one," Ian cried, leaping up to shake his hand.

"They wouldn't believe me when I told them about you," Ethel explained sheepishly.

"Well, I didn't do all that much," Brendan said modestly.

"You saved our mom's life!" Glenn insisted. And when he told Brendan what doctors had said, the young man sank into a chair. *Was this my mission, Lord?* he wondered. *Did you send me to Ethel?*

As Ethel recuperated, Brendan visited every few days, and they had plenty of time to share more tales of Ireland.

They also know that what Brendan did was ordinary— the extraordinary was all God's doing.

Steve Baal
Excerpted from Woman's World *magazine*

A Miracle of Love

Miracles happen in the most unlikely places. When the shepherds heard the angels proclaim, "Alleluia, hail the King," the star did not lead them to a palace. The shepherds found their prince of peace in a stable, lying in a manger.

My Christmas miracle happened in an even stranger place—a funeral home. But it wasn't strange to me. My husband, a funeral director like his father, built a branch office in the suburbs. In the apartment above it, between viewings and funerals, we raised two daughters and lived normal lives.

Through the years, I became fascinated by the endless accounts I heard of grieving people who received messages from God, assuring them their deceased loved ones were all right and still with them. Different as one circumstance was from another, a similarity in the messages gave them credibility.

At his wife's viewing, one man said, "I couldn't sleep and got up in the middle of the night feeling lonely and lost. I walked into the kitchen to brew a pot of coffee and wait for morning. But there, on the kitchen window sill, I spotted an enormous blossom on my wife's favorite cactus plant. Staring at it, a great peace filled me, and I felt as if I had witnessed a miracle. I understood that my wife was all right—and I wasn't alone."

One young woman said, "Yesterday afternoon, I wandered out to Dad's vegetable garden in the backyard. He'd been too sick to plant anything this year, but there, among the crabgrass and chickweed, I discovered one magnificent watermelon. Dad always said watermelon took up too much room, but he continued to grow them, because they were my favorite. When I rushed inside to tell my father about it, he was dead. I knew then the watermelon was a message from Dad—he'd probably had an angel deliver it—because there it was, all ripe and ready to pick. While I can't see my father, I know he's alive, and we'll be together again."

Over time, I heard hundreds of similar stories and when my mother died, a few days before Christmas, I desperately wanted one of those miracles for myself.

All her life, Mother grew magnificent roses and made a ritual of carrying in and savoring the last rose of the season. "If roses could last through Christmas, winter wouldn't seem so long," she said. In New Jersey, roses occasionally survived until Thanksgiving. Never had one made it to Christmas.

On December 22, I noticed that a scattering of leaves still clung to a rose bush nestled under the stairs to our apartment on the second floor. And there, at the top, like an angel on a Christmas tree, one bud waited to blossom. It was a tiny, fragile thing—like Mother at the end—but I knew that rose, lasting until Christmas, would be my miracle. When it blossomed, I would carry it inside and feel that wonderful sense of peace other people talked about.

For years, I had combed and styled women's hair for

viewings, and I was anxious to do this one final thing for Mother. As I finished Mother's hair, the office doorbell rang. The Snyder family had arrived for their appointment with my husband a half-hour early. Mr. Snyder and his daughter looked devastated, and something in the younger woman's eyes made me choke off the words, "You're early, and my husband isn't here. Why don't you come back in half an hour?"

As they stepped inside, I noticed that Mr. Snyder limped, and leaned so heavily on his cane that I wondered if it would support him.

"I don't want to see her," Mr. Snyder grumbled, as he dropped onto a chair. "She looked horrible. I don't want anyone to see her."

"Please, Dad," the daughter cried. "I don't think I can live with myself for not getting here in time unless I see Mother."

"No," Mr. Snyder snapped. "She wouldn't want you to see her like that. Her hair was all matted and she looked horrible. There will be no viewing and no one will see her."

The daughter's eyes pleaded with me. It was our policy to stay out of such matters, but as I turned away, something in that woman's eyes stopped me.

"Mr. Snyder," I said, "we do women's hair whether there is a viewing or not. Why don't you think about this? If your daughter would like to see her mother, come in fifteen minutes before the funeral."

My husband arrived then, and when Mr. Snyder lumbered into his office with his daughter, I stepped outside for another look at that rose bud. It would bloom tomorrow—the day of Mother's funeral—and I would feel the wonderful sense of peace others had spoken of when they received their message.

That evening, when my daughters arrived with their

families, they agreed. The delicate blossom that would be the Christmas rose represented the love and care Mother had given us, and the joyous moments we shared together. The thorns represented the difficult times, when her strength inspired us and bound us close together.

During the night, a cold front moved in. When we returned from the cemetery, the rose bud had withered from frostbite and died on the vine. "But it was there," my daughters assured me. "We all saw it."

To ease their grief, I agreed. Inside, I felt abandoned.

The next morning, December 24, I wondered how I would cope with Christmas. It was also the day of Mrs. Snyder's funeral. While I decided not to attend, I told my husband how much Mr. Snyder's daughter wanted to see her mother, and asked him to leave the casket open.

Breakfast was such a somber affair that I called my daughters into the kitchen and said, "There are children to think about. Mother wouldn't want to spoil their Christmas. She would want us to celebrate the way she taught us—with reverence and joy. So let's start with the Christmas tree." Silently, I asked myself how I would muddle through.

On Christmas Eve, while my daughters and I prepared the traditional dinner, a car pulled into the parking lot. From the kitchen window, I saw Mr. Snyder struggle from the front seat with his cane, and he spoke to his daughter in a voice that boomed up to the second floor.

"No!" he growled. "I can make it up those stairs, and I want to tell Mrs. Plum, myself."

Now, you've done it, I thought. *Will you ever learn to stay out of other people's affairs and let them make their own decisions? If Mr. Snyder wants to give you a tongue lashing, you deserve it.*

I opened the door, expecting the worst. Mr. Snyder huffed and puffed after his struggle with the steps, and he gasped as he said, "I want to thank you for what you did for my wife. She looked beautiful. I'm so grateful to have that last picture of her in my mind. I will carry it with me for the rest of my life. My daughter and I want to express our gratitude by sharing something of hers with you."

I knew by the velvet box in his daughter's hand that it contained a piece of her jewelry that she should keep for herself. "Thank you," I said. "But I don't accept gifts. . . ."

"Please," the daughter cut in. "We want you to have it. It's nothing of great value, but it meant a lot to Mother."

As I accepted the box, the daughter's hand touched mine. For a moment, our fingers clung as if we were sharing an emotion so powerful it paralyzed us. Our eyes met, and though no words were spoken, I knew an angel had touched me, and a miracle was about to happen.

As I lifted the lid and saw the pin, my heart swelled and tears of joy stung my eyes. On a bed of velvet lay a silver Christmas rose. The legend printed inside the lid read, "On a cold Bethlehem night, a little shepherd girl wept because she had no gift for the newborn babe. The Magi had brought rich gifts, but she had none. Suddenly, a rose appeared where her tears had fallen. A gift from an angel . . . a miracle of love."

As Mr. Snyder struggled down the stairs with his daughter, I clutched that box to my chest and cried, "It's here! My miracle."

As my family rushed to my side, the grief that shadowed our Christmas Eve celebration turned to joy.

While my husband clipped the silver Christmas rose to the tallest spike, God's message melded with angels, shepherds and Christmas itself. The first Christmas brought a gift of love for everyone, the old, the young, the great and the small. Mother's rose represented the miracle of it. Love is a gift that never dies; it lives forever.

Ellen Ingersoll Plum

The Miraculous Staircase

More things are wrought by prayer than this world dreams of.

Lord Alfred Tennyson

On that cool December morning in 1878, sunlight lay like an amber rug across the dusty streets and adobe houses of Santa Fe, New Mexico. It glinted on the bright, tile roof of the almost-complete Chapel of Our Lady of Light and on the nearby windows of the convent school run by the Sisters of Loretto. Inside the convent, the Mother Superior looked up from her packing as a tap came on her door.

"It's another carpenter, Reverend Mother," said Sister Francis Louise, her round face apologetic. "I told him that you're leaving right away and that you haven't any time to see him, but he says. . . ."

"I know what he says," Mother Magdalene said, going on resolutely with her packing. "He says that he has heard about our problem with the new chapel. That he's the best carpenter in all of New Mexico. That he can build us a staircase to the choir loft despite the fact that the brilliant architect in Paris who drew the plans failed to leave any space for one. And despite the fact that five master carpenters have already tried and failed. You're quite right, Sister; I don't have time to listen to that story again."

"But he seems like such a nice man," said Sister Francis Louise wistfully, "and he's out there with his burro, and. . . ."

"I'm sure," said Mother Magdalene with a smile, "that he's a charming man, and that his donkey is a charming donkey. But there's sickness down at the Santo Domingo pueblo, and it may be cholera. Sister Mary Helen and I are the only ones here who've had cholera, so we have to go. And you have to stay and run the school. And that's that!" Then she called, "Manuela!"

A young Native American girl of twelve or thirteen, black-haired and smiling, came in quietly on moccasined feet. She was a mute. She could hear and understand, but the sisters had been unable to teach her to speak. The Mother Superior spoke to her gently: "Take my things down to the wagon, child. I'll be right there." And to Sister Francis Louise: "You'd better tell your carpenter friend to come back in two or three weeks after I return. I'll see him then."

"Two or three weeks! Surely you'll be home for Christmas?"

"If it's the Lord's will, Sister. I hope so."

In the street, beyond the waiting wagon, Mother Magdalene could see the carpenter, a bearded man, strongly built and tall, with dark eyes and a smiling, windburned face. Beside him and laden with tools and scraps of lumber, a small gray burro stood patiently. Manuela was stroking its nose, glancing shyly at its owner. "You'd better explain," the Mother Superior said to Sister Francis Louise, "that the child can hear him, but she can't speak."

Good-byes were quick—the best kind when you leave a place you love. Southwest, then, along the dusty trail, the mountains purple with shadow, the Rio Grande a ribbon of green far off to the right, the two nuns traveled. The pace was slow, but Mother Magdalene and Sister Mary Helen amused themselves by singing songs and telling Christmas stories as the sun arched up and down the sky. Their leathery driver listened and nodded.

Two days of this brought them to Santo Domingo Pueblo, where the sickness was not cholera after all, but measles, almost deadly in a Native American village. And so they stayed, helping the exhausted Father Sebastian, visiting the dark adobe hovels where feverish children tossed and fierce Indian dogs showed their teeth.

At night they were bone-weary, but sometimes Mother Magdalene found time to talk to Father Sebastian about her plans for the dedication of the new chapel. It was to be in April; the archbishop himself would be there. And it might have been dedicated sooner, were it not for this incredible business of a choir loft with no means of access—unless it was a ladder.

"I told the bishop," said Mother Magdalene, "that it would be a mistake to have the plans drawn in Paris. If something went wrong, what could we do? But he wanted our chapel in Santa Fe patterned after the Saint Chapelle in Paris, and who am I to argue with Bishop Lamy? So the talented Monsieur Mouly designed a beautiful choir loft high up under the rose window, and no way to get to it."

"Perhaps," sighed Father Sebastian, "he had in mind a heavenly choir. The kind with wings."

"It's not funny," said Mother Magdalene a bit sharply. "I've prayed and prayed and prayed, but apparently there's no solution at all. There just isn't room on the chapel floor for the supports such a staircase needs. It's impossible."

The days passed, and with each passing day Christmas drew closer. Twice, horsemen on their way from Santa Fe to Albuquerque brought letters from Sister Francis Louise. All was well at the convent, but Mother Magdalene frowned over certain paragraphs. "The children are getting ready for Christmas," Sister Francis Louise wrote in her first letter. "Our little Manuela and the carpenter have become great friends. It's amazing how much he seems to know about us all. . . ."

And what, thought Mother Magdalene, *is that carpenter still doing there?*

The second letter also mentioned the carpenter. "Early every morning he comes with another load of lumber, and every night he goes away. When we ask him by what authority he does these things, he smiles and says nothing. We have tried to pay him for his work, but he will accept no pay. . . ."

Work? What work? Mother Magdalene wrinkled up her nose in exasperation. Had that soft-hearted Sister Francis Louise given that man permission to putter around in the new chapel? With a firm and disapproving hand, the Mother Superior wrote a note ordering an end to all such unauthorized activities. She gave it to a Native American pottery-maker on his way to Santa Fe.

But that night the first snow fell, so thick and heavy that the pottery-maker turned back. The next day at noon, the sun shone again on a world glittering with diamonds. But Mother Magdalene knew that another snowfall might make it impossible for her to be home for Christmas. By now the sickness at Santo Domingo was subsiding. And so that afternoon they began the long ride back.

The snow did come again, making their slow progress even slower. It was late Christmas Eve, close to midnight, when the tired horses plodded up to the convent door.

But lamps still burned. Manuela flew down the steps, Sister Francis Louise close behind her. Chilled and weary though she was, Mother Magdalene sensed instantly an excitement, an electricity in the air that she could not understand.

Nor did she understand it when they led her, still in her heavy wraps, down the corridor, into the new, as-yet-unused chapel where a few candles burned. "Look, Reverend Mother," breathed Sister Francis Louise. "Look!"

Like a curl of smoke the staircase rose before them, as insubstantial as a dream. Its top rested against the choir loft. Nothing else supported it; it seemed to float on air. There were no banisters. It made two complete spirals, the polished wood gleaming softly in candlelight. "Thirty-three steps," whispered Sister Francis Louise. "One for each year in the life of Our Lord."

Mother Magdalene moved forward like a woman in a trance. She put her foot on the first step, then the second, then the third. There was not a tremor. She looked down, bewildered, at Manuela's ecstatic, upturned face. "But it's impossible! There wasn't time!" she mumbled.

"He finished yesterday," the Sister said. "He didn't come today. No one has seen him anywhere in Santa Fe. He's gone."

"But *who* was he? *Don't you even know his name?*" the Mother Superior questioned.

The sister shook her head, but now Manuela pushed forward, nodding emphatically. Her mouth opened and she took a deep, shuddering breath. Then she made a sound that was like a gasp in the stillness. The nuns stared at her, transfixed. She tried again. This time it was a syllable, followed by another, "Jo-se." She clutched the Mother Superior's arm and repeated the first word she had ever spoken, "Jose!"

Sister Francis Louise crossed herself. Mother Magdalene

felt her heart contract. Jose . . . the Spanish word for Joseph. Joseph the Carpenter. Joseph the Master Woodworker.

"Jose!" Manuela's dark eyes were full of tears. "Jose!"

Silence fell, then, in the shadowy chapel. No one moved. Far away across the snow-silvered town, Mother Magdalene heard a bell tolling midnight. She came down the stairs and took Manuela's hand. She felt uplifted by a great surge of wonder and gratitude and compassion and love. And she knew what it was. It was the spirit of Christmas, and it was upon them all.

You may see the inexplicable staircase itself in Santa Fe, New Mexico today. It stands just as it stood when the chapel was dedicated over a hundred years ago—except for the banister, which was added later. Tourists stare and marvel. Architects shake their heads and murmur, "Impossible. Impossible." No one knows the identity of the designer-builder. All the sisters know is that the problem existed, they prayed and a stranger came who solved it then left.

The thirty-three steps make two complete turns without central support. There are no nails in the staircase, only wooden pegs. The curved stringers are put together with exquisite precision; the wood is spliced in seven places on the inside and nine on the outside. The wood is said to be a hard-fir variety, nonexistent in New Mexico. School records show that no payment for the staircase was ever made.

Arthur Gordon
Submitted by Rochelle Pennington

3

ON PARENTS AND PARENTING

Family stories that are told and retold at family gatherings . . . are important to the sense of family . . . stories aren't icing; they're basic ingredients in any group that claims to be family.

Delores Curran

Help Mom, I Need You!

Whatever is the matter with me? I ponder, standing outside on my deck. It's a beautiful evening in early spring, and there's no reasonable explanation for why I've abruptly canceled my plans to go away for the weekend. As I've just explained with some embarrassment to my friends (who have now left for a retreat without me), I simply have a strong feeling that I'm needed at home.

I run through a mental checklist of what might be compelling me to stay. My family is in good health. My older daughter, Lisa, called earlier in the day to wish me a good trip. My younger daughter, Katy, is expecting, but the baby's not due for three weeks. Still, Katy keeps entering my thoughts.

Katy is twenty-two years old and about to be a mother herself, but I sometimes feel as though she's still my baby. Right now things aren't too good between us. A few weeks ago we exchanged angry words after a mix-up about a get-together we'd tried to arrange. "You never have time for me anymore," she said, and I resisted the impulse to say the same. Katy and I had always been close. But lately we just haven't been connecting.

The cool quietness of the night helps calm me. Before going inside I take one last look overhead, staring up at the panorama of stars glittering in the vast darkness. Suddenly, so clear they seem almost audible, words come to mind:

"In everything, by prayer and petition, with thanksgiving, present your requests to God. And the peace of God, which transcends all understanding, will guard your hearts and minds in Christ Jesus." (Philippians 4:6–7)

Why did I think of these words now? I'm still wondering even after I go inside. When the phone rings, I reach for the receiver and hear Katy's voice, tight with pain: "Mom, I think I've started labor.

It's ten o'clock when I get to the hospital. Katy is in labor, and she's already in the birthing room, which looks almost like a bedroom with its rocking chair and comfortable recliner. There, too, are Katy's husband, Mike; her big sister, Lisa; and Mike's parents. We're all allowed to stay with Katy throughout the baby's birth.

Katy's IV is started, and a blood pressure cuff is strapped on. The fetal heart monitor is inserted. A machine alongside the bed now sounds with every beat, and a rapid beep, beep, beep fills the room. As Katy's labor becomes more intense, Mike and I take turns as breathing coach. "Katy, focus on the far wall . . . breathe in . . . hold it . . . breathe out. . . ."

At two o'clock in the morning, nurses and technicians come and go, checking machines, monitoring Katy. We joke, trying to keep Katy distracted. We can see from the rise and fall of lines on a screen that the contractions are fiercer and more constant. Katy asks for something for the pain.

By three o'clock in the morning, the anesthetic finally works. While Katy catches brief snatches of rest, I watch the monitor that shows in numerals the beats per minute of the baby's heart—155. The rhythmic beeps lull us. A nurse comes to suggest we all go downstairs to get some coffee. "Nothing much is happening here," she says, smiling at Katy's quiet form.

Our sleepy group straggles toward the door. But as I pass Katy's bed, she says, "Mom, don't leave me."

"Honey, what's wrong?" I send the others on.

"The contractions seem to be different," she says. I squeeze her hand and tell her to rest. "I'll wake you if anything happens," I tease.

I watch the machines. The contractions are less intense but lasting much longer.

And there's another change. Up until now, the digital readout of the baby's heartbeat has remained steady, never varying more than ten beats with each reading: 150 . . . 145 . . . 140 . . . But now, after each contraction, the beeps are further and further apart . . . 125 . . . 120 . . . The baby's heartbeat is slowing . . . 95 . . . 90 . . . 80 . . .

Katy's eyes open wide. "Mom! Something's wrong!" 70 . . . 65 . . .

Two nurses rush into the room. I hold Katy's hand, hoping my grip doesn't indicate my panic.

. . . 40 . . . 30 . . .

The beeps stop. No numbers flash on the screen; it's completely blank.

One long shrill wail fills the room. Suddenly white uniforms are everywhere.

"What's happening?" Katy's voice is jagged with fear as a nurse pulls an oxygen mask from the wall and slips it over Katy's mouth and nose. "Breathe," the nurse says firmly. More people crowd the room.

Tense voices ricochet around us. "Is her doctor in the hospital?" "Who's on call?" "Better set up for C-section." And then I hear words I hope Katy does not. "Tell the doctor to get here fast," someone calls out. "We're losing the baby!"

"Mama, pray! Please pray!" Katy's words are muted but distinct behind the oxygen mask.

I'm frozen with terror; I try to do as Katy says, but it's hard with all these strangers rushing around me. "Katy, Honey, I am praying." I lean closer to reassure her.

"I mean out loud!" Her hands twist frantically in mine.

I'd laugh if I weren't so scared. Katy's been known to roll her eyes when I even talk about praying, much less bow my head to say grace in a restaurant. She's often told me in great embarrassment, "Puh-leese, Mom, don't pray in front of people."

But now she repeats the request. "Pray out loud," she begs. I know I've got to keep her calm. But how to pray, what words to use?

In everything, by prayer and petition, with thanksgiving . . .

"Thank you, God," I say, "for this baby you've created, this little one we are so anxiously awaiting. Thank you for the hospital and the nurses." My voice starts off weak and unsure, but as more reasons for thanksgiving come to mind, my voice becomes confident and strong.

The piercing alarm fills the room, fills our ears, tries to fill our hearts.

"Louder, Mama!"

Present your requests to God . . .

"God, we want this baby. But we also want what you want. Help us through this, God, please! Be in the hands and hearts of the good people working here." Katy nods as I pray over the wailing of the alarm.

And the peace of God, which transcends all understanding, will guard your hearts and minds in Christ Jesus.

With each word, I see that Katy is relaxing, that the tension and fear are leaving her body and leaving the baby's body, too. "Thank you, God," Katy murmurs.

The alarm stops. There's complete quiet. And then we all hear it . . .

... beep ... beep ... beep ...
... 30 ... 40 ... 45 ...
The baby's heart beats again.
... 70 ... 75 ... 80 ...
No one speaks. Everyone listens to the blessed sound of that tiny heartbeat until it is healthy.

A soft cheer goes up in the room. The doctor pats Katy's arm. "We'll keep an eye on you, but I think you're going to deliver this baby normally. And soon."

Our unsuspecting family appears, bewildered by the crowded room. When I follow the doctor into the hall and ask what happened, he shakes his head. He can't explain what caused the crisis. And he has no idea why it reversed itself. "There are some things we'll never have answers for," he says.

Soon baby Caitlin is born. But since she's been deprived of oxygen, her skin is dark blue-gray. All eyes watch as an oxygen mask is used again, this time on the baby. I hold my breath, then watch in wonder as a pink glow suffuses the tiny body. A cheer goes up in the room once more: The baby is healthy!

A few minutes later, a nurse hands a blanket-wrapped bundle to me. In the early morning light I look long and wonderingly at the exquisite, wide-awake face of my new granddaughter.

"Mom?" Katy stretches her hand toward me. "I'm so glad you were there. I still need you, you know."

"Oh, Katy," I say, "I still need to be needed."

Trusting some inner instinct, I'd been home for Katy's call. And as we trusted in the power of His promises in a time of crisis, God had been there for us.

Ah, me and Katy and Caitlin. Yes, as the years pass, there will be moments when we do not connect.

But then will come the times when we're completely connected in ways that pass all understanding.

L. Maggie Baxter

A Father's Wisdom

My father died in Vietnam when I was five years old. The last thing I expected was to receive a letter from him seventeen years later. But that is what happened one winter day when I was twenty-two years old.

It was the day my fiancé and I announced our engagement. My mom was overjoyed at the news, as was my stepfather. Such an event is a milestone for the mother of an only son. As such, it occurred to her that I had "become a man." That realization sparked in her the memory that years ago she had been given a solemn duty to discharge.

I remember being in the kitchen alone one evening. My mother walked in and handed me a letter copied onto mimeograph paper, the likes of which I had not seen since kindergarten. The seven pages were still folded, evidence of an envelope since discarded.

"What's this?" I asked.

"It's something I should have given you years ago," my mother said. "It's a letter from your father. He wrote it to you from Vietnam soon after he arrived there, just in case something were to happen to him. You were little at the time, of course. He said that if he were to not return from the war, I was to give it to you when you became a man.

I forgot about it, to tell you the truth, although I thought I never would. When you and Claudia announced your engagement, it jogged my memory. It has been years since I had read or even thought about it. In reading it again, I realize that I should have given it to you a long time ago. I'm sorry."

It is hard to describe how jolting her words were. You would think I would have been ecstatic! Instead, I was in shock. It was too overwhelming. The letter in my hand seemed like a mysterious package with the potential to explode, depending on what it said.

While these things were racing through my mind, my body was having a reaction of its own. My face paled. I went a bit numb. My hands turned cold and began to tremble slightly. I took the letter and went to my room. I was completely unable to say anything to my mother beyond a quiet, "Thank you."

There's just something confusing about receiving a letter from your deceased father who has been gone so long that you have not one solitary memory of him. What I knew about him I had learned by asking questions of my mother, my grandmother and my aunts. I had read newspaper clippings and looked through scrapbooks. I had made peace with the fact that these tidbits were as much as I would ever know about my dad. There was no reason to expect more . . . certainly no reason to expect a personal letter seventeen years after a landmine ended his life.

I sat there stunned in my room. Finally, after a few minutes, I managed to unfold the pages. They were handwritten. I felt privileged to see the handwriting I had not seen before. Some words were hard to decipher, but it was worth the effort to see the personality in the handwriting that a typewriter would not have shown.

After only a couple of lines, I re-folded the letter. I wasn't ready. My head had not the slightest idea how to absorb the letter. Part of me was afraid to read it, afraid that with one quarter of my life behind me, my life would not have pleased him . . . that I would not have his blessing. By that stage in my life, I had adjusted to not having to take into account my father's approval or disapproval. Now, all of a sudden, I might have to.

At the same time, I felt humbled that I was even getting the chance to know my father's thoughts. *How many other boys,* I wondered, *would have this opportunity to read a letter from a father they never knew?*

I set the pages on my desk and went back downstairs. My mom noticed my melancholy mood and asked, "Did you read the letter?"

"Not yet," I replied, without offering an explanation. I wouldn't have known how. I hardly understood it myself.

That brief exchange was enough to drive me back upstairs where I sat down and read the letter straight through. The words took on an almost sacred quality to me. This is part of what I read:

Dear Doug:

Your old man is writing this letter tonight because he feels the urge to share some basic thoughts with his only son. You are a very little boy at this writing, but the years will pass rapidly and someday soon you will be a young man facing the realities of life.

I fully expect to be around in the years to come and hope to assist you on your path through life; however, one never knows what the future will bring.

. . . Someday, you will have to decide on a career. Many well-meaning people will offer their sincere advice and you will undoubtedly be quite confused. The choice of your life's work is equally as important as choosing a life's mate. Before you can do either, you must decide what you are yourself, as a person. As the years go by, you will soon discover whether

you are outward or timid, adventuresome or docile, ambitious or complacent. It is no sin to be one or the other; but, it is extremely important that you discover what you are—not what at some moment in life you may think you would like to be.

After you decide what you are, think about what you would like to be within the personality and innate intelligence you possess—and then, unless you lack all ambition, pick a goal several steps higher than what you think you can achieve and work like the very devil to achieve it. Remember, son, the tallest and straightest trees grow in crowded forests where they must each individually reach for the very sun that enables them to grow into large and proud trees—in competition with the other trees. Scrub oaks only grow by themselves where they have no competition to spur them on.

Many people . . . exist in a dream world. . . . I have heard ministers and teachers condemn the war in Vietnam on many grounds they sincerely believe to be unquestionably valid. Their words of complaint have scant meaning when I watch people going to the Catholic church nearby on Sunday and realize that until a few weeks ago, this was impossible because of Communist terrorism and military operations. I watch students, little boys like yourself, walk to school each morning under the protection of armed troops. I know that no schools or churches are allowed to operate in parts of this district I advise because they are under Communist control. . . .

It was said centuries ago that for every man willing to lead, one thousand wait to be led. Your father is very proud of this army green he wears and would not trade his life as an Infantry Officer for any other endeavor, whatsoever. I hope someday you can say the same thing about what you have done for the first dozen years after achieving manhood.

Doug, you are a very intelligent boy and you have an extremely kind disposition. Should something happen to me, and I hope to still be serving in the world's action spots when you are my present age, do not try to emulate a way of life that may not be suitable to your own particular makeup. I do hope you will choose a way of life that holds some potential for helping to make this a better world. . . .

Regardless of what career you choose, I do challenge you to do your part in defending the rights you have inherited. Do not rationalize and try to say you are doing your part if your conscience tells you otherwise. One must develop self-respect before he can hope to attain it from others.

Ten years from now, let's you and I sit down and discuss this far too wordy letter . . . and learn from each other, as I am sure that by then there will be much your old dad can learn from you.

Love,
Dad

When I finished reading the letter, it was as if the weight of the world had been lifted from my shoulders. I was not faced with trying to rebuild my life, after all. Instead, my dad had affirmed me, citing traits he had seen in me even when I was a little boy. His words were encouraging and motivating, not scolding or dogmatic. He did not lecture or warn me, but simply shared his thoughts. Instead of trying to persuade me to follow in his footsteps (which I had begun to do—even applying to West Point, only to withdraw my application), he held up virtues for which I could strive, no matter what career I chose. It felt good that, after all those years, I had some basis for thinking my dad would have been proud of me.

His letter had filled a place in my heart that I had only been partly aware of and had no idea was so large. I had received my father's blessing. It had come after many years, even from beyond the grave, but it had finally come. Until then, even though I had a wonderful stepfather, I had not fully appreciated the power of a father over his

children. This man was a virtual stranger to me, even
though I shared his genes. Yet, because he was my father,
his attention and affirmation in a letter mailed a week
before his death profoundly impacted the course of my
life as an adult. He gave me permission to proceed in a
direction I would have gone anyway, but now could go
with greater confidence.

I believe that God can "re-parent" us, filling in the gaps
left by imperfect or absent parents. The apostle Paul even
said, "You received the Spirit of sonship and by him we
cry, 'Abba (Daddy), Father.'" (Romans 8:15) But I also
believe that God does not usurp the place of a human
father or mother. When God established parent-child relationships, He gave them a power all their own. They have
an effect uniquely their own that even God can't replace. I
might not have believed that before, but I do now.

It is my wish that every father would realize the innate
and powerful impact he has upon his kids' lives . . . the
potential he can endow toward self-esteem or self-hatred,
toward confidence or insecurity. It is my wish that fathers
would never miss a chance to plant seeds of encouragement in young hearts. I hope that as the influence of the
father's role is increasingly appreciated in our culture, it
would become just as common to hear fathers say, "I love
you," or "Good job" as to hear those words from mothers.
A lot of fathers want to say such things, but they don't
sound so familiar, or the timing doesn't seem right, or
there is some other reason. . . .

Fathers, don't let anything stop you from saying the
things you want to say to your children. As my father
said: "I fully expect to be around in the years to come and
hope to assist you in your path through life; however, one
never knows what the future will bring."

J. Douglas Burford

A Farewell Gift

*After the pain of parting comes the happiness
of healing; rediscovering life, friends, self, joy.*
    Harold Bloomfield, Melba Cosgrove and Peter MacWilliams

My wife and I had just finished the 150-mile trip home
from our daughter's college. It was the first time in our
lives that she would be gone for any length of time. We
wondered how other people had survived it.

Later in bed, I thought of the time I started college. My
father had driven me too. We rode in the farm truck. In the
back was the trunk I had bought with money earned by
pitching hay that summer. My mother had to stay behind
to keep the cattle from getting into the crops. I, the fourth
in a line of brothers, was the first to go away to college.
My mother cried, and I cried; after we were out of sight of
the farm, I began to feel jellylike and scared.

The truck was slow, and I was glad. I didn't want to get
to the city too soon. I remembered how my father and I
stopped by a stream and ate the sandwiches my mother
had prepared.

My daughter's day was different, of course. We stopped

at a classy roadside place and ordered fried chicken. Then we went to the dormitory, and my wife talked with the housemother. When she came back, she was wiping her eyes. It wasn't until we were passing through the next town that she discovered our daughter had forgotten to take out the portable radio and record player. I told her she should have put it in the trunk with the other things, not in the back seat.

Now I heard a sob beside me. I knew that my wife was thinking about the new kind of loneliness before us.

My father didn't let me stay at the dormitory. A room in a private home was cheaper and better if a student wanted to work his way through. But I didn't have a room. My father told me that we'd leave my trunk at a filling station. I could come for it the next day after I had found a place to stay. We toured the town a bit, but the traffic confused him. I said maybe I'd better go on my own.

I shook hands with my father in the truck. For a long, haunting moment he looked straight ahead, not saying a word, but I knew he was going to make a little speech. "I can't tell you nothing," he finally said. "I never went to college, and none of your brothers went to college. I can't say don't do this and do that, because everything is different and I don't know what is going to come up. I can't help you much with money either, but I think things will work out."

He gave me a brand-new checkbook. "If things get pushing, write a small check. But when you write one, send me a letter and let me know how much. There are some things we can always sell." In four years, the total of all the checks I wrote was less than a thousand dollars. My jobs chauffeuring a rich lady, janitoring at the library, reading to a blind student and baby-sitting professors' kids filled in the financial gaps.

"You know what you want to be, and they'll tell you what to take," my father continued. "When you get a job, be sure it's honest and work hard." I knew that soon I would be alone in the big town, and I would be missing the furrowed ground, cool breezes and a life where your thinking was done for you.

Then my dad reached down beside his seat and brought out the old, dingy Bible that he had read so often, the one he used when he wanted to look something up in a friendly argument with one of the neighbors. I knew he would miss it. I also knew, though, that I must take it.

He didn't tell me to read it every morning. He just said, "This can help you if you will let it."

Did it help? I got through college without being a burden on my family. I have had a good earning capacity ever since.

When I finished school, I took the Bible back to my father, but he said he wanted me to keep it. "You will have a kid in school some day," he told me. "Let the first one take that Bible along."

Now, too late, I remember. It would have been so nice to have given it to my daughter when she got out of the car. But I didn't. Things were different. I was prosperous and my father wasn't. I had gone places. I could give her everything. My father could give me only a battered, old Bible. I'd been able to give my daughter what she needed.

Or had I? I don't really believe now that I gave her half as much as my father gave me. So the next morning I wrapped up the book and sent it to her. I wrote a note. "This can help you," I penned, "if you will let it."

Jim Comstock

The Hymnbook

I watched intently as my little brother was caught in the act. He sat in the corner of the living room, a pen in one hand and my father's hymnbook in the other. As my father walked into the room, my brother cowered slightly; he sensed that he had done something wrong. From a distance, I saw that he had opened my father's brand-new book and scribbled across the length and breadth of the entire first page with a pen. Now, staring at my father fearfully, he and I both waited for his punishment.

My father picked up his prized hymnal, looked at it carefully, and then sat down without saying a word. Books were precious to him; he was a clergyman and the holder of several degrees. For him, books were knowledge, and yet, he loved his children. What he did in the next few minutes was remarkable. Instead of punishing my brother, instead of scolding or yelling or reprimanding, he sat down, took the pen from my brother's hand and then wrote in the book himself, alongside the scribbles John had made: "John's word 1959, age two. How many times have I looked into your beautiful face and into your warm, alert eyes looking up at me and thanked God for the one who has now scribbled in my new hymnal? You have made the book sacred as have your brothers and sister to so much of my life." *Wow*, I thought. *This is punishment?*

From time to time I take a book down—not just a cheesy paperback but a real book that I know I will have for many years to come—and I give it to one of my children to scribble or write their names in. And as I look at their artwork, I think about my father, and how he taught me about what really matters in life: people, not objects; tolerance, not judgment; love which is at the very heart of a family. I think about these things, and I smile. And I whisper, "Thank you, Dad."

Arthur Bowler

Dear God

He stumbled on the little train,
Left out on the floor again—
The one he'd told his son to put away.
He'd have to have a "talking to,"
And as he headed for his son's room
He stopped to hear his little boy say:

"Dear God,
Please tell my mommy that I love her,
And that we wish she'd never gone away.
Daddy says that she's your special angel,
And that we'll meet in heaven someday!
And God,
Could you ask my mommy if she'd help you
Choose another mommy for our home?
Though we're doing fine, I think that it is time
We had another mommy for our own."

* * *

She locked the door, turned out the light—
Another day, another night,

Another year had come and gone.
She missed the child she'd never had
And the man who would have been a dad,
And she holds on to a faith that's nearly gone.

She prayed,
"God, please tell my darling that I love him.
And that I wish he'd never gone away."

* * *

He stumbled on the little train
Left out on the floor again—
The one they'd told their son to put away.
Taking his wife by the hand,
He said, "Let's go talk to him,"
And as they neared his room they heard him say:

"Dear God,
Thank you for the baby that you gave us;
She smiled when I gave her the new toy;
Mom says she's glad you sent a sister
'Cause she already has a little boy!
And God,
Please tell my first mommy that I love her
And that I think about her every day;
Mom and Daddy say that she's your special child
And we'll all meet in heaven someday!"

Cheryl Kirking

THE FAMILY CIRCUS®   By Bil Keane

"Make me be good. And if you don't get through to me the first time, please keep tryin' 'til I answer."

Reprinted with permission from Bil Keane.

The Wonder Years

One bleak day eighteen years ago, I was awash with self-pity. I was quagmired in the "terrible twos"—a parenting stage that started early and lingered long at our house—and there was no hope in sight.

The morning began with the usual activities, but I tried to rush my small sons through them. Company was coming that evening, and I wanted a clean house. I'd finished cleaning the living room and begun the family room when I heard whispered giggles coming from my boys. With a sense of foreboding, I tiptoed to the doorway and gasped in dismay at the sight before me.

"Doesn't the living room look pretty, Mommy?" Tyler, my then-four-year-old, held a giant-sized empty jar of silver glitter, while two-year-old Landon danced around in happy circles. The entire room—carpet, couch, coffee table, everything—glittered like a giant Fourth of July sparkler!

Banishing the boys to their room to play with Legos, I dragged the vacuum back into the living room. By the time it was restored to its original condition, my schedule was in shambles and I was exhausted.

Stepping up my pace, I returned to the family room. "Look, Mommy! We're helping!" my boys shrieked in delight. This time the empty container was an economy-size can of Comet cleanser I thought I had placed in a locked cabinet. I was too shocked even to gasp as I surveyed the scene before me. The floor and every book, plant, knickknack and piece of furniture were covered with a fine layer of bluish-white grit.

The worst was yet to come. The last room to be cleaned was the master bedroom that we'd recently recarpeted. As I walked into the room, my attention was immediately drawn to a large, black spot smack in the middle of the floor. Beside it sat an empty bottle of permanent black ink I'd inadvertently left out. I crumpled to my knees in tears.

That's how most of our days went during those preschool years. We bounced from disaster to disaster: perfume poured on my new satin bedspread; the phone cord cut with scissors while I was talking on the phone. If it could be poured, dumped, sprinkled or sprayed, Tyler and Landon found a way to do it. There was no shelf the two of them could not reach, no lid they could not pry off.

After I discovered the ink spot that morning, I called my mom, but she didn't provide the sympathy I expected. "Honey, I know it feels as though this time will never end but believe me, a blink of your eye and it'll be gone. You have to find a way to cherish this season of your life."

This is not what I want to hear, I thought. But I knew she was right. I just didn't know how to switch from surviving to cherishing. So from that morning on, I asked God for help. And in the process, I became aware of some patterns that had squashed my capacity for joy. Life in the Mathers home lightened up as I worked to change some of my habits.

First, I realized I overused the word "no." Some days it seemed I'd forgotten how to say "yes." One afternoon I jotted down everything to which I regularly responded "no." Looking over the completed list, I discovered I denied far too many of my sons' requests because they would make a mess or take too much time.

For example, the boys loved to pull their chairs to the kitchen sink and play in the water while I did dishes, but this slowed me down and made a sudsy mess. I decided to remove this activity from my "no" list.

The next morning, to the boys' delight, I filled the sink with warm water and told them to bring their chairs and have fun. This simple activity kept them so entertained, I finished my morning chores in record time.

Removing just this one "no" made a tremendous difference. The boys thought I was wonderful, and I was pretty impressed with them. As a bonus, my kitchen was cleaner than ever, thanks to all the splashed water.

But avoiding the word "no" hasn't always been easy. As Tyler and Landon grew older, I discovered that overusing it made them feel untrustworthy. The first time Landon asked to go camping overnight with friends, I refused to consider it. He angrily accused me of not trusting him. Although Landon was wrong, I couldn't really explain the fear that made me deny his request.

When my husband suggested my refusal was based on a reluctance to let Landon grow up, I knew he was right. We sat down together and laid out clear plans for the campout. Landon had a great time and I survived, thanks to several calls he made from a pay phone to reassure me he was okay. Several weeks later, when he asked to go to an unsupervised party, I again declined. This time Landon was disappointed, but not angry. He knew I trusted him—just not the circumstances.

I also realized I didn't laugh enough. Proverbs 15:15 promises that "a cheerful heart has a continual feast." During the preschool years, however, I was becoming emotionally anorexic. I'd forgotten there's something humorous to be found in almost every situation.

After one particularly trying day with my preschoolers, I escaped to a long, steamy shower, leaving my husband to oversee the boys. I'd just dressed when our neighbor dropped by for coffee. As she followed me to the kitchen, she stopped abruptly.

"Interesting," she murmured, studying the dining room floor. "We've always kept our catsup in the refrigerator." I followed her gaze to a giant red puddle circled neatly on the carpet. Husband and sons were nowhere to be seen. Instant embarrassment and anger inflated my chest. Then I caught the twinkle in my neighbor's eyes, and we both burst into laughter. Laughing can help shrink things down to manageable proportions.

I've definitely needed that healthy dose of humor in each stage of parenting. Learning to find the humor in difficult or embarrassing situations has often defused tension.

I compared my kids and my parenting to others. I routinely measured my success as a parent by this faulty yardstick—and came up short. As I scrutinized my friends' choices, I constantly second-guessed mine.

My insecurities increased as the boys grew older. One afternoon I was waiting in line to pick them up from school when I noticed a bumper sticker on the car in front of mine: "My child is an honor student at Pilot Butte School." Glancing around, I saw another vehicle with a similar sticker, then another. Suddenly, it seemed my car was the only one lacking a badge of success!

My temptation to compare raged strongest when it was time for my sons to pursue plans beyond high school. As I listened to other parents talk about the colleges to which their kids were applying or the scholarships they were receiving, my insecurities blossomed. I found myself being apologetic about Tyler's plans to work before going to school. Not until I caught the same tone in Tyler's voice did I realize I was passing my insecurities to him. That was the last thing I wanted to bequeath my son. Asking God's forgiveness, I determined to focus squarely on God—not on other people. That decision is one that I still renew every morning when I ask God for help.

Now as the parent of grown children, I see my mother was right. The preschool years passed in the blink of an eye. But it wasn't just those years that vanished in a moment— it was all of childhood! One moment we were reading Mother Goose together, the next, it was college catalogs.

As my sons have matured, I've found that everyday traumas that accompany each parenting stage come with valuable lessons. That became clear to me the day I found the ink on my new carpet. I called every cleaner in town for advice on removing the stain. The only solution was to cover it with a rug.

I just couldn't accept that. I had to try something. Getting a basin of water and a washcloth, I began soaking up the ink and rinsing out the cloth. Soaking . . . rinsing . . . soaking . . . rinsing. As I worked, tears spilling down my cheeks, chubby little hands patted me on the back.

"We're sorry, Mommy," they said. While Tyler ran to get more water, Landon brought a bar of soap. Together we worked and gradually, before our disbelieving eyes, the spot that should have been permanent disappeared.

That day I discovered God looks on mothers with a special kind of love. He knows our insecurities, our frustrations, our desire to be good parents. And some-times, when we need it most, He goes out of his way to prove his love. Tucked away with my cleaning supplies is a reminder of that. It's the cloth I used to clean the carpet. To this day it remains stained with permanent black ink!

Mayo Mathers

The Commandment

A Sunday school teacher was discussing the Ten Commandments with her five- and six-year-olds. After explaining the commandment to "honor thy father and thy mother," she asked, "Is there a commandment that teaches us how to treat our brothers and sisters?" Without missing a beat, one little boy, the oldest in his family, answered, "Thou shall not kill."

Richard Lederer

The Greatest of These

My day began on a decidedly sour note when I saw my six-year-old wrestling with a limb of my azalea bush. By the time I got outside, he'd broken it. "Can I take this to school today?" he asked.

With a wave of my hand, I sent him off. I turned my back so he wouldn't see the tears gathering in my eyes. I loved that azalea bush. I touched the broken limb as if to say silently, "I'm sorry."

I wished I could have said that to my husband earlier, but I'd been angry. The washing machine had leaked on my brand-new linoleum. If he'd just taken the time to fix it the night before when I asked him instead of playing checkers with Jonathan. *What are his priorities anyway?* I wondered. I was still mopping up the mess when Jonathan walked into the kitchen. "What's for breakfast, Mom?"

I opened the empty refrigerator. "Not cereal," I said, watching the sides of his mouth drop. "How about toast and jelly?" I smeared the toast with jelly and set it in front of him. *Why was I so angry?* I tossed my husband's dishes into the sudsy water.

It was days like this that made me want to quit. I just wanted to drive up to the mountains, hide in a cave, and never come out.

Somehow I managed to lug the wet clothes to the laundromat. I spent most of the day washing and drying clothes and thinking how love had disappeared from my life. Staring at the graffiti on the walls, I felt as wrung-out as the clothes left in the washers.

As I finished hanging up the last of my husband's shirts, I looked at the clock. 2:30. I was late. Jonathan's class let out at 2:15. I dumped the clothes in the back seat and hurriedly drove to the school.

I was out of breath by the time I knocked on the teacher's door and peered through the glass. With one finger, she motioned for me to wait. She said something to Jonathan and handed him and two other children crayons and a sheet of paper.

What now? I thought, as she rustled through the door and took me aside. "I want to talk to you about Jonathan," she said.

I prepared myself for the worst. Nothing would have surprised me.

"Did you know Jonathan brought flowers to school today?" she asked.

I nodded, thinking about my favorite bush and trying to hide the hurt in my eyes. I glanced at my son busily coloring a picture. His wavy hair was too long and flopped just beneath his brow. He brushed it away with the back of his hand. His eyes burst with blue as he admired his handiwork.

"Let me tell you about yesterday," the teacher insisted. "See that little girl?"

I watched the bright-eyed child laugh and point to a colorful picture taped to the wall. I nodded.

"Well, yesterday she was almost hysterical. Her mother

and father are going through a nasty divorce. She told me she didn't want to live, she wished she could die. I watched that little girl bury her face in her hands and say loud enough for the class to hear, 'Nobody loves me.' I did all I could to console her, but it only seemed to make matters worse."

"I thought you wanted to talk to me about Jonathan," I said.

"I do," she said, touching the sleeve of my blouse. "Today your son walked straight over to that child. I watched him hand her some pretty pink flowers and whisper, 'I love you.'"

I felt my heart swell with pride for what my son had done. I smiled at the teacher. "Thank you," I said, reaching for Jonathan's hand, "you've made my day."

Later that evening, I began pulling weeds from around my lopsided azalea bush. As my mind wandered back to the love Jonathan showed the little girl, a biblical verse came to me: ". . . now these three remain: faith, hope and love. But the greatest of these is love." While my son had put love into practice, I had only felt anger.

I heard the familiar squeak of my husband's brakes as he pulled into the drive. I snapped a small limb bristling with hot pink azaleas off the bush. I felt the seed of love that God planted in my family beginning to bloom once again in me. My husband's eyes widened in surprise as I handed him the flowers. "I love you," I said.

Nanette Thorsen-Snipes

Just Another Day

Think big thoughts but relish small pleasures.

Anonymous

Is it morning already? I rub my eyes and get up to ready myself for just another day.

It's just another day. . . . I look out my window to see the sun beaming down, caressing the Earth with its golden rays. Above, white clouds float in the brilliant blue sky. I hear a cardinal singing to his mate as he perches upon my back fence. And a bed of crocus open their purple heads to the heavens in joyful thankfulness.

It's just another day. My small daughter bursts into the room, her giggle ringing through the house as she hugs my neck tightly. Her small hand fits into mine as she pulls me to the kitchen to show me the card she has made. A stick figure with curly brown hair waves from the paper and beneath it, written in purple crayon are the words, "I love you, Mommy."

It's just another day as I stand quietly and watch a handicapped child. He struggles to get his special walker over the curb, but it won't budge. A well-meaning teacher offers assistance, but he brushes her away. With determination, he conquers the curb and is off to laugh and play with his friends. I weep inside for his handicap, but I am inspired by his courage. And I smile as I watch the children play, totally accepting their friend for who he is, not judging him for what he lacks.

It's just another day. My son proudly presents the report he did for school. He shares with me the hopes and dreams he holds for his future. His curiosity and excitement are contagious as we unfold the limitless possibilities that lay before him. I am encouraged that no dream is beyond our reach if we want it bad enough.

It's just another day. My beloved wraps his arms around me and surrounds me in love. I turn to look in the eyes that share my innermost feelings. What a special friend I have. Someone who loves me for who I am. Someone to lean on when I feel down. Someone to share my happiness. Someone to love.

Yes, it is just another day. A day to enjoy God's gracious beauty upon this Earth. A day to kiss the cherub cheeks of my children, and share in their hopes and dreams. A day to learn the value of determination and hard work. A day to learn the value of judging mankind for the quality he has, not what he has not. A day to learn the value of love.

Yes, it's just another day, I sigh. The stars dance in the velvet sky as a full yellow moon smiles cheerfully down. The house is quiet and still. The only sound is the soft even breathing of my spouse. I recall the scripture: "This is the day the Lord has made; let us rejoice and be glad in it." (Psalm 118:24) And as I lay at the side of my soul mate I pray that God will let me see "just another day"!

Charlotte "Charlie" Volnek

Who's Going to Stop Me?

Six-year-old Angie and her four-year-old brother, Joel, were sitting together in church. Joel giggled, sang and talked out loud. Finally, his big sister had had enough. "You're not supposed to talk out loud in church."

"Why? Who's going to stop me?" Joel asked.

Angie pointed to the back of the church and said, "See those two men standing by the door? They're hushers."

Richard Lederer

Special Children: Mine and God's

God could not be everywhere, and therefore he created mothers.

Source Unknown

Parenting a child with special needs presents unique challenges. And last summer, my daughter who has Down's syndrome taught me that God sometimes speaks amid those challenges.

That hot, July morning I awoke to the clicks of a broken fan blowing humid air across my face. That got me thinking about all the other things that had "broken down" in my life.

Sarah's heart surgery and many serious infections were over, but now we faced catastrophic hospital bills. On top of that, my husband's job would be eliminated in just a few weeks, and losing our home seemed inevitable.

As I closed my eyes to try to put together a morning prayer, I felt a small hand nudge my arm. "Mommy," Sarah said, "I-I-I g-g-g-got r-r-ready for va-va-va-vacation Bi-Bi-Bible school all by myself!"

Next to the bed stood five-year-old Sarah, her eyes

twinkling through thick, pink-framed glasses. Beaming with pride, she turned both palms up and exclaimed, "Ta-dah!"

I noticed her red-checked, seersucker shorts were on backwards, with the drawstring stuck in the side waist-band. A price tag hung from the front of a new, green polka-dot top, also on backwards. She had chosen unmatched red and green winter socks to go with the outfit. Her tennis shoes were on the wrong feet, and she wore a baseball cap with the visor and emblem turned backwards.

"I-I-I packed a b-b-backpack, t-t-too!" she stuttered, while unzipping her bag so I could see what was inside. Curious, I peered in at the treasures she had so carefully packed: five Lego blocks, a box of unopened paper clips, a fork, an undressed Cabbage Patch doll, three jigsaw puzzle pieces and a crib sheet from the linen closet.

Gently lifting her chin until our eyes met, I said very slowly, "You look beautiful!"

"Thank y-y-you," Sarah smiled, as she began to twirl around like a ballerina.

Just then, the living-room clock chimed eight, which meant I had forty-five minutes to get myself, two small children and a baby out the door.

As the morning minutes dissolved into urgent seconds, I realized I was not going to have time to change Sarah's outfit.

Buckling each child into a car seat, I tried to reason with Sarah. "Honey, I don't think you'll be needing your back-pack for vacation Bible school. Why don't you let me keep it in the car for you?"

"No-o-o-o-o. I n-n-need it!"

And so I surrendered, telling myself her self-esteem was more important than what people might think of her knapsack full of useless stuff.

When we got to church, I attempted to redo Sarah's outfit with one hand while I held my baby in the other. But Sarah pulled away, reminding me of my early morning words, "No-o-o-o-o . . . I l-l-look b-b-b-beautiful!"

Overhearing our conversation, a young teacher joined us. "You do look beautiful!" the woman told Sarah. Then she took Sarah's hand and said to me, "You can pick up Sarah at 11:30. We'll take good care of her." As I watched them walk away, I knew Sarah was in good hands.

While Sarah was in school, I took the other two children and ran errands. All the while my thoughts raced with anxiety and disjointed prayer. What did the future hold? How would we provide for our three small children? Would we lose our home? These painful questions caused me to wonder if God loved us.

I got back to the church a few minutes early. A door to the sun-filled chapel had been propped open, and I could see the children seated inside in a semicircle listening to a Bible story.

Sarah, sitting with her back to me, was still clutching the canvas straps which secured her backpack. Her baseball cap, shorts and shirt were still on backwards.

Watching her from a distance, I became aware of warm emotion welling within. One thought rushed through my mind, one simple phrase: "I sure do love her."

Then, as I stood there, I heard that still, comforting voice that I have come to understand is God's: "That's the way I feel about *you*."

I closed my eyes and imagined my Creator looking at me from a distance: my life so much like Sarah's backwards outfit, unmatched, mixed up. . . .

"Why are you holding that useless 'backpack' full of anxiety, doubt and fear?" I could imagine God saying to me. "Let me carry it."

I sensed that God was speaking not only to me, but to

all those who struggle with lives that seem backwards, inside-out and out of control. We all want to be financially secure, free from illness and immune to the inevitable pain that life brings. But God calls us to trust that what we need will be provided.

It is in these vulnerable times of weakness that we need to give our fear-filled backpack to the one who says, "You are precious in my eyes and I love you." (Isaiah 43:4)

That night as I once more turned on our crippled fan, I thanked God for the privilege of parenting Sarah. Through her, I realized, God had been revealed to me in a new way.

Nancy Sullivan Geng

4

GOING HOME

He spoke well who said that graves are the footprints of angels.

Henry Wadsworth Longfellow

A Chaplain's Gift

When World War II was declared in 1939, I was seven years old; my brother was five. For the next four years we paid little attention to world affairs and felt childishly safe on our parents' farm, just west of the Alberta town of Rocky Mountain House. War bond drives and ration coupons only slightly affected our young lives. Even the enlistment of our two older brothers—one in the Army, the other in the Navy—meant little. We were much too young to understand the anxieties the adults experienced every time they read the newspapers or heard the nightly news broadcasts.

Neither of us heeded media reports of the devastation taking place on the various battlefields in Europe. However, the death of our older brother on an Italian battlefield and the events that occurred on our farm that day have made a lasting impression on both of us.

That winter day—December 7, 1943—began no differently than any other. My brother and I ate breakfast in silence while our mother listened to the 7 A.M. news on our old battery radio. "Today marks the second anniversary of the Japanese bombing of Pearl Harbor," the announcer reminded us. Then he went on to update the progress the Canadian Army was making. Tears filled Mother's eyes as she thought of her son, who was undoubtedly in the midst of it. Angrily she exclaimed: "Leonard should have been sent home after he was wounded in Sicily. I hope he is strong enough to withstand the stress of combat so soon after being injured." Then, hoping to block out anything further that would intensify her fears, she reached up and turned off the radio.

We finished breakfast and completed last-minute preparations for school. After donning warm clothes we stepped outside, only to be greeted with a dreary day. There were ice crystals in the air and hoarfrost hung on the trees. Patches of fog drifted over the low-lying areas, making our one-and-a-half-mile walk unpleasant. School was even more depressing in the dimly lit one-room schoolhouse we attended. We were both relieved when the teacher dismissed us for the day.

We hurried home that afternoon, hunching our shoulders against the chill in the air. Along the way, we noticed our mother coming to meet us. That was unusual, and she explained: "I couldn't stay alone any longer. Something has happened that has upset me. After you left this morning, the dog began to howl. He has been howling all day." When she went out to water the horses at noon, she added, a white dove flew over her head. "I hope this is not a sign that something has happened to Leonard."

As we walked on, Mother continued to talk about my brother. She smiled a bit when she spoke of his love of music. Then she talked about his quiet ways, and the times he had been hurt because he had trusted the wrong people. "I have such an uneasy feeling about him."

Mother had been uneasy ever since Leonard's last leave before going overseas, when he had given away all his worldly possessions. I got the things he prized most—

some pictures, his camera and a pair of leather chaps. He handed my mother his one good suit of clothes, instructing her to make it over for my younger brother. With tear-filled eyes he kissed us good-bye and said: "This is the last time you will see me. I'm not coming home."

By the time we got home we were all uneasy. The dog followed us to the house and continued to howl. We did the chores early, ate supper and settled down for the usual quiet evening, avoiding discussion of the day's events. Mother turned up the volume on the radio, hoping to muffle any unexpected noise. My brother and I dawdled over homework, trying to delay bedtime as long as possible. When we did retire we had trouble sleeping, for the memory of our mother's experience kept recurring.

After a restless night we rose the next morning to discover the fog had lifted, making the previous day's events seem less eerie. As the days wore on and no telegram arrived with bad news, Mother began to relax. When two weeks had gone by, she appeared convinced that the events of December 7 were just a coincidence. Soon Christmas was four days away. Our brother Russell was home on leave from the Navy, his last before sailing overseas. We had planned a party for him and invited friends to come for the day. After our father had left to pick them up, we hurried with dinner preparations. In our haste to make sure everything was just right, we failed to notice Father returning sooner than expected.

Father's face was ashen and tears filled his eyes. Everyone knew he had bad news. The telegram the local station agent had handed him just a short distance from our home was unopened. Mother took the envelope from his hand and tore it open. It read: *Regret deeply M102186 Private Walter Leonard Brierley officially killed in action 7th of December, 1943. Stop. Further information when received.*

Silence fell. Only Mother's quiet sobbing could be

heard. My brother disappeared to his room; I hid behind the dining-room door so no one could see my tears. It was some time before Mother regained her composure. When she did, she told the rest of the family the puzzling events of that date. She sighed as she added, "I knew something terrible had happened. I believe God was preparing me for it."

On Christmas morning Mother was the first to rise. She lit the fire in the cookstove and prepared the bird for the oven. When breakfast was ready, the rest of us straggled to the table. Everyone tried to make the day special for Russell's sake, but we lacked enthusiasm. We opened our gifts quickly, trying not to think of the items so carefully chosen for Leonard's parcels.

Mother seemed to be in a trance as she prepared dinner. She made the usual generous portions—even though she knew little would be eaten. Knowing there would always be someone missing from her table in the future devastated her. Tears filled her eyes as she decorated the Christmas cake with tiny silver balls. Usually she had lots of help with the decorating, but that day she did it alone.

A subdued group gathered around the dining-room table for dinner. Everyone was trying to come to grips with what had happened. The usual non-stop exchange of noisy conversation gave way to periods of uncomfortable stillness. Father sat silent at the head of the table, no doubt remembering the many disagreements he and Leonard had had. My sister and older brothers recalled all the fun times they had had with Leonard. Then, with downcast eyes, they expressed regret for the times they had made his life uncomfortable. For the first time, everyone admitted that, when it came to a showdown, no one had ever gotten the better of Leonard. My younger brother ate quickly, pretending he was grown-up enough to understand why everyone was so quiet.

I sat beside Mother and picked at the food on my plate, tormented by what had happened. My mind raced with memories; the days my brother drove me to school in our old horse-drawn cutter, him waiting for me outside when classes were dismissed. Then I recalled warmer days when he had pulled me up behind him on his saddle horse. I remembered how Leonard had helped care for me when I became ill with scarlet fever and had to spend two months in bed. Then, when I developed rheumatic fever, he rode for the doctor and held me on his lap when the doctor sent me to the hospital.

Soon feelings of anger began crowding out my memories. I wanted to cry out and ask why we had wars, why Leonard had to die. But the words stuck in my throat like a foreign object. *It's not fair*, I thought. *Leonard was my hero. We shared secrets. We played Bluebird records on the gramophone and sang Wilf Carter songs together. He promised that one day he would teach me to yodel. Now it's too late. He's gone and we never said good-bye.*

My mother broke down and wept. "Poor Leonard. He always seemed so alone. He was too young to die. If only I could have been there to hold him and tell him one more time how much I loved him."

On Boxing Day we exchanged tearful good-byes with Russell as he boarded the bus to return to his ship. Unlike Leonard, he assured us the war would be over soon and he would be coming home unharmed.

Mother then began the double task of trying to come to grips with one son's death and another's leaving. Just when she was beginning to make progress, Leonard's letters written just days before his death arrived. They opened wounds just beginning to heal, but the assurance of his love for us and his wishes for a Merry Christmas made them a special bonus. The days that followed failed to lessen my mother's grief. She sewed a black ribbon on our coat sleeves and wore black when she went out. Neighbors came to visit. Friends wrote letters of sympathy and sent cards. The letters of condolence that arrived from the Department of National Defence, the prime minister and King George VI only seemed to deepen her sorrow. Then, one day, a letter arrived that brought a measure of peace.

The envelope bore the familiar "Passed by Censor" stamp and contained a neatly written letter from the chaplain of the Loyal Edmonton Regiment. Its contents assured her that her twenty-seven-year-old son had not died alone but was surrounded by caring, compassionate people. Dated December 12, 1943, it read:

Dear Mrs. Brierley,

It is with deep regret that I confirm the news of the death of your son, Pte. W. L. Brierley, M102186, who was killed in action on Dec. 7th, 1943, and was buried the same day. He was waiting to go over the top when a long-range shell burst near and he was mortally wounded in the abdomen. Nothing could have saved him although medical attention was near at hand, and he soon passed away. Pte. W. Barnett of the Edmontons was hit at the same time.

We buried him at a cemetery near (San) Leonardo with his comrades there to pay their last respects. It was a brief service conducted by myself as a unit chaplain. We were still under shell fire, but he was given a decent burial, and we put a cross at his head and some flowers for you.

He died so that others may live and peace come more quickly to a war-weary world. At the graveside we prayed that God might strengthen you in the days of your sorrow. All is well with him now, but you must bear the burden of his passing as part of the world's sacrifice for the evil that has been brought upon us.

May God bless you until the day of reunion.
Yours sincerely,
Edgar J. Bailey, Chaplain

My mother read and reread that letter, each time thanking God for the courage and compassion of the chaplain who, under shell fire, was able to write such words of comfort. After many months, Mother decided to let go of the past. She placed the letter with my brothers', tied them neatly, and stored them in her cedar chest. But she never forgot the chaplain's words or the events of December 7, 1943. She rarely spoke of it, except to those close to her, but insisted until her death in 1973 that what had happened on our farm that day was no figment of her imagination.

My mother's grief was most evident on special occasions: December 7, Christmas, my brother's birthday, and especially Remembrance Day. Every November 11 she took the Silver Cross from her jewelry box and pinned it on her lapel. Then, with heavy heart, she joined other Silver Cross mothers at the cenotaph to pay tribute to all who had given their lives for their country.

I, too, continued to grieve. While walking to school on cold winter days I would close my eyes and imagine Leonard was driving me. I longed to feel the warmth of his body beneath our mother's old patchwork quilt. And every time I rode horseback in the rain, I felt dry and protected in his worn leather chaps. I still miss him. Not a day goes by that I don't think about him, about how handsome he was and how I would have enjoyed having him around as I was growing up. I think about how wonderful it would have been for my children to have known their uncle.

In early 1991 I read a newspaper article about chaplains at war. It contained interviews with three army chaplains, two of them then leaving for the Persian Gulf War. The third was Rev. Edgar Bailey, the World War II chaplain of the Loyal Eddies. After reading the article I contacted him and expressed as well as I could my thanks for the letter he had written my mother. The eighty-seven-year-old remembered my brother and related various events that had preceded his death. We talked and cried, then arranged to meet at the lodge in Edmonton where he now resided.

A month later, my husband and I visited the old gentleman. It was incredible! When we entered his room he immediately drew our attention to family pictures and war medals hanging on the wall. We chatted briefly about ourselves, then he handed us a scrapbook filled with notes and clippings covering nearly sixty years of his life. I could have spent the afternoon poring over its contents, but time was running short. Reluctantly, I put the scrapbook aside and started my tape recorder as he began to talk.

"Some people have asked what chaplains do in the war and why they are there. I think the best way to explain it is to tell you what General (Bernard) Montgomery said to me one time. He said, 'I would as soon go into battle without my artillery as without my chaplains.' Guns are of no use without the men behind them. The chaplains show the men that someone cares about them and is concerned about their loved ones back home."

When it was time for us to leave, he put his arms around me and kissed me tenderly on the cheek. His voice broke as he whispered, "That's from your brother." It was a time of sadness but also of joy. After forty-seven years I had finally been given an opportunity to properly say good-bye to Leonard. I thanked God for Edgar Bailey because He had provided that opportunity.

Dawn Philips

Luke's Truck

God's finger touched him, and he slept.

Alfred Lord Tennyson

Eyes wide with terror peered at me from the hospital bed. "You must be Luke Hatten," I said, as I scanned the name on his identification bracelet. His work-roughened hands nervously fingered a pamphlet. Its bold, red letters shrieked *When You Have Cancer*.

I cleared my throat uneasily. "I'm Roberta Messner, a registered nurse. Your doctor and wife thought it might be helpful if I visit you when you're discharged. If it's okay, I'll stop by Saturday."

Mr. Hatten stared blankly out the window at the barren view. In a couple of months, the hospital grounds would be awash with a carpet of crocuses, vibrant azaleas and hyacinths in Easter-egg hues. But this was the cancer ward, where time is measured in moments—not months.

Mr. Hatten's roommate caught up with me by the elevator. "You've got your work cut out for you, Nurse," he stated flatly. "They say it's terminal. Ever since Luke got his sentence, he walks the floor all night. He told me, 'I can't sit for long. When I sit, I think.'"

I felt whipped from the start. Here it was the eve of spring, with the promise of new life, and *my* patient was dying. How could I help him?

On Saturday morning, a short, stout woman met me at the door of the Hattens' tidy rural cottage. "I'm Ida. Do come in," she said, tugging the hem of her apron.

Luke sat in a frayed wing chair in a corner of the living room. He forced a smile. Just two weeks before, Luke had undergone surgery for colon cancer. But the relentless disease had spread. Once a hard-working handyman, a now-weary Luke clutched his abdomen in a spasm of pain. *Lord, help me know what to do,* I silently prayed.

"Luke just took a pain pill," Ida explained. "Why don't we have some coffee out in the kitchen while the medicine takes hold?" I followed her to the gingham-curtained kitchen window. A look of desperation stole across her deeply-lined face. "This is all such a shock," she said, tearing up. "He worked so hard—always tinkerin' on something. And just when he thought he was ready to retire, *this* happens."

Ida bit her lip, then pointed to the shining red truck in the driveway. "He wanted that truck so bad. Drove it straight from the showroom over to the clinic. His belly had been painin' him a little, but we never dreamed it was . . . cancer. Next day, the doc just cut him open and sewed him right back up."

I walked back into the living room. "That's quite a truck you have out there, Luke," I said.

"Never even got to show it to the crew down at the hardware store," came his faint words. "Doc says I can't drive. I'm on too many pills."

"Sometime when you feel up to some fresh air, I'd love

to take a look at it. My husband has a truck, too, but it's an old clunker."

Luke's brown eyes lit up. "Had old junk heaps all of my life. Always kept hopin' to get a new one. Then I did—just before this thing hit." He struggled out of the chair and pressed a kiss to Ida's cheek. "Gimme my coat, Hon."

With marrow-deep determination, Luke led me to the driveway. He pointed to a row of brittle, lifeless bushes. "There'll be yellow blossoms like you never did see on them come spring. Sure would like to see spring come one more time." Dusting the glistening truck with the sleeve of his plaid flannel jacket, he cautiously peeped in the windows as if it belonged to someone else.

"Would my husband ever love this beauty!" I exclaimed. "Just look at those chrome bumpers and black leather seats."

"Well, climb up in 'er and have a seat," he urged. Luke settled himself behind the steering wheel, reaching in his pocket for keys. "Feels funny not havin' a floorboard full of old rags and oil cans," he chuckled.

"Better start it up to charge the battery," I suggested.

Luke turned the key in the ignition. "Gotta let it run a minute to lube the engine," he explained, honking the horn with the fervor of a three-year-old.

A neighbor tapped on the window. "Hey Luke, what's a pretty young nurse doing in that truck of yours?" he chided.

Luke toyed with the power seats, the electric mirrors, the quartz clock, the heater. My idle hands longed for a stethoscope. A thermometer. *Anything* to avoid the inevitable discussion. But all my gadgets were in the Hattens' living room.

"How'd you ever decide on the color, Luke?" I asked, opting for small talk.

"Same color as the bike I got the Christmas I turned

seven. Pa made me wait 'til after supper to ride it up the holler. Seemed like forever."

Once in the driver's seat, Luke emerged strong, in control, and finally opened up to me. "One day I was drivin' this truck off the car lot, and the next thing I knew, they were sendin' a nurse to help me die," he said softly. I nodded and reached for his hand.

"Doc says I don't have long. I gotta put things in order, Nurse. I'm tellin' you this 'cause I don't wanna worry Ida."

I visited Luke several times each week. He'd be waiting in the driver's seat with a thermos of coffee and two mugs. We talked freely of our shared faith, his fear of dying and leaving Ida alone, and God's promise of eternal life. As Luke learned to face his pain, he grew more peaceful. After our "truck talks," we'd head back to the kitchen where Ida waited. There we'd discuss the details of Luke's care and help Ida prepare for an uncertain future.

On Palm Sunday, I attended church before checking on Luke. The pastor spoke about how Jesus became a man so that we could know God. He closed with the story of Jesus facing death in the Garden of Gethsemane. Jesus had told his disciples: "My soul is exceedingly sorrowful, even unto death: tarry ye here, and watch with me." (Matthew 26:38) Even Jesus had not wanted to face death alone.

That afternoon I found Luke leaning on Ida by a budding forsythia bush. His old leather belt curled about him, gathering his trousers in loose folds. He handed me some freshly cut branches, wrapped in wet paper towels and newspapers. "Put these in a jug of water when you go home, and they'll take root. Someday you'll have a yard full of forsythias."

I smiled, but deep down I doubted his wisdom. With what little I knew about gardening, I was sure a budding branch had a slim chance of taking root.

Over the next few days, Luke's condition rapidly worsened. At our last visit, he lay ashen and listless, his breathing rapid and labored. I leaned over to give him a hug.

"I'm not afraid anymore," he whispered. "Jesus is right here, reachin' his arms out to me. I'll live again . . . just like my Lord."

Luke died that evening. I drove over to be with Ida. "Oh, how I'll miss him," she wept. "But how could I drag my Luke back to this Earth? He's livin' with Jesus. One day I'll see him."

As I left their home, I paused by Luke's truck. Gazing into the window, I studied the empty seats where the two of us had so often sat. The air was fragrant with the scent of spring flowers. With the sleeve of my sweater, I buffed the red gem as Luke would have done, then lifted the windshield wipers to release a wayward cluster of golden forsythia blossoms.

To really make a difference in the lives of others, we have to meet them where they are, I thought. I might never have known the real Luke in his bewildering, antiseptic hospital room—my secure environment. There, in the rush, I might have patted his hand, offered reassurance and gone on about my duties.

But sipping coffee in that truck—Luke's Garden of Gethsemane—the barriers were broken. Two strangers experienced the promise of Easter.

If I ever forget that, I'm reminded each spring by my yard full of Luke's forsythias.

Roberta L. Messner

"The way I figure it, heaven's a place where there's no soap, or vegetables, or corners to sit in."

DENNIS THE MENACE® used by permission of Hank Ketcham and © by North American Syndicate.

There's No Place Like Home

I have many wonderful and vivid images of my parents from my childhood. I can clearly picture them holding hands as they sat in front of the television, Mom crying "uncle" through her laughter as Dad tickled her. I remember the soft murmur of their voices, with laughter sprinkled in, coming from their bedroom. It was their joy and love of one another that set the tone for our home.

I can only recall one bad moment. Literally hours before they were to leave for a vacation in Hawaii, my mother backed out. Now Dad, who had been living for the trip was understandably angry. Even now I shudder to think of the money he must have lost as a result. Needless to say, they had a few strained, unhappy weeks. Eventually, they worked it out. The love they shared would allow nothing else.

About a year later, Mom was diagnosed with cancer. As the chemotherapy and radiation therapies came and went, it became apparent that her cancer was winning the battle. And it was on a crisp, late fall afternoon that she and I sat on the picnic table in our backyard and talked of that trip.

"If I could change anything I've done, I would have gone to Hawaii," she said softly.

I don't care a bit about seeing Hawaii, Vicki. I don't regret the trip at all. What I do regret is the hurt it caused your father." She sighed and reached down to pick up our little dog.

"Oh, Vicki, I love my home. If someone gave me the choice of being anywhere in the entire world, I'd always choose to be here with my family. I've never minded having to work. It's just that I was away from home so much more than I would have liked. I'm just saying that if I could have done something for your dad, it would have been Hawaii."

Mom had always worked to help Dad provide for my brother, sister and I. She never complained and my parents always adjusted their hours so that one of them was home with us when we needed them. And even if she worked an all-night shift, she never went to bed in the morning until we were dressed, fed and out the door to the bus. Some mornings her exhaustion was a palpable presence. But never did she give in to it until she had seen us off for the day.

As the fight for life wound down, her physicians suggested that we consider putting her in a nursing home. Her health had deteriorated to the degree that she would require a lot of care. When we explained that it wasn't an option, the doctors said they didn't feel we understood what would be involved in her care. But it was the doctors who didn't understand.

This woman had devoted her whole life to her family. And as her words came back to me: "If someone gave me the choice of being anywhere in the world, I'd always choose to be here with my family," I realized that we had, in essence, been presented with just such a choice. Our last gift would be to allow her to die in her home with everything she cherished around her.

The holidays were upon us, and we were all painfully aware that this would be our last Christmas together. Despite the heavy sadness that hung over our home, Dad bought the largest, most beautiful Christmas tree he could find for her. He adorned it with ornaments that they had accumulated over the years—ornaments her children had made in their first years in school: a bird in a nest, a circular clay plaque with a tiny handprint in the middle, a construction paper wreath with the words, "I love Mom and Dad" in red glitter.

With the fireplace blazing and carols playing softly on the stereo, we spent a heart-wrenching final Christmas together. Mom sat for hours before the tree letting each ornament take her somewhere we couldn't see, each memory testifying to a life dedicated to her family.

It was in the snowy, early morning hours of a brand-new year, at the age of forty-seven, that Mom lost her battle with cancer. She was in her own bedroom—with the familiar sounds of her beloved home, with her family and her dog tucked familiarly in their beds—that she left us.

But she gave us one last gift as she departed. She stood silently at the base of my bed, outlined in a bright, white light. I can remember feeling tremendous love and even sadness emanating from her as she watched my sister and me for the last time. But the woman I saw there was not the emaciated, disease-ravaged person I had kissed good-night hours earlier, but the whole, healthy woman she had been a short year ago.

In making it possible for her to spend her last days in her own home, my mother had given us a gift in return. She gave us proof that our souls live on. I will never doubt the existence of God, because my mother loved us enough to show Him to us on her way to heaven!

Vicki L. Kitchner

Grammy and God

Pleasant words are a honeycomb, sweet to the soul and healing to the bones.

Proverbs 16:24

A little girl gave a wonderful explanation of the final years and death of her grandmother. She said to her mother after the funeral: "Mom, you always said that Grandma walked and talked with God. What I think happened is that one day God and Grandma went for an extra long walk, and they walked on and talked on, until God said to Grandma, 'You are a long way from home and are so tired, you had better just come home with me and stay.' And Grandma went."

"Dear Abby," April 22, 1993
Submitted by Linda Lum

Kisses from Heaven

"Not too far!" Gwen called as she watched her children, Joe, twelve, and Nicole, eight, playing in the surf.

But as the wind blew her hair off her face, bittersweet tears filled her eyes. *I wish you could be here with us, Dad,* she thought. *If it weren't for you, this day might never have been. . . .*

Fifteen years earlier, a knot had twisted in Gwen's stomach when her boyfriend Nick took her to meet his parents. But the minute she walked into Joseph and Mary's, she felt at ease. In the months that followed, Gwen not only fell in love with Nick, but with his family too. When they got engaged, tears of joy filled Gwen's eyes when Joseph whispered in her ear, "Welcome to the family."

A few weeks later, Nick tentatively told Gwen that his parents had offered to remodel the basement for them. "That sounds great!" she said. "They always make me feel so welcome—I know it's going to work out!"

And it did. Soon Gwen felt like she had two sets of parents. As the years passed, their two children were born, and from the moment they opened their eyes in the morning, they couldn't wait to race upstairs to see Nawnu, Italian for grandpa, and Nana, grandma.

When they outgrew their basement quarters, Nick and Gwen bought the house across the street. "I wouldn't want to live anywhere else," Gwen insisted.

In his own quiet way, Joseph—now "Dad" to Gwen— became a source of strength to her. While not a man of many words, when Gwen's grandma passed away, he took her in his arms. "Life's too short," he whispered, and when Gwen looked up, she saw tears in his eyes too.

Then one day, Dad began having severe chest pains. "He had a heart attack," the doctor said. "It doesn't look good."

With his wife and children holding his hands, Gwen stood at the foot of the bed. *I'm only a daughter-in-law,* she told herself. But when Dad saw her, he motioned for her to come close too. *He's letting me know I'm one of his,* Gwen realized. When he passed away, her heart nearly broke.

The next day as arrangements were being made for his funeral, Gwen noticed she was bleeding slightly when she used the bathroom. But she was so grief-stricken that when the bleeding stopped on its own, Gwen put it out of her mind.

But the day after the funeral, Gwen was washing her face when suddenly, blood started gushing from her. *What's going on?* she thought. Feeling faint, she cried out to Nick.

"I'm taking you to the hospital!" he gasped.

"What could it be?" Gwen asked the doctor.

"We'll need to do some tests," he said. Seeing the concerned expression on the doctor's face, Gwen sensed it was something serious. "It couldn't be cancer, could it?" she whispered, her voice quavering.

"I don't know yet," he confessed. Gwen burst into sobs. *Please God, she prayed, don't let it be. . . .* But the moment the doctor came into her room the next day, Gwen knew the news was bad.

"I have cancer, don't I?" she asked.

The doctor nodded. "It's rectal cancer."

Surgery, chemotherapy, radiation, colostomy . . . Gwen heard the rest of what the doctor had to say through a fog of fear. *This can't be happening!* she thought.

And though he tried to be strong, she could see that Nick was scared too. Walking down the corridor, his mind raced. *I just lost Dad,* Nick agonized. *I can't lose Gwen, too.*

Then, as he choked back a sob, he felt a hand on his shoulder. But when he turned to see who was there, he was alone—except for the unmistakable sense of his father's presence. Suddenly, a wave of peace washed over him. *Dad! You're here with us!* he thought.

"I know this sounds crazy . . ." Nick said when he told Gwen what had happened. Usually, he was a skeptic. But this had been so real.

"Everything's going to be all right!" Gwen wept. "Dad's watching over us."

Later that day, when Dr. David Kaufman checked on her, his face grew pale as he read her chart. "This is incredible," he said. "If we'd found this two months later, you wouldn't have had a chance. Usually rectal cancer has no early symptoms," he explained. "But thanks to your bleeding episode, I think we caught it just in time. The CAT scan and blood work look good—the cancer hasn't spread."

Tears of relief filled Gwen's eyes.

"What caused the bleeding?" she asked.

Dr. Kaufman pointed heavenward. "It's what we call a heralding episode—some people are just meant to be saved."

"This is Dad's doing!" Gwen gasped, clutching Nick's arm.

Still, Gwen had a lot ahead of her. In a few days she'd have surgery to remove the cancerous tissue—and install a colostomy bag which she'd have to wear for the rest of her life. Then she'd face months of chemotherapy and radiation.

But the next day, Dr. Kaufman brought more good news. He'd arranged for Dr. Alfred Cohen, a top surgeon at Sloan-Kettering Cancer Center, to do an operation using a new procedure that reconstructs a new rectum out of stomach tissue. "If you need a colostomy, it will be temporary," he said.

"I can't believe it!" Nick's sister Nancy cried when she heard the news. "When I went to the bank today to settle Dad's affairs, they told me that just one check he'd written had yet to clear," she said. "Gwen, it was a contribution to Sloan-Kettering."

"It just confirms everything I've been feeling," Gwen breathed. "Dad is making sure God is looking after me!"

And as they wheeled her to surgery, Gwen whispered, "Dad, I know you're orchestrating this whole thing from heaven!"

A few hours later, Gwen woke in recovery to find the surgery had gone so well that she didn't need even a temporary colostomy. And the next day when Gwen saw Dr. Cohen, he was grinning from ear to ear. "Every pathology report came back negative," he said. "In a few days, you can go home."

"What about chemo? Radiation?" Gwen asked.

"There's no need," Dr. Cohen said.

"Thank you, God!" she wept. *And thank you too, Dad,* she silently added.

Today, almost a year later Gwen is cancer-free. And as she spends the day at the beach with her family, she can't help thinking about her guardian angel.

"You know what, Mommy?" Nicole says. "Sometimes when I feel the wind in my face, I think it's Nawnu kissing me."

"I know just what you mean," Gwen says as she hugs her.

Meg Lundstrom
Excerpted from Woman's World *magazine*

Saying Good-Bye to Bubba

All I have seen teaches me to trust the Creator for all I have not seen.

Ralph Waldo Emerson

Parents can appreciate the anticipation and excitement of their children's first words. Some parents even work hard every day to ensure they are the first to be summoned and to encourage those long-awaited sounds: "Da Da" or "Ma Ma."

The day came for Derek's first word. We heard it and were thrilled that all our efforts, coaching and hours of repetition had finally produced the desired results. Even the dog was excited to hear a recognizable word and ran to share a wet kiss! As we laughed and carefully noted this milestone in his baby book, I have to admit my husband and I were a little heartbroken. We knew there was no way to contort the word into "Ma Ma" or "Da Da" as our baby sat on the floor calling "Ubba." Yes, he was definitely calling for Bubba, our beloved family dog. It had been love at first sight for the two of them. As any friend would, Bubba was teaching Derek many things: love, caring and responsibility, and along with a nightly ritual of feeding Bubba dog bones, Derek was learning to count.

Derek was now twenty months old and I lay in the hospital awaiting the arrival of our second son. I began to get a little concerned because my husband and mother had not made it to the hospital yet. Finally, they arrived and I saw it in their faces. They didn't want to tell me but I knew something had happened, and a feeling of sadness in my heart told me it was Bubba. It was true, they had found him dead that morning and buried him before Derek woke up. The next few months were very hard. Bubba had been with me for many years and the bond between a little boy and his dog was broken. I now had the responsibility to somehow explain to Derek in a way he could understand that Bubba was gone, forever.

For weeks Derek faithfully continued his nightly feeding rituals. He would search the house and stand at the door calling for Bubba. We struggled with ways to help his young mind understand.

A few months later we had flown to my hometown for a visit, and on our return flight Derek scrambled across the seats and into my lap. Always looking for a learning experience in everything we do, I began talking about the clouds and how we were on top of them and would soon be flying through them and then would be underneath them. Derek pressed his face against the window, shook his head and exclaimed, "No, Mommy!" Then I heard him softly calling, "Bubba." As my heart broke and eyes filled with tears, my baby looked at me for help in finding his lost friend amongst all the clouds. I prayed, "God, help me know the right things to say and please help his little heart mend." Derek was now pointing out the window and saying, "God-Heaven-Clouds-Stars-Bubba." At that moment, I realized in his own little way he understood.

The flight captain came on and announced our final

descent. As I worked to get us both buckled in, Derek again pressed his face to the window, called for Bubba and patiently waited. As the last cloud passed our window, he lovingly looked upward, waved and said, "Bye-bye, God! Bye-bye, Bubba!"

We landed that afternoon with pieces of our hearts left drifting in the clouds. Derek never searched or called for Bubba again.

Shelly D. Dunford

Missing My Mother

It happened today as I passed a full-length mirror while shopping in the mall. Rather than my usual brief glance to check my hair and makeup, I was brought up short. It suddenly seemed as if I was looking at my mother—her face, her hair color, her body shape and her kind of shoulder bag. For one brief moment, I thought about calling to tell her about it. Then my mind cleared and I remembered that heaven is farther away than the best fiber optics can reach.

Getting used to being motherless is taking longer than I thought possible. Even though it's been six years since my mother died, many things still trigger thoughts of her: seeing her birthday or anniversary date on the calendar, wearing her wedding ring, dusting the brass candlesticks she bought overseas, sniffing the aroma of meat loaf in a cafeteria (it's not as good as hers), or glimpsing an intensely pink sky at sundown, a near duplicate of the one that appeared the day she was buried.

Common sense tells me these reminders will lessen in frequency and intensity as the years pass. Or will they? My friend Frances recently told me, "My mother died over thirty years ago, and I still miss her so much."

Why does the loss of a mother seem different than other losses? Maybe it's the unique mother-daughter relationship that causes motherless daughters like me to feel our grief for years while concealing it like a box of old love letters high on a shelf. The immense expectations connected with a mother's role leaves us struggling with the void she's left behind. The one we thought would always be there for us—nurturing, loving, caring—now no longer is. Suddenly we find ourselves measuring the future in terms of mother-absence. *Mother won't see her grandchildren born. Mother won't attend her oldest grandson's graduation. Mother won't be escorted down the aisle first in her granddaughter's wedding.* But even those painful thoughts are clung to because they represent a connection, a remembrance.

Jeanette, a friend who lost her mother three years ago, calls her difficult moments "grief points"—times when she suddenly feels the loss of what was or what could have been. With the realization that her mother, an excellent seamstress, would no longer be there to make a wedding dress for her someday, Jeanette was left with a poignant sense of future loss.

My grief points usually involve past losses, regrets over the times my mother and I failed to communicate. If I could pick up the phone today and reach her, would we get beyond small talk to deeper issues? Because she lived seven hundred miles away (and often seemed intimidated by the phone), we postponed those conversations for our semi-annual visits. Then there never seemed to be enough time or privacy—until she was dying.

During that seven-week period, our conversations went well beyond the books we were reading or current events. We talked about life and death, past and present hurts. The mother-daughter bond grew stronger (better late than not at all). I thank God for those times, at the same time wondering what might have happened if He'd chosen to grant miraculous healing.

Why didn't we communicate better earlier? I was simply "too busy." While I was caring for a growing family, the years rushed by in a flurry of activity. My mother said she understood because she'd been there. She even boasted to her friends about how complicated my life was. But after finding a packet of my old letters in her bureau drawer while emptying her house, I regret not writing her more. I, too, often played that foolish game of "I'll write her when she writes me." A game where nobody won. My mother frequently described herself (pretty accurately) as "the world's worst letter writer." This was evidenced by a note she wrote me in college that included a sentence about having the cast taken off her leg. I called home immediately and found out she'd broken her ankle two months earlier but neglected to mention it!

Although physical distance kept us apart most of our adult lives, I wish I'd been better at bridging the emotional distance that sometimes separated us. Now I realize I shouldn't have expected it to be a fifty-fifty proposition; one person usually needs to give more in order to keep communication open.

Ironically, I've come to understand my mother better now that she's gone. It recently occurred to me that I never saw her cry. She undoubtedly had many reasons to cry: a traumatic childhood with an abusive father, the loss of her first husband in World War II, a turbulent marriage to my father (an alcoholic), and multiple health problems and surgeries.

After she died, I found a poem in her Bible that spoke of accepting what comes into our lives without complaint ("whatever is, is best") because it comes through the hands of a loving God. Apparently, she believed that.

Even though she didn't come to a personal relationship with Christ until several years before she died, she never harbored anger against God for the way her life turned out. Thinking of her perseverance and strength gives me a fresh appreciation for her attributes.

On this continuing grief journey, I'm learning not to look at the past through rose-colored glasses, to succumb to the temptation to make a martyr of my mother (she would have hated that!), or to idealize her with a perfection no human being merits. Neither do I blame her for any childhood deficiencies, not even the ones for which she apologized. She gave me what she was capable of giving at the time. And I've forgiven her for the times when that wasn't enough, as I hope my children will forgive me.

When I was about five years old, I used to climb onto my mother's lap and say, "I love you. I have the best mommy in the whole wide world." It seemed to embarrass her because she never knew exactly how to respond. The reason became clear when she explained to me on her deathbed that, for some unknown reason, the words "I love you" had always been hard for her to say.

Sometimes when I think of her now, I don't see her as I last did—in her sixties, frail and bedridden as she lost her second battle with cancer. Instead, when life knocks me around and I find myself suddenly inexplicably wanting my mother, I picture her as the beautiful twenty-eight-year-old woman she once was and myself as a child again. I climb onto her lap and say, "I love you. I have the best mommy in the whole wide world."

But this time my mother puts her arms around me and says, "I love you, Honey. I have the best daughter in the whole wide world." And it is enough.

Maybe when I join her in heaven, we'll have a chance to try it again.

Vicki Huffman

When Fireflies Wink

Let your conversations be always full of grace, seasoned with salt, so that you may know how to answer everyone.

Colossians 4:18

It is at twilight that I remember Mama best. I can still see her chasing fireflies, her skirt swinging below her knees. As the fading sun slips behind Georgia pine trees, it leaves the sky blanketed with a sunburst of orange. A glow radiates from Mama's face and laughter dances in her hazel eyes as she gathers fireflies in her hand and shows them to me.

Until I was about five, Mama caught fireflies and put them, still blinking, into an empty mayonnaise jar. Later, she tucked me into bed and I pretended those pulsating little bugs were a nightlight. Sometimes, they seemed to be winking at me. Even at that young age, I was painfully aware that Mama never once told me she loved me. It troubled me that she never kissed me good night, or at any other time for that matter.

But I believed she cared. She just showed it in a unique

way—through humor. I remember her humor being especially poignant as she battled terminal lung cancer. In
1980, the first inkling my husband and I had of trouble
was the day Mama began experiencing chest pains. After
a few days of pain so severe she had trouble talking, she
let me drive her to the doctor.

Once in the examining room, Mama pulled the white
paper gown over her head as she was instructed. She held
the paper out for my inspection. "I hate these things," she
said, a sparkle of mischief growing in her eyes. "I feel like
an overgrown paper doll." Though deeply concerned, I
laughed out loud. That was Mama.

Later, the X-rays confirmed there was a tumor in her
left lung. I had hoped it wasn't malignant, but after a
biopsy the results came back positive. The doctor gave
her a year to live. During that year, Mama battled the cancer by staying busy. With my husband's help, she planted
a small garden outside her mobile home on the south side
of Atlanta. As soon as the sun blinked upon the horizon
each morning, Mama dragged her three-legged stool outside and sat among the green beans, tomatoes and
cucumbers to weed the garden, which blossomed with
life. After a half hour in the blazing sun, perspiration
beaded her forehead and upper lip. She'd come in
gasping.

Once, with a familiar twinkle in her eyes, she said, "You
know, my breath keeps coming in short pants." Then she
laughed. I knew what she was imagining—puffs of air
dressed in a pair of short pants.

In April 1991 Mama lay in a hospital bed, her long battle
almost at an end. One day after radiation therapy, the
nurse wheeled Mama's gurney back into her room.

Although she was a shell of her former self, a smile
twinkled in her hazel eyes. "My mouth is so dry," she said.
"I thought they'd have to shave my tongue." Not only did

I laugh out loud but the nurse smiled as well. Thankfully, Mama's humor made accepting her illness a little easier.

One day as I left the hospital room I couldn't hold back the tears. I felt a comforting touch on my shoulder as I neared the nurses' station. I turned to see a nurse whose eyes showed deep concern. "Why can't you cry with your mother?" she asked. I shook my head trying to regain composure. "It's a shame," she went on, "because every time you leave, your mother cries too."

I wanted so much to let Mama know I cared, but it was impossible since I'd never received outward affection from her. I simply didn't know how to show her that I loved her. As an adult with four children of my own, it was beyond my comprehension how a mother could not kiss her child or say, "I love you."

As I pondered our lives together, questions formed in my mind. *Why can't I tell my mother that I love her? Was it because of the betrayal I felt when she left my father?*

Perhaps it was Mama's growing alcoholism. Maybe she just couldn't handle love and was incapable of giving it. I didn't know. I only knew the words "I love you" never came from her lips and the same words remained stuck in my throat. I also grieved the fact that I could not kiss her.

With the rebirth of spring and the resurrection of the once-dormant azaleas and dogwoods, I found myself thinking of the Easter season and the sacrifice of God's son over two thousand years before. Although I was alienated from God during this season of sorrow, I remember pleading with him, *Please help me say good-bye to my mother before it's too late.*

Every day I brought my barely used Bible to Mama's room and curled up on a vinyl chair partially hidden behind the hospital bed. One evening when twilight shadows filled the room, I sat in my usual place silently reading from the Psalms. I don't know who the dark-haired nurse was who interrupted my thoughts, and she had no idea I was sitting there in the shadows. I held my breath as she walked up to Mama. Watching in silence, I saw the nurse gently brush Mama's chestnut hair from her face. She held Mama's face in her hands in the most tender way. I knew she must be an angel sent by God because she did the one thing I couldn't: she leaned down and kissed Mama's forehead. As I gently exhaled, the woman tiptoed from the room.

The next day doctors were forced to increase the dosage of morphine to ease Mama's pain. Through the veil of drugs, Mama's eyes glazed and I feared I had waited too late to say good-bye. Beneath the green oxygen mask, she struggled for every breath. I struggled with her. *She probably won't hear me, I thought, but I have to tell her.*

I picked up my mother's spindly hand and held it. I took a sharp breath, and for all the times I couldn't speak, I whispered, "Mama, I love you." For a heartbeat in eternity, Mama's eyes cleared. She looked at me and a smile traced her lips. The presence of God in that room was inexplicable. It was as though God himself winked at me—the way fireflies wink at children on warm, summer nights.

Nanette Thorsen-Snipes

The Bridge Builder

"America! I'm really here," Ursina had murmured. "If only my family could visit this wonderful land. My dream all my life is to come here." Her eyes glistened slightly with tears. "I'm really here!" She opened her arms as if to hug someone. When she talked about America with such intensity, I would look around at my small hometown of Elberton, Georgia, wondering if Ursina saw something I had missed.

She often spoke about her mother, brother and sister, and her country fondly, but if she suffered from home-sickness, she never let any of us know. Ursina's father had died in a Russian prison in 1945.

She knew a lot about American history, but she never flaunted her knowledge. Always though, she wanted to learn more about our land and customs. She listened enraptured as we answered her never-ending questions.

"I want to learn all about America." Ursina pronounced "America" in a special, almost reverent way. Nothing ever seemed too small to captivate her attention.

Ursina's accent fascinated me. I hadn't met many people from other countries, and no one my own age. I watched her mouth closely as she pronounced my name precisely.

Sometimes now I don't think about her for months—even years. Then something stirs my memory—an old song, a ballerina skirt pulled out of mothballs, or a photograph of our graduating class. Then I recall vividly my senior year of high school in 1953, and Ursina Stahnke, the German exchange student who had come to live in America for a year and to graduate with our class.

The stubborn memory has remained in my heart all these years, and with bittersweet fondness, I remember Ursina. She could have easily been a beauty queen with her long, thick hair and dark eyes. Her flawless complexion seemed to be as perfect as a doll's. When she smiled, it happened slowly, like a velvet curtain being drawn back. She seemed completely unaware of her deep beauty.

The Halls, the family she was living with in Elberton, fell in love with Ursina almost instantly. Mrs. Hall sewed beautifully, and as a school party approached, she began making Ursina an exquisite formal gown. Ursina told me about it. "So lovely, new, green net, wonderfully soft . . ." she had whispered, with tears sparkling in her eyes. "I'm going to have my picture made in it for my family."

One bright September day when Ursina had been here only four weeks, some of us girls in the senior class decided to have a party for her. We called it a Coca-Cola party. We planned to have the get-together at Shirley's home. We all brought something special we had baked and there was an air of excitement.

Ursina came into the room a bit breathless, a little nervous, looked around at us, then slowly smiled that wonderful smile of hers, obviously pleased at our efforts. She tasted the cakes and cookies with great fanfare, as though she was judging a cooking contest, and she raved over each morsel. I watched her lift a Coke bottle to her mouth. She swallowed slowly, then smiled approvingly. Ursina got the most out of everything. I had gulped mine down without even tasting it. When all of her Coke was gone, she shut one eye and looked into the empty bottle with the other eye as though she peered into a microscope and saw something fascinating.

Ursina planned to ride Shirley's pet horse that afternoon. She was a skilled rider. As I left the party, she called out, "Bye. See ya tomorrow." Ursina had started to pick up our Southern slang, and it pleased us all.

That night I received a telephone call. One of my girl-friends spoke in a strange, tight voice. "Marion, Ursina fell or was thrown off the horse this afternoon. She's in the hospital, unconscious. They're going to operate, I think. They—they—shaved her head."

Back in bed I rationalized and hoped. *Since they've shaved her head,* I thought, *they surely will operate and she will be fine.* I went to sleep imagining a smiling Ursina with short, curly hair.

The next morning I learned the agonizing truth as the grim news spread throughout our shocked town.

Ursina had died.

I shut my eyes, remembering her peeping down into the empty Coke bottle and grinning. I recalled how her eyes sparkled when tears threatened. I thought about how coming to America had been her life's dream. My small hometown had been America for Ursina.

I couldn't cry. I ached inside, unable to shed tears. Then I began to think about her mother—what bitterness she must have for people in Elberton, America.

Elberton mourned. At the funeral home, Ursina's body was never left alone. They had dressed her in the new green evening gown she had never gotten to wear. Later at a memorial service, a granite statue of Ursina, chiseled

by a gifted artist from Elberton, was placed in the school-
yard and a well-known columnist from Atlanta spoke. She
wrote about Ursina and Elberton in her column. Our
senior class dedicated the annual to Ursina's memory. We
used the picture of her in the new green dress. She would
never see that photograph. Underneath the picture it
said, "Ursina Stahnke, beloved German exchange student
who was accidentally killed while horseback riding on
September 17, 1953—to know her was to love her."

Many people from Elberton sent messages of sympathy
to Ursina's family in Hamburg, Germany. I couldn't write
a letter. It seemed incredible to me that her mother
wanted to hear from Americans. How she must hate us!

I tried to pray for them. Maybe prayer is an attitude of
the heart after all and God understands a silent, aching
heart that doesn't know the exact words to say to Him.

A prayer that I hadn't known how to express was
answered through a letter from Ursina's mother. Our local
newspaper published it. Reading the letter, feelings I
couldn't put into words welled up inside me and I finally
cried for a long time.

> *The weeks in America were the crown of Ursina's life. She
> loved America before she had seen it. America had always
> been the goal of her thoughts and desires. I had only jubilant
> letters from her. She seemed to live in a dream; she was drunk
> with joy about the lovable people in Elberton. Ursina drank
> in all the beauty and was enjoying life in a manner that she
> never had been able to in our narrow circumstances. It could
> not have become any more beautiful perhaps—therefore, my
> beloved child had to go. She came home very much differently
> from what we had pictured. On the 25th of September we
> saw the child once more—like Snow White lying in her cof-
> fin, but already quite distant and sublime. We became quiet
> and prayerful at her sight.*

The chapel had been turned into a sea of sunflowers at my wish and it was filled with music, 'Andante' by Hayden. I chose the twenty-third Psalm for the minister to read, and later learned that you also had chosen that Scripture for her in Elberton.

I don't feel anything but gratitude for the people of Elberton for helping Ursina realize her dream. How beautifully and how lovely you sent me my child! Your acts of love are a wall around my heart. I have become quiet. God would have taken her here too—I know this for certain.

Please give Ursina's clothes to poor children in Elberton.

I will by and by write more letters to Elberton. We don't ever want to miss the love of friends that spoke to us from letters. My children and I greet all the dear people of Elberton. We are more often with you now than here, as if we could still reach Ursina there. There shall remain a bridge of affection which my beloved child has built between our people.

Ursina's family later crossed that bridge and came to Elberton for a visit. I was out of town and didn't meet them. But I already knew them. They were people, like Ursina, with amazing love for my country. They were people who simply would not turn their backs on my town, my country.

As time passed, I often caught myself looking for beauty in the simplest places, expecting happiness out of heartache, and experiencing forgiveness where bitterness might have grown.

Marion Bond West

5

ACTS OF KINDNESS

The best portion of a good man's life is his little, nameless, unremembered acts of kindness and love.

William Wordsworth

The Vote Was Unanimous

If there is any kindness I can show, or any good
thing I can do to any fellow human being, let
me do it now, and not defer or neglect it, as I
shall not pass this way again.

William Penn

Bob Leverenz couldn't figure out what all the fuss was about. As president and board chairman of Leverenz Shoe Company in southeastern Wisconsin, he was just proud that his employees were willing to help out the world-famous Allen-Edmonds Shoe Company when their factory burned to the ground. Allen-Edmonds lost everything in the multimillion-dollar fire: fifty thousand pairs of men's dress shoes, sales records, files and machinery.

After a planning session with his management personnel, Bob took to a vote with the union workers in their New Holstein plant the idea of sharing their own Leverenz factory space with Allen-Edmonds. They presented a plan whereby the Leverenz workers would condense their work week into four ten-hour days. This would free up the factory for the Allen-Edmonds people to use their facilities to make their shoes on Fridays, Saturdays and Sundays.

When the union vote was taken, every hand in the place shot up. The members of the local United Food and Commercial Workers Union voted unanimously to share their factory space and machines with their competitors.

That's when the media descended upon the Leverenz Shoe Company. The wire services called. Radio, TV stations and newspapers nationwide wanted to know about the shoe company that had opened its doors to help out a burned-out competitor. Even Dan Rather at CBS cast them in the national limelight during his evening TV news broadcast. Bob received congratulatory letters from people all over the country, but quite honestly he couldn't understand what the fuss was all about. To his mind, it was simple. Someone was in trouble and they were able to help.

One of the interviewers from CBS asked Bob, "How is it that if Macy's burned down, other department stores would rejoice in the added business it would bring their way? How could you be so different? How could you help someone who is competing with you for the consumer's shoe dollar? How could you actually let them come in to your factory, and use your machines and equipment to make their shoes?"

Bob told the interviewer that the answers to those questions began in 1970 when he attended a layman's leadership institute in Miami. After three days of talks by prominent business, political and sports figures, Leighton Ford, vice president of the Billy Graham Evangelistic Association, challenged the participants. "I don't have any idea of the depth of your commitment to the Lord. Perhaps you want to renew your commitment or make one for the first time."

At that moment Bob knew that everything he'd been

doing for God, the church and his community he'd actually been doing to elevate himself in the eyes of his
friends, family, coworkers and fellow citizens. Suddenly
he knew he'd just been going through the motions of
being a Christian.

At home Bob paged through his Bible and found a verse
in Romans:

"Then what can we boast about doing, to earn our salvation? Nothing at all. Why?

"Because our acquittal is not based on our good deeds;
it is based on what Christ has done and our faith in him.
So it is that we are saved by faith in Christ and not by the
good things we do." (Romans 3:27-28)

That was it! All his life, Bob had been headed in the
right direction, knowing that God was real. He chugged
along, teaching another Sunday school class, raising a
little more money for various organizations and thinking
he was a Christian. But when he read that verse in
Romans he understood that all those actions and good
deeds must be the outgrowth of his faith, rather than a
substitute for it.

His interest in people—their hurts, needs and wants—
intensified. At last he was trying to minister because of his
allegiance to God and not because it was a good thing to
do, because it was expected of him, or because it made
him look good.

Soon after Bob had a chance to put his new commitment to work at the Leverenz Shoe Company. Because of
the major recession in this country in 1974, it was ques-
tionable whether he could continue to operate their New
Holstein plant. Division in the ranks, jealousies, high
emotions and back-biting among employees were
destroying them. Bob had never seen these attitudes in
the company before.

One day at the factory he shut off the main switch,

called all the workers together and asked them to pray with him. In that tiny town of New Holstein, Wisconsin, 150 workers and Bob prayed their way out of the doldrums of low morale.

Bob spoke aloud. "Lord, remind me how much I depend on my fellow workers to make my job go smoothly. Help me to remember that without the person next to me my job would have no meaning. Lord, help us work together and respect each other."

No one can ever tell Bob Leverenz that prayers aren't answered. The transformation in that factory was miraculous. After they prayed together those people in New Holstein started helping each other in a constructive way. They corrected things done by previous operators on machines that were detracting from a quality product. Attitudes changed.

Now the emphasis was on making a better pair of shoes instead of climbing over the next person to get ahead.

One other time Bob brought his workers together to pray. In November 1983 they were faced with the grim fact that two-thirds of the shoe companies in this country had gone out of business because of the influx of imported shoes. They desperately wanted to keep their company together, but to do this, they'd have to lay off thirty percent of the people from the New Holstein and Valders factories.

But something just wasn't sitting right. Bob wondered, *Are we really supposed to take this drastic measure?* He thought about the verse from Romans and wondered if this is what Christ would have done. Did he have the right to put 30 percent of his employees out of work? Instead of ending the meeting and moving ahead with the plan, Bob asked his management committee to pray with him about the decision. The discussion that followed brought about a solid feeling that they should scrap the factory reorganization and cutback plan, and talk to the workers instead.

That afternoon they visited both plants, New Holstein and Valders. They explained how dismal the prospects were for the future. Then Bob asked all the employees to pray with him. After the prayer, the discussion that followed brought out all sorts of money-saving suggestions.

Just two months later, in January 1984, business started to zoom. Salesmen brought in orders from new customers. Previous customers reordered in huge quantities. By mid-March, sales figures were forty to fifty percent higher than they'd been the previous year. In many respects business was the best it had been in ten years.

During this wave of success came the Allen-Edmonds fire. Some say that could have been the frosting on the cake for the Leverenz Shoe Company. With Allen-Edmonds, one of the leaders in high-quality men's dress shoes, out of business even temporarily, the Leverenz shoes could have seen even greater sales. But that's just not the way the folks at the Leverenz Shoe Company did things anymore.

Bob admits that when the Allen-Edmonds people moved into their plant on weekends he wondered if they'd misuse their machines, if they'd know how to lubricate them, if they'd leave messes that his employees would have to clean up. Would their special equipment get in the way of the Leverenz machines?

He needn't have worried. Two Leverenz employees offered to come in that first weekend on their own time to help adjust the machinery to meet Allen-Edmonds' needs and to help their workers place their raw materials in a convenient location.

Then workers from both companies started leaving notes for each other, little greetings, words of appreciation. On Valentine's Day the Allen-Edmonds people left a jar of candy and a cute card for the Leverenz people.

The second week one of the Leverenz workers left them a note, "You don't have to take all those packages of laces home with you each weekend. Leave them here. I've cleared off a shelf for you."

Heartwarming relationships developed among the workers of the two shoe companies . . . workers who never met each other face to face.

When Bob said he couldn't figure out what all the fuss was about when the media descended upon their little factory after the fire, it's because what they did came so naturally. Bob believes that his union workers in New Holstein probably read that verse in Romans even before he did.

It's a simple story, really. Everyone at the Leverenz Shoe Company believed that helping each other is what true faith in God is all about. And when you're really working for the Lord, you can't do anything less than help out a competitor when the opportunity arises. Just ask the folks at the factory in New Holstein. They voted on it unanimously.

Patricia Lorenz

The Cookie Lady

Rain droned against the office window, matching my mood. I should have known that my new job at the hospital was too good to be true. Throughout the day, rumors warned that the newest employee from each department would be laid off due to a drop in census. I was the newest one in the training department.

My boss appeared at the door of my cubicle, interrupting my thoughts. "Got a minute?"

My neck chilled as if he'd shoved ice under my collar. I figured a minute would be all he needed to say, "You're fired!" Would it matter if I told him about my roof leak and overdue notices?

"You probably know we're cutting back," he began. "Administration wants us to offer outplacement classes to help those employees find other jobs. Show them how to write a resume, make a good impression in an interview and so on."

Apprehension made a fist in my stomach. I might as well have been an executioner sharpening her own ax. "Fine," I mumbled, not knowing what else to say.

After he left, I decided to go home early. If someone saw

my tears, I'd pretend I had allergies. Through my blurry eyes, I noticed a paper plate of peanut butter cookies, crisscrossed with fork marks, on the secretary's desk.

"Who brought the cookies?" I asked.

"Some lady leaves them every Friday," she said. "Help yourself."

I blotted my eyes with the back of my hand before taking two. *Life's so ironic,* I thought. I was expected to teach a job-hunting class before I got my own pink slip while some rich volunteer donated cookies so she wouldn't feel guilty about not having to work. Her maid probably baked them.

"See you tomorrow," I said, wondering how many more times I'd have the chance to say that.

In the hall, the elevator door opened, revealing a gray-haired woman about the height of a third-grader. Only her head and the top of her green apron were visible over the cart loaded with cleaning supplies. At least she had a job!

All the way home, I fought self-pity, finally giving in to the tears when I reached my driveway. I couldn't remember feeling so alone. And scared.

The next morning, I considered telling my boss to teach the classes himself. I didn't have the nerve, though, so I drove to the library for books to help me prepare my classes.

Later at the hospital, when anyone mentioned my leaving, I joked about taking early retirement and living in the barn on my father's farm.

I kept up the pretense of not caring for the next two weeks until the Friday of the final meeting with the personnel staff in the basement. Personnel employees handed out final paychecks and collected office keys while I waited at a table with my class schedule for those interested in help. Laid-off workers formed a line at the door, most of them crying. I'd be just like them in a couple of weeks.

The chaplain took the seat next to me, probably so he could comfort those who wanted to talk. He opened his Bible, worn and marked with yellow highlighter.

While he greeted the first employee to reach us, I glanced over to see what he'd highlighted. It was Romans 12:5: " . . . so we, though many, are one body in Christ, and individually members of one another. Having gifts that differ according to the grace given us, let us use them." I read the rest of the passage before he reached for the book. "He, who teaches, in his teaching."

It was one thing to have a gift; another to have the chance to use it, I thought. My throat tightened against the tears that threatened.

Out of the corner of my eye, I noticed a woman in a green apron shuffling to the table. The chaplain leaned over and whispered, "Good heavens! I can't believe our Cookie Lady is being laid off. We'll miss her as much as we'll miss her peanut butter cookies on Fridays."

Cookie Lady? I stared at the woman, noticing that her fingers were crooked, probably from arthritis. She certainly didn't fit the description of the wealthy volunteer I'd imagined.

Settling in the chair in front of us, she folded her hands in her lap like an obedient child waiting for instructions. When the chaplain spoke to her in Spanish, I knew my classes were useless for her.

She smiled and reached into the pocket of her apron to offer us cookies from a paper sack.

"Gracias," I mumbled, wishing I knew more of her language. Suddenly, my self-pity turned to shame as I realized how much better off I was than this poor woman who still thought of others despite her problems. The cookies seemed to emphasize the words from Romans—

we belong to each other and each needs the other.

I knew I had to do something for her, even before I examined the classified section of the newspaper for myself.

At noon, the last of the workers filed past our table. I grabbed the cookies, all I planned to eat for lunch, and returned to my cubicle.

Grateful for the midday silence, I wrote and revised until I was satisfied I'd expressed how I felt about the unselfishness of the Cookie Lady who needed a job. Finally, I slid my article into an envelope and asked the boss for permission to leave for awhile, not explaining I was headed for the newspaper office.

Maybe my efforts wouldn't work, but at least I tried. *This would be my cookie for her,* I thought as I pulled into the newspaper building's parking lot.

After I located the appropriate office, the features editor agreed to see me for just two minutes because he was on deadline.

"I don't know if you print freelance material," I told him. "And I don't expect to be paid for this if you use it. . . ."

"I'll look at it later," he promised, then returned to his work, so I knew my time was up.

Days went by and no story appeared. Why had I felt so sure that my story would interest the editor who had plenty of staff to write features? Several times I started to telephone but decided that if God wanted it to happen, it would.

I scanned the classifieds daily, but found no jobs I felt qualified for. Then after I decided that my article never would be published, I found it by accident.

Obviously, I wasn't the only one who noticed it; messages were in my slot on the secretary's desk. One was from the bakery down the street.

I held my breath as I dialed the bakery's number. This

had to be a job for the Cookie Lady. . . . Within minutes, I had an appointment to bring her in for an introduction to the bakery's owner. Excitement turned to anxiety when I realized I shouldn't have been so presumptuous.

Footsteps startled me and I glanced up to see the chaplain, newspaper in hand, and the Cookie Lady behind him.

"Good piece," the chaplain said. "Just wanted to tell you before we went to the employment agency."

"Maybe you can skip that," I said, smiling. "The bakery down the street has an opening. The owner read my article and thought she. . . . Will you take her down since I can't translate for her?"

He grinned. "Be happy to, but she won't need a translator. Those folks are from Mexico, so she'll fit in just fine."

After they left, I couldn't concentrate on my search through the classifieds, wondering if she got the job. After all, she taught me to think of others in spite of my own problems.

I took the other messages from my pocket. At least I could answer the rest of my calls before I left. One seemed so unlikely that I read it twice. "An editor of a local magazine liked your piece and wants you to call her next time you're looking for work. Here's her number and the name of her magazine."

Surely I couldn't have found a job so easily before I'd even mailed out a resume. No question about it—we are all one in body with Christ and I intended to remind others, just as the Cookie Lady had reminded me.

Kathryn Fanning

God's Love in a Baseball Card?

We get in return exactly what we give. It all comes back. Incredible echoes mirror our actions to an empathic degree, sometimes in greater measure than we give.

Charles Swindoll

It is August 1999. We are in a small town in Northern Michigan at our son's wedding reception. The best man, Doug, is about to make a toast. I look at our son, Ben, and I marvel at the man he has become. My mind drifts away for a moment, reflecting on some events from the last twenty-five years.

It is late March 1974. It is 2 A.M. and I have fallen momentarily asleep. We are at the hospital waiting on the birth of our first child. The doctor nudges my shoulder. "We're going to have to do a C-section. Labor has not progressed in several hours. The baby is in fetal distress." Okay. I am worried. There is a blur of activity. My wife only wants relief from the nauseating pain. The surgery is quick. In 1984, most fathers still waited in the fathers' room. Shortly, the doctor returned. "You have a son.

Mother and child are fine." My mind races with a flood of thoughts: *Is he healthy? Will his mother recover? What will he become? What will we do together?* Soon life returns to normal, and we are grateful to God for his gift to us.

As I begin to listen to the best man's toast at the wedding, more memories fly by in my thoughts. There was the first fish he caught. Though only a small sunfish, it was an incredible marvel to a four-year-old watching it slowly rise out of the water's depth. Hunting and fishing were to become his passions. Over time he devoted most of his spare time and money to these pursuits. We approved. Young people have a difficult enough time growing up in our contemporary society. Because of his love for the outdoors, we never really had to worry about him.

One other interest area captured some of his time between the ages of seven and twelve. Like most boys his age, he loved to collect baseball cards. By whatever means were at his disposal and with great gusto and passion, he collected these cards representing his boyhood heroes. Over time, he amassed a rather large collection. The cards themselves represented carefully saved and spent allowance money, chore money, gifts from friends, holiday stocking stuffers, vacation souvenirs, birthday presents and, of course, the product of intricately planned trading sessions with his buddies. Special cards dating back to the early 1950s were purchased or received as gifts.

Then, like many things in life, his interest in sports cards and collecting began to wane. The large box with the card collection found its quiet resting place in the back of a closet as if it were waiting for better days. It was a box of memories and a repository of connections with the past.

Back to the wedding. I am looking at Ben's new bride,

Andrea. She is beautiful and full of pride for her new husband. It is a special moment. I wonder if she knows how much she means to Ben. A few months earlier Ben had shared his intent with us to marry Andrea. We were pleased but a little taken aback that he was ready to make one of life's most meaningful commitments. His pursuit of his interest areas had not left him well-positioned to buy an engagement ring. As parents we felt that it was important for Ben to find the means to purchase the ring. Our hope was that it would help him realize the extent of the commitment he was making, and it would help him experience the self-sacrifice that goes into making a relationship work.

The process of saving for the ring quickly became tedious. The passions of young love seemed frustrated by the process. Ben came up with the idea of selling his sports card collection. After all, it was worth quite a bit of money by now and it was only gathering dust in the closet. What could be more important than solidifying his relationship with Andrea? After cataloging the cards and getting some idea of their worth, Ben set a price for the collection. A friend's father seemed to see the value in the collection as an investment and he purchased it. Ben couldn't have been happier. Though there was some sense of loss for the collection, he could now go about the business of forming a permanent relationship with Andrea.

Back to the wedding toast. . . . The best man, Doug, had just finished describing some of the good times he and Ben had experienced hunting together. He then began telling the story of a young boy's love of his baseball card collection and his ultimate willingness to sell the collection to buy a diamond ring for his wife-to-be. A light hush fell over the reception as the guests began to realize the significance of the sacrifice Ben had made. As Doug proceeded with his toast, many eyes began to well up with tears. Perhaps those listening identified with the loss of something meaningful as part of pursuing a loving relationship.

And then the incredible happened. It was Doug's father who had purchased the card collection several months earlier. In an unbelievable moment of kindness and grace, Doug gave Ben's card collection back to him. It was a stunning reminder of how God's love can be mirrored through us to others.

We will never forget that moment. It was as if time stood still. Briefly, we were able to glimpse part of the true significance of life—through baseball cards!

Now it is October 1999. Ben has his new wife. Their marriage is a joyful thing to behold as they live out their young love for each other. He also has his baseball cards—probably gathering dust in a new closet. You see, it is not the cards and their memories that count. In this instance, these simple sports cards were a clear example of God's unconditional love and grace for us—a gift we can never fully repay. The marriage will grow. The sports cards will be a legacy to pass on. The message of God's awesome grace that they represent will, hopefully, be repeated many times over by those who chose to see it on a summer evening in a small town in Northern Michigan.

John Nielsen

Giving Life

Nothing seemed out of the ordinary when m᾿ husband, Marvin, walked in with mail in hand. As he began
sorting through the usual envelopes, he came to a r᾿nde-
script envelope addressed to him. He opened it to᾿nd a
generic card with a picturesque scene adorning the᾿ont.
Opening the card, he read what must be the most p᾿ent
words anyone has ever written him: "Thank you for᾿av-
ing my life."

Several years ago, Marvin and I were in church w᾿en
someone made a plea to the congregation for bone m᾿r-
row donors. A young boy in our community was dy᾿g
and his only hope was to find an unrelated bone marro᾿
donor. When we left church, Marvin suggested we go t᾿
the drive and register to be donors. And so we did.

Unfortunately, neither of us matched the young boy
and he died soon after. However, years later Marvin
received a letter stating that he was a possible match for
someone else. Marvin called the telephone number, and
so began our experience with the National Bone Marrow
Donor Program.

Marvin completed several more blood tests to confirm

that he was a match to this anonymous patient. Every time he was contacted it was to continue to the next step, until November 1998 when he was notified that he was a near perfect match and they scheduled an operation date.

This was an exciting time for our family as my husband, eleven-year-old daughter and I prepared to welcome our first son into this world—due date, November 25. The first date suggested to my husband for the operation was on our son's due date, so he declined and scheduled it for two weeks earlier. Marvin left, beeper in hand, along with my father to drive three hours to the out-of-state hospital. All of their expenses were covered, including the large steak dinner they treated themselves to.

I talked to Marvin on the phone after his surgery to assure him I was not in labor and he could relax. Marvin described the experience and the royal treatment he was given. He felt fine, a little sore. He told me about the nurses that were brought to tears when they learned why Marvin was at the hospital and about the doctors that so diligently cared for him. He told me about the note he wrote to his recipient wishing him well and sending our prayers. Marvin recovered very quickly during the day and so they drove home that evening.

Since the donor and the recipient are kept anonymous, we don't know whose life Marvin helped to save. For all I know, it could be you or your husband, brother, father or son.

Our son was born on his due date. As we watch him grow and mature, we know that somewhere there is a man who began his life again and is continuing to grow and mature. Men sometimes ask women what it is like to give life. Now I just say, "Ask my husband."

Kimberly White Kerl

The Easter Bunny

When I was a little girl, every Sunday my family of six would put on their best clothes and go to Sunday School and then church. The kids in elementary school would all meet together to sing songs, and then later divide into groups based on their ages.

One Easter Sunday, all the kids arrived with big eyes and big stories about what the Easter Bunny had brought. While all of the kids shared their stories with delight, one young boy, whom I shall call Bobby, sat sullenly. One of the teachers, noticing this, said to him, "And what did the Easter Bunny bring you?" He replied, "My mom locked the door on accident so the Easter Bunny couldn't get inside."

This sounded like a reasonable idea to all of us kids, so we kept on going with the stories. My mom knew the true story, though. Bobby's mom was a single parent, and she suspected that they just couldn't afford the Easter Bunny.

After Sunday school was over, everyone went off to church. When my dad came to meet us my mom announced that we were going home instead. At home, she explained that to make Bobby feel better, we were going to pretend to be the Easter Bunny and make a basket of our goodies for him and leave it at church. We all donated some of our candies to the basket, and headed back up to church. There, mom unzipped his coat, hung the basket over the hanger, and zipped up the coat and attached a note.

Dear Bobby,
  I'm sorry I missed your house last night. Happy Easter.
Love,
The Easter Bunny

Beth H. Arbogast

Reprinted with permission of Stephen Nease.

John's Heart

The house was strangely quiet when Linda Greaves opened the front door one evening last April, keys in one hand and a bag of groceries in the other.

"John?" she called, but there was no reply from her twenty-seven-year-old son.

The message light on the answering machine was flashing. *Maybe that's John calling to say he's running late,* Linda thought, pressing the rewind button.

There were three messages, but they weren't from John. They were about him. "Oh dear God, no!" Linda exclaimed, dropping the steaks as the messages began to play, each more urgent than the last.

"This is the hospital. John Greaves has been admitted to the trauma center. His condition is critical. Please call immediately."

With trembling fingers the Downingtown, Pennsylvania, single mother of three dialed and redialed the number, but the line kept ringing busy. Hysterical with panic, she called John's older brother, Jim.

"John's in the hospital!" she sobbed. "I can't get through! Please come quick!"

At the trauma center Linda learned that John had crashed his new red motorcycle when he failed to stop in time to avoid the car ahead. John had suffered a punctured lung and numerous broken bones in the wreck, and despite wearing the best helmet money could buy, he'd sustained a massive head injury and was now in a deep coma.

"His brain is peppered with tiny hemorrhages," the ER doctor told Linda and Jim. "It's as bad as it gets. I can't tell you what will happen."

John's entire life flashed through Linda's mind. The little boy who used to collect frogs from a nearby creek and act in homespun plays with his big sister, Janice. Then, as a teenager, the endless happy hours he and Jim had spent in the garage working on friends' cars and motorcycles.

Growing up without a dad, John had always given his mom such strength and comfort. Linda couldn't hold back the tears as she recalled all those Saturday mornings when she'd wakened to his question, "Hey Mom—what do you want in your omelet?" Or the many times she'd come home after a long day to find John beaming with pride, waiting to show her a formerly squeaky cabinet hinge or the patio door lock he'd repaired.

"Please, God, don't take him away," Linda prayed as the doctor led her and Jim to see John. "I can't imagine my life without him."

John was on life support and he looked so terrible that Jim hung his shoulders in despair. "I know he's gone. This is it," he murmured, but the instant the words crossed his lips Linda exploded in anger.

"I don't want to hear that from you!" she shouted in helpless fury. "As long as there's a chance John will get well, you or anyone else who wants to have negative thoughts can just take them outside because I refuse to have anything but love and positive thinking in this room."

The doctors could repair John's body, but there was little they could do for his head injury. "IIe has no detectable brain activity," the surgeon told Linda later that night as she sat at John's bedside praying to the angels for a miracle. But there was a slight chance the medicines they were using to help John rest might also be masking some faint brain activity. "For now we'll have to watch and wait," the doctor said.

Several days passed, but John's brain scans remained flat. Linda pinned a collage of photos of John to the bulletin board behind his bed. She wanted his doctors and nurses to know that he was more than just a patient. "He's my son, and he's going to get well," she insisted.

In one photo John was a teenager holding a twelve-foot python. In another he was only two and sitting on his very first riding toy; a shiny red motorcycle. John had always loved motorcycles, and he'd ridden them ever since he was seventeen. Linda's son had always been extremely safety-conscious, but clutching his limp hand she couldn't help but wonder, "Was I a bad mother for letting him ride them?"

On the fifth and sixth days John's physical condition began to rally. His lion's heart beat regular and strong. "You're going to make it," Linda told him, certain he could hear her.

The doctors withdrew the sedatives, and after they had cleared his system they ran another brain scan. "I'm terribly sorry," the neurosurgeon said when he met with Linda on the seventh day to review the results. "There's absolutely no brain activity. I'm afraid John is brain dead."

Linda burst into gasping tears. "That's it," she sobbed. "It's all over. I've lost John."

A while later, while Linda and other family members were talking about final arrangements, a Gift of Life representative approached and broached the difficult subject. "John checked the box on his driver's license to become an organ donor," he said tentatively, and the instant he spoke the words a vivid image of Carol Hagan, a friend from work, appeared before Linda.

There were tears in Carol's eyes, and Linda knew why. Last September Carol's husband, Christopher, had come down with a virus that had all but destroyed his heart muscle. Christopher was a carpenter, a volunteer fire fighter and rescue worker. But today Carol's husband was confined to home, too ill to work. Without a new heart the man who volunteered to save lives would soon lose his own life.

Linda had never met Christopher, but her heart went out to Carol. Linda now knew how agonizing it was to watch helplessly as someone you love slipped away. And Carol had two young children to raise. *How would she manage?* Linda wondered.

Before, at work, there was nothing Linda could do but listen when Carol shared her troubles and count her own blessings. But now maybe there was something she could do to make a real difference.

Linda asked the transplant representative, "Can it be done?" and when he answered affirmatively she reached for a phone and called her friend at work.

"How's John?" Carol blurted when she recognized Linda's voice.

"He's not going to make it," Linda replied. "We're getting ready to take him off life support. That's why I'm calling. I want your husband to have John's heart."

Carol was numb with shock. "I must be talking to an angel," she finally managed.

By now both women were in tears. Linda handed the phone to the transplant representative so he could get some information. Miraculously, both John and Christopher were blood type A, and they were each six feet, one inch tall.

"We'll have to run tests, but it looks like a good match," the representative told Carol. "Get your husband to the hospital as soon as possible."

A while later Linda and the others gathered at John's bedside to say their final good-byes. "You were always so giving, I know this is what you would want us to do," Linda said. Kissing her son, she told him one last time, "I will always love you."

At that very moment Carol and Christopher were on their way to the hospital. "I can't believe Linda would think of us at a time like this," Carol said, wiping away tears of sorrow and hope.

Linda was home later that night when the hospital called to tell her John was a perfect donor match for her friend's husband. His kidneys and liver would also help others to live.

In the morning Linda received a second call. Christopher's transplant was a resounding success. Hanging up the phone, Linda turned her head heavenward and whispered, "Thanks, John. Because of you there are at least two little children who won't have to grow up without a dad."

Four days after the transplant Linda was invited to visit Christopher in the hospital. "Hi," he greeted her from the waiting-room doorway, and Linda could hardly believe he was already strong enough to walk on his own. Linda leapt to her feet and threw her arms around her friend's husband, trying hard not to squeeze too tight.

"Feel this," Christopher said, taking Linda's hand and pressing it to his chest.

"It feels just like John's heart beating," she wept.

"I can't even remember my own heart beating so strongly," Christopher told Linda.

"My son had a lion's heart, and now it belongs to you," Linda explained.

"Thank you, from all of us," said Carol.

"I'm the one who's grateful to you," Linda replied. "Because of you, a piece of my son gets to live on."

Poring through Linda's photos, Christopher observed, "I feel like I have a new family. Do you have any advice for me?"

Linda thought for a moment, then, with tears spilling down her cheeks, she told him, "Have fun and laugh a lot. Love your wife and say your prayers . . . and talk to me once in awhile."

Bill Holton
Excerpted from Woman's World *magazine*

"The heart from a donor must already be full of love."

Reprinted with permission from Bil Keane.

Warts and All

Whatever you did for one of the least of these brothers of mine, you did for me.

Matthew 24:40

In the fifth grade, I fell madly in love with a new girl named Barbara. She had moved to our town from the city and possessed a sensual, sophisticated glamour I found most alluring. We sat alphabetically, and since her last name began with a D and mine with a G, she was placed next to me.

I would sit in my chair and inhale Barbara's perfume, thanking God I was born to a man named Gulley and not Zelinski. David Zelinski sat four rows away, also awash in love, bemoaning his cruel fate. Halfway through the year, Barbara's stepfather adopted her, her last initial changed from D to W, and she moved four rows over next to David. Thus was David's faith in a benevolent God reborn, while I teetered on the edge of atheism.

This was the first in a chain of curses during what turned out to be a Job-like year. On the heels of her name change, I contracted a virus which caused twenty-six warts to grow on my hands. On Sunday mornings at Saint Mary's, I would lift my wart-rounded hands heavenward and implore God to heal my affliction. On Mondays, Barbara would steal glances at my hands, speculating on what repulsive deed I must have done to merit such a leprous condition.

Doctor Kirtley spoke of a miracle worker in the city, a man who burned warts off. My mother drove me to his office, where he painted my warts with his formula. Within a week my warts fell off, though in a month's time they grew back even more profusely, much like a meadow razed by fire regenerates fourfold a season later. Then Doctor Kirtley sent us to a man who froze my warts off. I had to wear bandages on my hands for several weeks. I would stand Napoleon-like on the playground, my bandaged hands thrust under my jacket. That cure, too, was short-lived, and I resigned myself to a life of privation.

The summer following that horrific year, my father took me to visit Harvey Ellis. Mr. Ellis worked at the town park and enjoyed a reputation as a man of virtue. My father was forever dragging me to meet people like Mr. Ellis, hoping their Christian values would rub off on me. Today, I return to my hometown and old-timers talk about Mr. and Mrs. Such-and-so and then say, "You probably don't know who I'm talking about; they were before your time." But I always remember and can tell of Saturday mornings on front-porch swings while Judge Helton and Harvey Ellis and Loren Ruthledge dispensed their timeless wisdom.

The Saturday I met Mr. Ellis, he shook my hand and then said, "I notice you have warts."

"Thirty-five of them," I told him, "and increasing by the week."

He eyed me up and down and then pulled a fifty-cent piece from the chest pocket of his overalls. "I'll buy them from you," he said. What an odd thing. My parents had spent upwards of a hundred dollars to have my warts removed, and Mr. Ellis wanted to pay fifty cents for them. I took the half-dollar from his workworn hand.

"Keep that money," he instructed, "and when your warts go away, use that same money to buy someone else's warts."

By the time our county fair came, my warts had vanished. Incredible, but true. I prowled the midway looking for Barbara, eager to make myself available for hand-holding if she had a mind to. But that summer she was holding hands with David Zelinski. Still, to be wart-free was such a blessing that her indifference scarcely mattered.

When I recall how Mr. Ellis brought me back into the human fold, I remember that Jesus once took ten lepers in hand and did the same. For years, they'd stood outside looking in. Then with a touch and a word and a healing, Jesus unlatched the gate and welcomed them home. Kindness is always looking to swing wide the mercy gate.

Mr. Ellis died the next year. I tucked the fifty-cent piece away in a box, and every now and again I pull it out to hold it. I've read somewhere that warts are genetic, so I'm saving it against the day my sons' warts stand betwixt them and their Barbaras.

Just before Mr. Ellis died, we named the park for him. I drive by and recall a Saturday morning, long ago, when a kind old man took an awkward young boy in hand and gifted him with a healing, warts and all.

Philip Gulley

A Brand-New Pair of Shoes

The teacher was young and enthusiastic, in her first year of teaching. The school she was assigned to was in one of the poorest towns in the province of Havana. Water was scarce. Most of it came from wells located on one side of town. She saw people around the school carrying buckets of water every day for use in their houses. The children were always clean no matter how old, tattered or patched their clothing was.

The teacher's favorite pupil was a nine-year-old girl with brown hair and expressive eyes. She smiled all the time. She was always tidy and her hair well-combed. Her dress was washed and ironed but her shoes were almost gone. The teacher didn't believe much more could be done for them. By the beginning of the second semester, the little girl's shoes were nothing more than rags wrapped around her feet. That weekend the teacher bought a brand-new pair of shoes for the little girl. They were made of genuine leather and had a bow on top. They looked lovely on the girl's feet.

At the end of the school year, the teacher was successful in her bid to transfer to the city of Havana to a school where most children came from a better background. She taught there for over thirty years until she retired and began devoting her time to reading and writing.

One day she was taken to a small private clinic with double pneumonia. She had been paying her membership quota at the clinic for years but had never used it. She was surprised at the good services and attention she received from the clinic's personnel. It seemed as if the doctors and nurses were going out of their way to please her. One day, she told another patient how satisfied she was with the care she was receiving at the place.

"You can certainly say so," the other lady said. "I will say, since you've been coming, the rest of us have been treated more kindly, also."

"What are you trying to imply?" the teacher asked. "I'm nobody important, and I don't know anyone here. Why would they give me more attention?"

"Well, ask if you don't believe me."

That evening, when her favorite nurse came to see her, the teacher asked, "Is it true that I have been given special attention here?"

"Yes, it is," the nurse answered. "The director, Dr. Mendez, asked us to take good care of you."

Mendez was a very common name, and the teacher didn't remember anyone in particular with that name. Upon dismissal, she decided to thank Dr. Mendez personally. She knocked at her door.

"Come in," a voice said.

Upon entering, the teacher saw an attractive lady in her forties, who smiled at her.

"Dr. Mendez, I came to thank you for ordering your staff to take care of me in such a wonderful way. How can I repay you?"

"You repay me?" the director said. "I'm the one trying to repay you."

"I don't understand. I don't remember having met you before."

"Oh, but you have, my dear. You were my inspiration, my role model. You were the motor which propelled me to strive for a better future. You gave me the desire to improve myself and my lot. I owe you everything I am and have achieved in life."

"But I don't see how...."

"You don't remember me, do you? I'm that poor girl for whom, one day, you bought a brand-new pair of shoes, the most precious leather shoes in the whole wide world."

Graciela Beecher

Sharing with the Preacher

My first year at seminary, I did my field work at the state penitentiary in Richmond, Virginia—a cold, creepy place with steel doors that clanged shut. In the infirmary was a young man about my age. His eyes were hard, angry and showing hurt like a cornered animal. Loudly he welcomed me with, "Here comes another one of them preachers. You're all a bunch of hypocrites."

"You're right. And so are you. Welcome to the club," I fired back.

He flung all the usual accusations at me. My answers were not what he expected. Thus began a weekly ritual in which we would talk while those in the other beds listened closely. Soon his story came out.

His family fell apart and he lived in the streets, supporting himself by stealing cars. He was in prison for multiple car thefts. To avoid work detail, he injected his foot with gasoline. He overdid it and his foot was now permanently damaged. He might even lose it. No wonder he was furious. My heart ached for him.

Gradually we learned to respect each other and even had some laughs together. Soon we were discussing our purpose in life. His tone softened. We became friends. He began to think of himself as a Christian.

Then it was time for me to move to my summer field-work in a rural church. I felt sad and I noticed the same feeling in him as he asked, "Preacher . . . this our last day?"

"Yeah. I'm gonna miss you, guy," I replied.

He beckoned me to come to the side of his bed. He put his hand behind my neck and abruptly pulled me down so my ear was next to his mouth. In a whisper, he explained to me in detail the two best ways to hot-wire a car, which cars were easiest to steal and which method worked best on which make of car.

I almost laughed. *Me, a minister, stealing cars?* Then I realized what he was doing. He was giving me his most precious possession, the one skill he had developed in life.

My eyes filled with tears. All I could do was stammer, "Thanks. If I ever lose my car keys, I'll know what to do. Take care of yourself, buddy." I left hurriedly so people wouldn't see the tears running down my face.

At that moment, I learned that love is expressed in many different ways.

Robert J. McMullen Jr.

Mother Teresa, the Wino and Me

*Now abideth faith, hope, charity, these three;
but the greatest of these is charity.*

1 Corinthians 13:13

I will never forget the day I met Mother Teresa. More
than that, I will never forget what she taught me about
loving other people, especially the poor.

She wasn't nearly as famous in the late seventies as she
is now, but she already had hundreds of thousands of
admirers around the world. I was the editor of a Catholic
newspaper in Rhode Island and when I heard she would
be speaking in Boston I decided to go.

I arrived at the auditorium early to get a good seat, but
I discovered that I'd already been granted a seat in the
press section. As I waited for the lecture to begin, I passed
the time by chatting with another reporter, who turned
out to be, like Mother Teresa, a native of Albania. As we
were talking, a priest walked over and said to my companion, "Mother Teresa would be happy to meet you right
now."

With uncharacteristic boldness, I rose to my feet and

tagged along. So did a handful of other reporters. We were ushered into a room where a little old lady wrapped in a blue-and-white sari was chatting with the Cardinal Humberto Medeiros, then archbishop of Boston.

I couldn't believe how tiny she was. But what I remember most is her smiling, wrinkled face and the way she bowed to me, as if I were royalty, when I was introduced.

She greeted everyone that way. I thought that if Jesus Christ walked into the room, she would greet him in exactly the same manner. The way she did it conveyed a message that said, "You are holy."

But meeting her wasn't as memorable as what she taught me about loving people. Until that day, I had always thought of charity as simply being nice to people. For Mother Teresa it was much more.

During her talk, she told us how she and the members of her order, the Missionaries of Charity, seek to recognize Christ in the poorest of the poor.

She told a story of how one of the sisters had spent an entire day bathing the wounds of a dying beggar who was brought to them from the streets of Calcutta. Mother Teresa's voice dropped to a whisper as she told the hushed auditorium that, in reality, the nun had been bathing the wounds of Jesus.

She insisted that Christ tests the love of his followers by hiding in grotesque disguises to see if we can still see him.

A few nights later, I was leaving my office after dark when a drunk accosted me. He was dirty and ragged and smelled bad.

"Did the bus leave yet?" he asked.

The only bus that ever stopped on that corner was a van that carried street people to a soup kitchen.

"You've missed it," I told him. Then I thought about Mother Teresa. I didn't exactly buy the idea that this old bum was God in disguise, but I could see a person in front of me who needed a meal. The soup kitchen wasn't very far out of my way.

"C'mon, I'll drive you," I said, hoping that he wouldn't throw up in the car.

He looked surprised, delighted and a little stunned. He studied me with bleary eyes. His next words floated to me on the smell of cheap wine and they seemed to confirm everything Mother Teresa had taught me.

"Say," he said, "you must know me."

Robert F. Baldwin

Mrs. Tree and Her Gentleman Caller

*God has given us two hands—one to receive
with and the other to give with.*

Reverend Billy Graham

Mrs. Tree had lived alone since becoming a widow a quarter-century before. Like most people in our neighborhood, she had little. But what she did have was enough for her meager needs—rent, a little food, electricity and a donation each week to her church.

But she had not attended services for some time. Mrs. Tree was almost blind and, once her husband died, could not manage the two-block walk alone. One of her friends did her shopping, and Mrs. Tree's occasional trips to the doctor were made possible by a visiting nurse who came and picked her up.

We called her Mrs. Tree because her German name, *Baum*, she told us, meant tree. "*Tannenbaum* is a Christmas tree," she taught me patiently when I delivered papers with my brother Kevin on his paper route, "and *Rosenbaum* means rose tree."

Kevin had met the old woman one day while collecting

for his route. She was sitting on a back stoop enjoying the sun. Of course she had no need for a newspaper, but Kevin's outright friendliness did not depend on whether one was a customer.

"What do you do by yourself, Mrs. Tree?" he asked, realizing how lonely she was.

"I listen to my radio," she replied. "I love some of the stories on it, like *Ma Perkins* and *Helen Trent*. Then there is fine music in the evenings or sometimes a play or a show with that funny gentleman and that little wooden puppet, Charlie McCarthy."

To be sure, Mrs. Tree was a proud woman who seldom asked for help with anything. But Kevin had a way about him that invited confidences, and, one day after finishing his paper route, he announced he was accompanying Mrs. Tree to church on Sunday.

"You'll have your hands full!" Mama laughed. "I still remember when the Ladies' Guild went to see if they could help her and she told them to mind their own business!"

Mrs. Tree, Mama added, had been a very attractive woman; her husband, a dapper gentleman, had worked for the gas company in the office. Though they were not wealthy, they enjoyed a social life, and Mrs. Tree sort of considered herself the belle of the ball.

"Perhaps," Mama speculated with a light laugh, "being helped by ladies was not her cup of tea!"

"She seems nice enough to me," Kevin said quietly.

I giggled, secretly referring to the coming Sunday as "Kev's date."

When the first church date grew into a second and then, a third, Kevin showed no sign of quitting. Nor did Mrs. Tree. Each Sunday, she'd be ready and waiting, dressed in her best, for the walk to church. For his part, Kevin, in his Sunday clothes, would help her with her coat—which she always wore, even in the heat of summer.

All the way to church, Mrs. Tree clung lightly to Kevin's arm. Once inside, she insisted on sitting in front where she'd sat with her husband.

When Kevin led Mrs. Tree out of the church, the crowd on the sidewalks parted politely. They did not, however, disguise their interest in seeing the mysterious parishioner on the arm of my older brother.

During the week, Kevin told us that Mrs. Tree had invited him in for tea and they'd sat at a comfortable old table covered with a linen cloth. They drank the tea from china cups, he said, and ate little cookies made of shortbread. Kevin promised to ask Mrs. Tree next time if he could bring some cookies home for us to enjoy, too. The dates continued through the summer and into fall.

Though Kevin was not very talkative about his friendship with the elderly widow, he did confide that she often told him stories of her husband and how they had wished for children but had not been so blessed. She also showed him photographs of herself and her husband in their younger days. Kevin told us she was a "Corker indeed," which meant, in his practiced eye, she was very attractive.

As the leaves began to fall in earnest, Mrs. Tree seemed to slow a bit. Kev said she remarked more often about "these tired old bones" and how the winter days seemed to hang in her loneliness.

"I'll still come here for you!" Kevin protested. "And my brothers can come, too."

She smiled and told him he was a kind lad, and she thanked God for bringing him to help her.

As Kevin got up to leave, Mrs. Tree pointed out a crumb on his lip and handed him a handkerchief. He dabbed his lip and went to the door, absentmindedly taking with him the lace-bordered cloth.

"I forgot to give her the hanky!" he said, still clutching the sweet-smelling lincn when he got home.

"How did she know you had a crumb there," Mama asked, "with no eyes to see?"

Kevin stood thunderstruck. He turned to go out the door, intent on returning the hanky. But Mama told him she thought perhaps it was all right to stay put, and so he stashed thc handkerchief in his drawer, planning to return it on Sunday.

A few days later, Father O'Phelan informed us that Mrs. Tree had passed on the night before. Mama, though, was not surprised when we brought her the news. Indeed, she seemed to think that the handkerchief was the old woman's way of saying good-bye to my brother.

A funeral was held on Saturday morning, and Kevin sat next to Mama in the pew usually reserved for family. He was, for what it was worth, all she had.

It turned out that, shortly before she died, Mrs. Tree had bundled a few books and an old framed picture of her and her late husband with a note to give the items to Kevin. But the remembrance he cherished most was the old woman's sweet-smelling handkerchief. It was, he's said in the years since, her personal good-bye and a thank you far and above anything he ever expected.

Sean Patrick

Winter Morning Guest

The Lord helps those who help others.

Anonymous

One winter morning in 1931, I came down to breakfast—and found the table empty.

It was cold outside. The worst blizzard on record had paralyzed the city. No cars were out. The snow had drifted up two stories high against our house, blackening the windows.

"Daddy, what's happening?" I asked.

I was six years old. Gently Dad told me our fuel and food supplies were exhausted. He'd just put the last piece of coal on the fire. Mother had eight ounces of milk left for my baby brother Tom. After that—nothing.

"So what are we going to eat?" I asked.

"We'll have our devotions first, John Edmund," he said, in a voice that told me I should not ask questions.

My father was a pastor. As a Christian he'd been chased out of his Syrian homeland. He arrived as a teenager in the United States with no money and barely a word of English—

nothing but his vocation to preach. He knew hardship of a kind few see today. Yet my parents consistently gave away at least 10 percent of their income, and no one but God ever knew when we were in financial need.

That morning, Dad read the scriptures as usual, and afterwards we knelt for prayer. He prayed earnestly for the family, for our relatives and friends, for those he called the "missionaries of the cross" and those in the city who'd endured the blizzard without adequate shelter.

Then he prayed something like this: "Lord, Thou knowest we have no more coal to burn. If it can please Thee, send us some fuel. If not, Thy will be done—we thank Thee for warm clothes and bed covers, which will keep us comfortable, even without the fire. Also, Thou knowest we have no food except milk for Baby Thomas. If it can please Thee. . . ."

For someone facing bitter cold and hunger, he was remarkably calm. Nothing deflected him from completing the family devotions—not even the clamor we now heard beyond the muffling wall of snow.

Finally someone pounded on the door. The visitor had cleared the snow off the windowpane, and we saw his face peering in.

"Your door's iced up," he yelled. "I can't open it."

The devotions over, Dad jumped up. He pulled; the man pushed. When the door suddenly gave, an avalanche of snow fell into the entrance hall. I didn't recognize the man, and I don't think Dad did either because he said politely, "Can I help you?"

The man explained he was a farmer who'd heard Dad preach in Allegan three years earlier.

"I awakened at four o'clock this morning," he said, "and I couldn't get you out of my mind. The truck was stuck in the garage, so I harnessed the horses to the sleigh and came over."

"Well, please come in," my father said. On any other occasion, he'd have added, "And have some breakfast with us." But, of course, today there was no breakfast.

The man thanked him. And then—to our astonishment—he plucked a large box off the sleigh. More than sixty years later, I can see that box as clear as yesterday. It contained milk, eggs, butter, pork chops, grain, homemade bread and a host of other things. When the farmer had delivered the box, he went back out and got a cord of wood. Finally, after a very hearty breakfast, he insisted Dad take a ten-dollar bill.

Almost every day Dad reminded us that "God is the Provider." And my experience throughout adult life has confirmed it. "I have never seen the righteous forsaken nor their children begging bread." (Psalm 37:25) The Bible said it. But Dad and Mom showed me it was true.

John Edmund Haggai

Ali and the Angel

A few days after Thanksgiving, the pastor of a small church in South Milwaukee, Wisconsin, was shopping at a large mall north of Milwaukee. He wandered into a temporary store set up just for the holiday season, which contained one-of-a-kind statues and sculptures purchased from museums all over the world. Most of the stunning brass and bronze statues were life size. Some were over eight feet tall.

As Pastor Ron wandered down the first aisle, he looked at the prices, thousands of dollars for each. He wondered who could possibly afford to put one of those statues in their home. *Certainly no one from my small church,* he mused. *I doubt if there's a house in South Milwaukee big enough to do justice to one of these enormous statues.*

Pastor Ron wandered up another aisle when he saw it. The angel. An incredible angel . . . approximately four feet tall, cast bronze, with a six-foot wing span and the most beautiful face the pastor had ever seen.

Thinking about the memorial/hospitality room he was dreaming about for the back of his church, he stepped forward and turned over the price tag. He gasped when he saw $7,000 in neat black letters.

Whew! Too steep for our church, Pastor Ron muttered. His church only had about eight hundred families, mostly blue-collar workers struggling from paycheck to paycheck.

Just then a tall, striking gentleman who seemed to be of Middle Eastern descent walked up.

"May I be of help? The angel, she is beautiful, yes?"

"Oh, without a doubt. The most beautiful angel I've ever seen," Pastor Ron said wistfully. "But unfortunately I need to look at something much smaller."

He followed the dark-haired man to the rear of the store where he pointed out another angel, this one only eighteen inches tall.

"No, this is too small," Pastor Ron said. Even the little angel was beyond the price range for his church.

"We want to build a memorial," Pastor Ron began, "but we don't have that much money to. . . ." He stopped talking when he realized the salesman was no doubt of a different faith and perhaps wouldn't understand.

Pastor Ron followed the man up the aisle toward the front of the store where the first angel, the most beautiful one, stood with arms outstretched. Once more Pastor Ron paused to admire the delicate beauty of the sculpture and the peace radiating from the angel's face. He took a deep breath and started to thank the man for his time, when the salesman spoke.

"Tell me again. What is it you need the angel for?"

"Our church. I'm the pastor of a small church in South Milwaukee. We want to build a memorial, a sort of hospitality room in the back of church. A place where we can remember all of our deceased members. A place to celebrate the living as well. We'll have a bulletin board for photos of weddings, baptisms, confirmations . . . and I, well, I've been hoping to find an angel to preside over this place of prayer and hospitality."

"I see," said the tall, serious man as he pulled a calculator out of his pocket. "My name is Ali," he said. "I am the owner and manager. We travel all over the country with these exquisite museum pieces."

Ali punched numbers on his calculator. Then he cleared the total and started over.

Pastor Ron felt his shoulders sink as he thought to himself, *Even if he gives us a discount of twenty, thirty or even fifty percent, we still can't afford this angel. What am I doing here in a place where original, one-of-a-kind pieces of artwork are on display?* He began to feel uncomfortable, wishing he'd passed by this store during his visit to the mall.

Finally Ali finished fiddling with the calculator. "How does this look?" he said as he held the calculator in front of Pastor Ron's eyes. "I will even deliver the angel to your church for you personally," he said.

Pastor Ron's head jerked back a bit when he saw the figure. "Sixteen hundred dollars? Are you sure? You do mean the large angel, this one, the one priced at seven thousand dollars?"

"Yes. The artist signed this cast bronze angel. It is a museum masterpiece."

"But why?" It was all Pastor Ron could mutter.

Ali spoke softly. "Because I, too, am a spiritual man. I am a Muslim. I would rather see this angel in a house of prayer than in someone's home. All I ask is that on the day you put this angel in your church you ask your people to pray for Ali."

On the day Ali and his father delivered the angel to the little church in South Milwaukee, Pastor Ron began to understand a little more about angels. He learned that not all angels are gilded with copper and bronze. Not all of them have wings and small delicate faces. Some of them are tall with dark hair and black mustaches. One of them is a Muslim named Ali.

Patricia Lorenz

6

THE POWER
OF BELIEVING

*People of all ages of history have fought their
fears in one way or another, but the only
thing that really conquers fear is faith in the
Lord: "I will trust and not be afraid."*

Isaiah 12:2

Letters to a Stranger

For happiness brings happiness, and loving ways bring love, and giving is the treasure that contentment is made of.

Amanda Bradley

On a bitter January evening in 1992, the phone rang and my fifteen-year-old son Tajin hollered, "Mom, it's for you!"

"Who is it?" I asked. I was tired. It had been a long day. In fact, it had been a long month. The engine in my car died five days before Christmas, and I had just returned to work after being out with the flu. I was feeling overwhelmed by having to purchase another vehicle and having lost a week's pay due to illness. A cloud of despair hung over my heart.

"It's Bob Thompson," Tajin answered.

The name didn't register. As I walked over to pick up the phone, the last name seemed vaguely familiar. Thompson . . . Bob Thompson . . . Thompson? Like a computer searching for the right path, my mind finally made the connection. Beverly Thompson. In the brief time it took me to reach the phone, my mind replayed the last nine months.

As I drove to work last March, some patches of snow were still on the ground, but the river, winding on my left, had opened up and was full of swift-moving water. The warm sun shining through my windshield seemed to give hope of an early spring.

The winter of 1991 had been a hard one for me as a single working mother. My three children were in their teens, and I was finding it hard to cope with their changing emotional needs and our financial needs. Each month I struggled to provide the bare necessities.

I faithfully attended church and a Bible study but had very little time for anything else. I longed to serve the Lord in a way that had some significance. So that day I again apologized to him that I had so little to give back to him. It seemed I was always asking him to meet my needs or answer my prayers.

"Lord, what can I do for you? I feel like I'm always taking from you because my needs are so great." The answer to my own question seemed so simple. Prayer.

"Okay, Lord, I will commit this time that I have during my drive to work to prayer. Will you give me some people to pray for? I don't even have to know their needs, just let me know who they are." My heart lifted as I continued to speak to him during the remainder of my forty-five-minute trip from New Hampshire to Vermont.

I arrived at work and proceeded to open the mail and prepare the deposit. I was in charge of accounts receivable for the Mary Meyer Corporation, a company that makes stuffed animals. I opened one envelope and attached to the check was a note that said, "I'm sorry this payment is late. I have been seriously ill. Thank you, Beverly Thompson."

I can't explain it, but I instantly knew that this was the person the Lord had given me to pray for. "You want me to pray for her, don't you Lord?" I asked him silently. The answer came in a feeling of peace and excitement combined—I knew he had just answered my prayer from less than an hour ago!

So began my journey of prayer for Beverly Thompson. At first I found it very awkward to pray for someone I didn't even know. I did know one thing besides her name. She owned Chapter 1 Bookstore in Presque Isle, Maine, and she ordered bulk quantities of our plush animals to sell. I didn't know how old she was. Was she married, widowed, single or divorced? What was wrong with her? Was she terminally ill? Did she have any children?

The answers to these questions weren't revealed as I prayed for Beverly, but I did find out how much the Lord loved her and that she was not forgotten by him. Many days I found myself in tears as I entered into prayer for her. I prayed that he would give her comfort for whatever she would have to endure. Or I pled for strength and courage for her to accept things that she might find hard to face.

One morning, as my wipers pushed the spring rain off my windshield, I saw muted tones of browns and grays. I prayed that the Lord would give Beverly eyes to see that the same drab landscape would be transformed into the greens and yellows of spring by a single day filled with sunshine. I prayed she could find hope, even though it might seem covered up in the muted tones of her life, and rely on a God who can transform winter into spring.

In May, I felt that I should send her a card to let her know I was praying for her. As I made this decision, I knew I was taking a risk. Because I had taken her name from where I worked, I could possibly lose my job. I wasn't in a position to be without any income.

But, God, I told him, *I've grown to love Beverly Thompson. I know you'll take care of me no matter what happens.* In my first card, I told Beverly a little bit about myself and how I had asked the Lord for specific people to pray for. Then I mentioned how I had come to get her name. I also told her that the Lord knew all about what she was going through and wanted her to know how much he loved her.

I certainly knew how much God loved me. When I first moved into this new town, it had been difficult, especially as a single mom. But only a few weeks after arriving, I bought a Bible for fifty cents at a yard sale. When I got home, I found a folded note inside.

When I opened it, I couldn't believe my eyes.

"Dear Susan," the handwritten note began, "he who began a good work in you will carry it on to completion until the day of Christ Jesus." (Phil. 1:6) Obviously, the writer was encouraging another Susan, since I had randomly picked up the Bible. But for me, it was assurance that God was personally interested in me!

Summer came and went, and I continued to send Beverly cards and notes. I never heard from her, but I never stopped praying for her, even telling my Tuesday night Bible study group the story. They also upheld her in prayer.

At times I had to admit to God that I really wanted a response, I wanted to know what Beverly thought about this stranger and her steady stream of notes. Did she think I was completely crazy? Did she hope I'd stop?

I took the phone from my son's hand and immediately my hand went clammy. *I know why he's calling,* I thought. *He's calling me to tell me to stop bothering his wife. They probably think I'm a religious kook.* A million scenarios flew through my mind.

"Hello, Mr. Thompson," my voice squeaked nervously.

"My daughter Susan and I had just been going through my wife's things and found your cards and notes and your phone number. We wanted to call and let you know how much they meant to Beverly and to fill you in on what happened."

My heart loosened as this grieving husband continued to tell me about Beverly's last days.

"While we were going through her things, we found your cards and notes tied up with a red ribbon. I know she must have read them over and over because they looked worn."

Then he said quietly, "My wife had been diagnosed with lung cancer at the age of forty-eight."

I winced at the thought of Beverly's physical setback, but Mr. Thompson's next words comforted me. "She never suffered any pain at all. I know now that this was a result of your prayers."

Then he answered one of the questions I had nagged God about. "The reason you never heard back from her was because she also developed brain cancer," he said.

"Our relationship with God amounted to going to church once in a while, but it was nothing that had much effect on our lives," Mr. Thompson explained. "I wanted you to know that my wife asked to be baptized two weeks before she passed away. The night before she died, she told me it was okay for her to die because she was going home to be with her Lord."

As Bob Thompson continued to share his wife's story with me, the drab landscape of my own life was transformed. As insignificant as my life had appeared to be to me, God used it to shine His love upon another life, resulting in a gift that no one could take away.

The experience increased my faith significantly. God took one of the lowest points in my life and added glints of his glory. It made me realize that when we're willing to be obedient, God works in profound ways.

Susan Morin

A Beacon of Light

The nonbeliever says: "Show me God and I will believe in Him." The believer answers: "Believe in God and He will show himself to you."

Michal Paul Richard

In Tulsa, everyone who has ever driven downtown at night has experienced the breathtakingly brilliant light glowing from the fifteen-story church tower of Boston Avenue Methodist. The warm beacon of light burns brightly every night. But that was not always the case.

Up until 1950, the tower was lit for only two weeks a year—during the Christmas season—because the cost was so steep. One bitterly cold, windy night of that year close to Christmas, the church's minister, Dr. Paul Galloway, decided to catch up on some paperwork. So, after dinner, he returned to the church. As he walked up to the heavy sanctuary doors, he glanced up at the beautiful building whose art deco style had made the church a landmark since it opened in 1929.

As he unlocked the doors, he looked up at the tower's light glowing in the sky and, as always, felt warmed within.

The minister walked through to his office and began to work. He was soon so lost in thought that he did not hear the sanctuary door open or the footsteps coming through the carpeted church. He was startled when his office door opened, and he looked up to see a young woman in an elegant fur coat close the door behind her and swiftly turned to face him. Framed by wind-blown bleached hair, a bleak despondent face he'd never seen before turned defiant eyes on him. "Are you the pastor of this church?" she demanded, slumping against the door.

"Yes," he answered.

Suddenly she straightened and blurted out belligerently, "What do you have to say to someone who's going to commit suicide?"

Thus a dialogue started which revealed that the woman had come to town to see her brother, a professor at Tulsa University, for the last time. Then she'd rented a room at a downtown hotel where she planned to end her life. But, as she'd started to close the green drapes of her hotel window facing Boston Avenue, a great shining light had caught her attention. She'd stood staring at the beacon of light in the sky. It called to her somehow, as if offering a hope she'd so longed for these last three years.

She'd thrown on her coat and rushed downstairs to the hotel desk. There she'd inquired of a clerk, "Where is that big light in the sky coming from?"

"Boston Avenue Methodist Church," he'd answered.

"How do I get there?"

"Go out the front door, turn right, go to the traffic light and turn left," the clerk said. "That church is only a few blocks away."

Now, sitting in the office of Paul Galloway, she found the heavyset, graying minister to be a warm, friendly man who did not try to dissuade her from her determined task. Instead, he listened carefully with only gentle comments to her reasons for committing suicide (none of which is known to anyone to this very day except those two). When they had talked together for some time, the minister asked, "Would you be willing to read two little books before you destroy yourself?" After some talk about the books, which spoke of a meaningful life, she agreed.

He handed her a small volume and said, "The other book is at my home. Would you be willing to ride there with me to get it?" After several moments of hesitation, she said, "Okay." The minister was hoping that once they got to his home, his warm caring wife could help him better relate to the young woman.

But, when they arrived at the parsonage on Hazel Boulevard, she refused to go inside. So the minister went in, got the book, and asked his wife to ride along with him and the woman to her hotel. After they saw the woman into the attractive lobby of her hotel and she left them, the minister told his wife as much as he could (which was little) about the strange encounter.

The next week, Paul Galloway's wife noticed how relieved he looked when he received one of the books in the mail. After another few weeks, the other book arrived.

A year later during Christmas season, a special delivery letter came from the woman. She wrote that the warm reception she'd received on that bitterly cold winter night, when the tower's light had brought her to the church, was so great that she had not only survived her terrible depression, but she had since entered a training school to serve as a medical missionary.

At the next meeting of the church stewards, Dr. Galloway told them the story and asked that the budget include the cost for lighting the tower every night of the year. The stewards enthusiastically agreed after their minister read them the letter's last sentence. The young woman wrote, "I want to serve as a ray of hope to others as your tower's beacon of light reached out to save me that night."

Jeanne Hill

Beach Encounter

Little deeds of kindness,
Little words of love,
Help to make earth happy
Like the heavens above.

Julia Fletcher Carney

One crisp, early November morning, I took a brisk walk on a beach near my home. Except for the gentle surf and some screeching seagulls, the beach was silent and deserted. Emotionally, I was reeling under the stress of a recent difficult divorce. How was it possible that a family like ours could totally disintegrate? We already had our two daughters when I was diagnosed with cancer. Treatments followed with the usual sickness and loss of hair. They were unsuccessful, and eventually I had major surgery. Miraculously, I recovered from this ordeal and was given a clean bill of health.

During the following months I began to lose my balance and tire easily. After many doctors' appointments and tests, I was diagnosed with multiple sclerosis. My HMO offered no treatment or hope. I coped the best I could, had hand controls put in my car, used crutches on bad days and even a wheelchair at times. My husband was unable to cope with all these illnesses. He began to show symptoms of manic-depression and eventually became abusive, even to the point where he once beat me unconscious.

God had been my strength and anchor during these ordeals. I knew He was walking with me, that He would never leave me or forsake me, and knew all about my wounds and hurts. It was His peace that had carried me thus far. Some days, when my legs were strong enough to carry me unaided, I enjoyed my beach walks like on this crisp November morning.

In the distance, I spotted a man sitting quietly on the sand, gazing at the ocean. Yet, as I passed him from behind, I saw his shoulders shaking and realized that he was sobbing, apparently in great agony. Should I stop and talk with him? A perfect stranger? Who knew if he was a fugitive or an ax murderer? I walked on.

However, something about those agonizing sobs pulled me back. I slowly turned and walked toward him. He was still crying and hardly seemed to notice me. I took a closer look and saw a man in his forties, dressed in jeans and T-shirt, short hair and cleanly shaven. Certainly not a dangerous-looking man. Gently, I sat down beside him. For a moment, no one spoke, then I asked softly.

"Are you all right? Can I help you with something?"

He kept staring at the ocean.

"I have melanoma," he said. "They are going to amputate my leg."

Taken aback, I was silent for a moment, then began to ask him general questions, hoping to calm him down and get his mind on something else. I learned that his name was John, he was single and alone in the world. I noticed a necklace he was wearing, made out of old string fashioned into a cross. Wanting to keep the conversation going, I asked him:

"Where did you get that, John?"

"I made it in Vietnam," he began. "My buddies and I were in a foxhole. They all got killed, except me. The enemy was still around so I could not move or let them know I was alive. To get my mind off the danger, I took the strings of my buddies' gear and started to knot it into a necklace. I prayed for safety while I was doing this and put a cross at the end. I have never taken it off," he finished.

"When you were praying," I asked softly, "did you believe God heard you?"

"I don't know," he said, "my life was spared, but what for? Now I have a deadly disease. Look at all the thousands of people who were killed during the war. How can a good God allow all this?"

I explained as best as I could what the Bible has to say about good and evil, war and disease. As I spoke I was strangely aware that somehow these weren't my own words pouring out of my mouth. They came with a compassion and conviction that weren't my own. God was there with us, explaining His love and care to this desperate young man.

"John," I said gently, "you've been through a lot and you are facing a lot more. You need someone to lean on, to support you. You need Jesus as your friend. You can trust Him, and He loves you, John. God is there for you. Jesus, His son, died, so that we may have peace and eternal life. We need this peace to go through life," I stressed.

I told John a little about my own life's struggles and illnesses.

"I could not have made it without God's help and support. Even today, as I was walking on the beach, I felt His presence and his strength. Without Him, I could never have survived. But look, I'm still alive and I still have hope. You can too, John."

Our conversation continued. John had many questions. The gentle surf kept rolling toward us, and I knew God was at work in John's heart. Finally, I asked him if he wanted to pray. Slowly, he nodded his head.

Gently, I led him in a prayer of forgiveness and surrender to the Lord. We both wept, but this time John's tears were not tears of sorrow but tears of relief and peace. Deeply moved, I was amazed at this transformation and in awe that God had used me in this way so unexpectedly.

"John," I finally warned him, "you're going to have a hard time. You're a child of Christ now, and there are going to be some roadblocks ahead of you. It's very important that you find a good church, get a Bible and start reading it."

I suggested a local beach community church.

"People dress informally there, John. You can come just as you are."

I got up to leave and rummaged through my bag for a business card but found none. Finally, I tore a deposit slip from my checkbook, wrote down my phone number and handed it to John.

"Call me," I said. "We'll talk and I can also get you a Bible."

Then I got up to continue my walk. I hadn't gone far, when he got up and ran after me, calling me back.

"You know," he said, when he caught up with me, "you are an angel who dropped in from heaven."

I smiled and said, "No, John, you've watched too much TV. I'm not an angel." I turned away again, but he stopped me. Slowly he took his necklace off and handed it to me.

"I want you to have this," he said.

Tears came to my eyes again. Overwhelmed, I knew I

couldn't refuse his gift, so I carefully accepted it and pulled it gently over my head.

When I returned home I hung John's necklace over my desk lamp. Every time I saw it there, I prayed that God would keep him safe and in the center of his will.

I did not hear from John again, but the following spring a letter arrived. There was no return address. Inside was a small card. Taped to it was a crumpled piece of paper from my checkbook with my address. On the back of the card was one sentence: John went to be with the Lord.

When I read it, I cried and removed John's necklace from my lamp and put it with other treasures in a safe place. I knew I would see John again in heaven. But the story did not end there.

Three years later, last December, I received a mysterious Christmas card. Again, there was no return address. Inside was a handwritten note that said: *I'll be eternally grateful for my son's eternal life. I'm John's mother, and I now attend his church.*

P.S. I'm glad to report that today my multiple sclerosis is in complete remission. I have given away my crutches and wheelchair and recently had the hand controls in my car removed. To God be the glory.

Mia Watkins
As told to Aubrey Beauchamp

When I Say I Am a Christian

When I say, "I am a Christian"
I'm not shouting "I am saved"
I'm whispering "I was lost!"
"That is why I chose His way."

When I say, "I am a Christian"
I don't speak of this with pride
I'm confessing that I stumble
Needing God to be my guide.

When I say, "I am a Christian"
I'm not trying to be strong
I'm professing that I'm weak
And pray for strength to carry on.

When I say, "I am a Christian"
I'm not bragging of success
I'm admitting I have failed
And cannot ever pay the debt.

When I say, "I am a Christian"
I don't think I know it all
I submit to my confusion
Asking humbly to be taught.

When I say, "I am a Christian"
I'm not claiming to be perfect
My flaws are too visible
But God believes I'm worth it.

When I say, "I am a Christian"
I still feel the sting of pain
I have my share of heartaches
Which is why I seek His name.

When I say, "I am a Christian"
I do not wish to judge
I have no authority.
I only know I'm loved.

Carol Wimmer

How Prayer Made Me a Father Again

I can't begin to count the number of times that prayer has played an important part in my life. As often as God has answered my prayers, I realize it's important to pray for others, too. So when our church started a Tuesday night prayer service, I became a regular participant. The pastor sometimes would begin with a short devotion, and then we'd sing a couple of praise choruses before getting down to serious conversations with God. From the beginning we knew we were there to pray.

During the first few months, attendance was sparse. Those who came gave their prayer requests and there'd still be plenty of time to bring them to the Lord. However, as prayers were answered, more people joined and the number of requests multiplied. It took most of the service to hear all the requests.

The pastor solved the problem. Now when we arrive for the service, we write down our prayer requests on a sign-in sheet in the foyer. During our praise time, the pastor makes a copy of these requests for each person. With list in hand, we find a quiet place to pray individually.

One Tuesday evening our prayer list was short. I

prayed for each need listed. I prayed for the church, our community, our state and our country. Then I prayed over the list again.

I looked at my watch thinking the hour ought to be up. *I still have fifteen minutes left! There has to be something more I can pray about,* I thought.

Then my son came to mind. I had not seen Teddy in twenty-seven years. When he was less than a year old, his mother and I divorced, and she moved with Teddy out of state. I smiled to myself as I thought back to those months with my firstborn son. I would get off the bus from work and could hear him crying half a block away. As soon as I walked into his room, his cries turned into laughter.

After the divorce, I made an effort to keep in touch, but my first letters were returned unopened. Later they were marked, "Addressee moved, left no forwarding address." I had no idea where either Teddy or his mother lived.

When Teddy was about five, I learned through an attorney that my ex-wife had remarried and her new husband wanted to adopt my son. I agonized over my decision.

The attorney wouldn't disclose Teddy's whereabouts unless I chose to seek custodial rights. But a custody battle might forfeit any chance for Teddy to enjoy a stable life. I reasoned: *Teddy doesn't know me. Would it really be fair to deny him a father to satisfy my own need to see him? Would my selfishness cause more emotional damage?*

I loved Teddy and missed him terribly, but I decided I couldn't interfere with a chance for happiness in his life. I waived my rights, hoping it was the best thing to do for my son.

Now years later, I simply asked prayerfully, "Lord, my son is a grown man now. I love him and miss him. Please just let me know what kind of a man Teddy has turned out to be. Anything more than that I leave in your hands. In fact, Lord, I don't even know where to start looking for him, so I am truly leaving it all up to you. Please, let me know my son. Amen."

As I left that prayer service, the Lord gave me peace from the words of Malachi 4:6—"He will turn the hearts of fathers to their children, and the hearts of the children to their fathers."

The rest of the week I went about my normal routine and forgot about my prayer. But God hadn't forgotten.

The Saturday after the prayer meeting, I ran into our pastor at the post office. After I collected the mail from my box, we started to chat. As I scanned through my mail, a letter caught my eye.

I couldn't place the name or the return address. As the pastor commented on Sunday's church activities, I started reading the mysterious letter.

"Are you okay?" he asked me. Tears were rolling down my face. I couldn't speak; I handed him the letter I had just read—from Teddy.

Teddy explained that he had decided to search the Internet for me. This letter was one of forty-seven letters that my son had written to Richard Whetstones all over the country. Then I noticed the postmark: It was dated Wednesday, the day after my Tuesday night prayer. This wasn't a coincidence. This was a direct answer to my prayer.

When I told my wife, Rose, she was excited because she had encouraged me to try to find Teddy. Since I hadn't mentioned my Tuesday night prayer to her, she was even more thrilled when she learned the whole story.

I decided to call Teddy that day, but I was nervous as I dialed the phone number in Amarillo, Texas. When he answered the phone, I said I had received the letter and I was his father. We agreed to pursue the relationship further.

So I sat down and wrote him back, enclosing a photo I had of him—a color snapshot taken by a family friend at Teddy's christening. In the photo, Teddy was in his mother's arms while my dad and I stood proudly beside him.

In Teddy's return letter, he enclosed the exact same photo—the only family photo he had! That was the confirmation we both needed. I had found my son—or rather, he had found me.

When I told my sister Donna about Teddy, she began corresponding with him, secretly arranging a person-to-person reunion for the two of us at her wedding in May. Teddy and I had time to slip away for breakfast, then walked on the Clearwater beach, talking the whole time.

Teddy had a lot of questions. He had had suspicions about being adopted early on, but didn't learn the truth until he was fifteen years old. His mother hadn't mentioned me at all; I was thankful she hadn't painted me as a terrible person. Having heard all kinds of horror stories about reunions that turned bad, I was reminded once again that God remained faithful.

In October 1997, Teddy and his family—wife Dana, and their children Hayden and Jorden—visited Rose and me in Florida. Teddy's wife couldn't get over how similar Teddy and I were—in looks, mannerisms, speech and ideals—even though we lived completely separate lives.

My Tuesday night prayer wasn't the first or the last prayer that God has answered in my life. But it is one of the most wonderful and satisfying blessings He has ever given me. All I did was simply ask, trusting for His answer.

Richard Whetstone

A Child's Prayer

The family that prays together, stays together!

Al Scalpone

"Don't you remember me, Nurse?"

When people ask me if I remember them, I get a sinking feeling in my stomach. This was no exception. I was new to that particular school district, but I'd been all over Amsterdam doing school nursing as well as public health and infant childcare. How was I to remember all those mothers over the years?

I must have shown my embarrassment at not recognizing this mother. She chuckled before she said: "I don't blame you, Nurse, for it was so long ago that we met. You were still a student nurse working in the barracks with the diphtheria patients, and you nursed my son, Henk, then only five years old."

"Yes, oh yes. I remember my little Henky." He'd been such a lovable little boy, but so very sick when he came from the holiday camp. He'd been homesick and sad, being so far away from home.

My training-school hospital was close to the seaside and we often treated children from these camps. That was before the war. Yes, I remembered Henky, and even his mother . . . only too well.

His files had said that he was Roman Catholic, so that night I prayed with him before and after supper and again just before I tucked him in for the night. I slept in the barracks, too, and my bedroom window looked out on the children in the glass cubicles. He was only one of ten patients, one I never forgot. His throat was very sore; therefore, I didn't think too much of it that he didn't pray with me or say the responses. Nevertheless, I kept on praying with him for several days. One day, he began to talk. But even though he folded his little hands and closed his eyes devoutly when I told him that we were going to pray, he never prayed with me.

One day I asked him: "Come on, Henky, pray with me; you know how, don't you?"

His big blue eyes looked up at me earnestly, and he only shrugged. I thought then that he'd forgotten about prayer, since he was in strange surroundings and it was not a Christian camp. One had to keep reminding the children; otherwise they would forget to pray, I'd thought.

From then on, Henky prayed with me—haltingly at first. But soon he was most eager to pray. Before long he was leading me in the Lord's Prayer and soon he was proud to say all the prayers by himself.

Travel was expensive, and it was difficult for the parents to visit. One day his mother came for a visit. She could not come in and had to talk to Henky through the window on the veranda. They shouted back and forth most cheerfully, and I smiled to myself when I heard Henky boast about his prayers. He was indeed a religious boy, never forgetting his prayers—even at naptime. It was always a moving moment when I saw his little hands folded and his eyes closed as he knelt beside his bed. I hoped his mother would stay to see him at his prayers.

Suddenly an angry knocking at the door startled me. I, too, was in quarantine, so I could only talk to the visitors from a distance. It was Henky's mother. Her eyes flashed as she snapped: "Who told you to teach Henky to pray?"

It was obvious that she objected to prayer—and strongly. "But he is Christian," I said lamely. "It is on his files."

She snorted angrily: "That's his father, of course. He filled in the forms and he had to write that down even though he never goes to church or prays."

I wanted to comfort her and said timidly: "A little prayer never did any harm."

"No, of course not," she agreed hesitantly. Then with a rueful smile she added: "That'll put him to shame when Henky comes home with prayers of his own." She shrugged and said almost sadly: "It won't last though; Henky's too small to keep it up. And no one will encourage him—certainly not his father. As for me. . . ." She turned around in mid-sentence and stomped off.

She hadn't told me to stop praying, and so Henky and I cheerfully went on praying and singing the religious songs. My parents prayed and sang for every reason or season. It was part of our life. Henky loved to sing and pray, and soon he knew my whole repertoire.

When his parents came to take him home, he cried— much to their amazement. Yes, I remembered Henky.

All that flashed through my mind as I looked at the woman before me. Eleven years had gone by. I had often thought of Henky, but only as the five-year-old.

"How is Henky?" I asked eagerly.

His mother laughed. "You should see him. Thin and tall—a marvelous boy. Everybody loves him. He always talks about you."

She put a hand on my arm and said earnestly: "But you did something quite wonderful when you gave Henk religion."

I wanted to protest that I had done very little in the six weeks he was with me. But she was so excited, she gave me no time to speak. She had come to see me to tell her story and was bursting to share it.

I listened in amazement as she continued. "You know, I never expected Henky's prayers to last. But he kept up and taught his little sisters to pray as well. He wouldn't eat or go to sleep without his prayers. By that time, my husband felt that he should go to a Christian school and the girls as well. Soon we both joined the children when they prayed.

"Then the war came, and we needed prayer to give sense to our lives and our suffering. We prayed and sang together as Henky taught us day after day.

"Needless to say, we all joined the church and were strengthened in our most difficult times. God has been good to us. He must have sent Henky your way to get us all into his stable. Henky's prayers went a long way."

Lini R. Grol

Zachary

The Lord is my strength and my shield; my heart trusts in Him, and I am helped; therefore my heart exults, and with my song I shall thank Him.

Psalm 28:7

"Good morning, the Logan Hotel!" I glanced at my watch, hoping that it was still morning.

The woman on the other end of the line spoke softly. "Hello, this is Diane Fillman."

"Hi, Diane. How are you?"

"Not so well, Joyce." Her voice trembled. "Our family is going through a very hard time right now."

"Tell me, Diane, what is wrong?"

"Our son Dennis and his wife Michele have been trying to have a baby for several years. They've been disappointed so many times. After resigning themselves to the fact that they couldn't have children of their own, they decided to adopt a baby.

"Four months ago, they adopted a precious baby boy. They named him Seth. He instantly captivated all our hearts. The church family has prayed for this child for so long; they love him as their own." I listened intently as she continued.

"A couple of weeks ago, the caseworker called. The kids received a crushing blow when she informed them that the birth father's name had been forged on the legal documents. He is aware that he has a son now, and he wants his baby! Legally, Seth will have to be given over to his biological father!" Her voice broke.

"Oh, Diane," I said with tears streaming down my face, "what a heartbreaking story! Is there anything we can do to help?"

"Well, that's why I am calling. Dennis and Michele will be going to Philadelphia next week to hand Seth over to this total stranger!" She swallowed hard before she could continue. "I know they will need to go somewhere to regroup before going back to the empty house. They just love Ocean City, New Jersey, and I immediately thought of the Logan. Would you have a room for four days starting on Tuesday?"

"Of course," I said, trying to regain my composure. I cleared my throat. It was time to think about the business of being an innkeeper again. Looking on the reservation chart, I said, "There is a room available with toilet and shower. I'd be glad to reserve it for them."

"Thank you so much. I'll put a deposit in the mail this afternoon."

"We certainly will be praying for your family, Diane. During times like these we really have to white-knuckle God's faithfulness!"

"We sure do," she replied. "Joyce, I can't tell you how grateful I am that the kids have a haven to come to during the storm. Thanks again. Good-bye."

"Good-bye, dear." The receiver felt heavier than usual as I put it back into the cradle. It felt like the heaviness in my heart. I wrote the name "Fillman" on the chart. If only I could have written "crib" in the space as well. . . .

The night before they were to arrive, I tossed and turned. I prayed for them into the wee hours of the morning. *Lord, you said that you would never give us more than we can handle. As Dennis and Michele's Good Shepherd, restore their souls. Carry them on eagles' wings through this valley of trouble.*

The next day, I was the manager on duty at the front desk. I will never forget seeing the Fillmans coming through the door that day. The agonizing grief that gripped their hearts stared at me through vacant eyes. Not wanting to make it any harder for them, I tried to be as businesslike as possible. "You must be the Fillmans," I said. They nodded.

There were things they needed to know about staying at the Logan. I knew that the last thing they wanted to hear was a long orientation. I frantically looked over the list of check-in information. This day, so many of those things seemed unimportant. I proceeded to acquaint them with the hotel. Halfway through, I almost lost it. I kept picturing them handing over their baby to a complete stranger! *They'll probably never see him again,* I said to myself silently. I kept pushing those heart-wrenching thoughts away. Only by God's grace did the Fillmans and I make it through the preliminaries.

I showed them to their room. After I came down to the kitchen, I fell apart. One of the chambermaids asked, "Are you all right?"

"No," I sobbed, still feeling so much of the couple's pain. She put her arms around me and hugged me until I regained my composure. (There is such healing in hugs.) I thank God that the phone didn't ring and for sending chambermaids with the gift of mercy.

One question kept plaguing my mind. *Did I do the right thing by not mentioning Seth? They might think I don't care.*

I decided to write a note: "Dear Dennis and Michele: We just want you to know that we love you. Our prayers are with you during this difficult time. If you need a hug or someone to talk to, we are here for you. Love in Christ, the Logan Staff."

I quietly slipped it under their door, hoping not to disturb them.

Every morning, we saw this sweet little couple sitting in the wicker chairs on the Logan's front porch. They seemed to be soaking up God's strength as they read their Bibles. The note wasn't mentioned. However, they did smile at me every time they passed by.

On the day they were to check out, Dennis and Michele came up to the desk. I introduced them to my husband, Larry, who had been in Maryland when they checked in. I had already filled him in on what had taken place in Philadelphia.

They started by thanking me for my note, saying how much it had meant to them. Then, as if we were old friends they shared from the depths of their hearts. We could see that God had truly become their anchor in the storm. The strength they had drawn from him was very evident.

"We aren't mad at God," said Michele. "We are just so thankful that we could have Seth for four wonderful months. We may have only held him in our arms for a short time, but we'll carry him in our hearts forever." She looked up into the face of her husband standing next to her.

"We don't understand how it will happen, but we know God will bring good out of it somehow," added Dennis with a strong sense of conviction.

Larry and I hugged them as we said good-bye. We cried as we watched them leave, knowing in our hearts that God would help them to face the empty crib and little toys. He would also carry them through the difficult days ahead. We were amazed that those we had hoped to encourage had encouraged us even more. . . .

The next Christmas, we were pleasantly surprised to hear from Dennis and Michele. The following excerpt is from their newsletter:

We received a call from our caseworker on November 9— would we be interested in showing our profile to a birth couple? After a day's consideration, we called our case worker. YES! Show our profile. On November 16 (it seemed much longer than just a week's wait), we learned that we were to be the parents of a beautiful son who was born October 30, weighing 7 lbs., 10 oz. He was declared "beautiful" by the pediatrician who saw him ten days after his birth. The next few weeks were filled with evidence of God at work in making us into a family.

The letter went on to tell that after much prayerful consideration, they picked a name for their new baby. "We will call him Zachary, because it means, 'Jehovah has remembered.'" As Dennis and Michele went to the agency to pick up their new son, the caseworker told them that the birth parents had already named him. She said, "His name is Zachary!"

Now, each year when Dennis and Michele come back through the Logan door for their yearly vacation, they are accompanied by an adorable little blue-eyed, curly-haired boy. His name is a constant reminder to those of us who know the story that God is still in the business of turning "valleys of trouble" into "doors of hope."

Lord, you do remember. Let us never forget!

Joyce A. Coffin

Christ's Healing Power

I tell you most solemnly, whoever believes in me will perform the same works as I do myself, he will perform even greater works, because I am going to the Father. Whatever you ask for in my name I will do, so that the Father may be glorified in the Son.

John 14:12–13
The Jerusalem Bible

It was an unusually balmy, spring-like day for the last week of March 1968. Our family had recently moved into our "new" 100-year-old home in Oakville. Winter had held us captive in the house long enough. Tanya, age seventeen months, Jay, age three and a half, and I had spent all day in the yard. They had played while I raked and removed the debris that had collected during the fall and winter months.

The arrival of the school bus and our other two children, eight-year-old Cindy and six-and-a-half-year-old Robin, alerted me to the fact that I'd become so absorbed in the yard work that I'd neglected to start dinner on time. Oh well, hot dogs were quick and one of the kids' favorite meals.

While waiting for the hot dogs to come to a boil, I went into the living room to talk to my husband, Gorden. He had just come home from work at the Farmer's Elevator. In a matter of minutes, our quiet conversation about the day's events was broken by screams from our four children in the kitchen.

Tanya, hungry from playing outside in the fresh air, had grown impatient and decided to help herself to the hot dogs, which by then had come to a rapid boil. The pan of scalding water had emptied itself on her face, neck and chest.

Cindy was already pulling off the white sweater Tanya wore when Gorden came through the doorway. He yanked off her corduroy shirt so quickly that buttons flew across the room. Next came the little white tee shirt, also wet and steaming.

Hearing the commotion, a neighbor from across the street came through our front door as we were wrapping Tanya in a clean sheet. I sat rocking our crying baby back and forth on my lap, trying to soothe away the pain. While assuring me that everything would be all right, the friend removed the curlers that I'd placed in my hair early that morning. Her husband, a county policeman, arrived home as we were going out the door; he whisked us into his car. Within minutes, we were at the hospital.

The emergency room doctor and nurses seemed cool and brusque. Perhaps the sight of Gorden in his dusty work clothes and me in my soiled jeans, flannel shirt and rumpled hair gave them the wrong impression. The expression of "negligent parents" written on their faces and in their tone of voice made my already unbearable guilt even heavier.

When I heard the doctor instruct the nurses to admit

our crying baby, my heart sank. I had prayed they would treat her and then we'd all be on our way home. The doctor's caustic parting words rang in my ears: ". . . if she lives." There had been no doubt in my mind that it was a serious injury, but the idea that it might be life-threatening never occurred to me until that moment.

They moved Tanya into a room, and then the charge nurse informed me that I would not be permitted to stay with her. The thought that I was expected to simply walk away from my baby's side, believing she might die during the night, was almost more than I could handle.

While Gorden returned home to comfort the other children, I stood in Tanya's room, crying and praying that God wouldn't let our precious baby die. As I did so, some men appeared at the doorway.

Since we had not yet been attending the Oakville Brethren Church regularly, it's not surprising that I barely recognized the men in the doorway as being from the church. They were trying to convince the nurse to let them enter Tanya's room. This nurse, who resembled a Marine Corps drill sergeant, asked if one of these men was my minister. Eagerly, I answered, "Yes!"

Begrudgingly, she admitted them, adding curtly that they had "only a few minutes!"

I saw three men enter the dimly lit room and stand across from me beside Tanya's bed. I can't remember what was said, only that they—and I silently with them—prayed that God would heal this child. Then, all too quickly, they were gone.

My pleas to stay with Tanya were to no avail. A uniformed security guard escorted me to the lobby. The twenty-minute drive through the dark countryside seemed to take an eternity as I traveled home, continuing to plead with God to watch over Tanya and to forgive me for allowing such a terrible thing to happen to her.

At eight o'clock the next morning, I could hardly believe my eyes as I entered Tanya's room. The third-degree burns on her face were gone! Not one trace of the blazing red skin, so prominent just hours earlier, remained. Only clear, soft, white skin. Her neck and shoulder were the only areas that bore the scars of that boiling water. She was not only alive, but healed.

It wasn't until after Tanya's release from the hospital that we learned the identity of the men who had prayed over Tanya that first night. It was Deacon Richard Smith and Deacon Jerry Covington.

"But who was the third man?" I asked.

"What third man?" they replied.

"There were *three* men. I saw them," I said.

Dick smiled. "Yes, I believe you did."

Do you suppose? Was it really *Him*?

Marie Clowdis-Coon

Communion Blooper

A father sat in the morning worship service of the local church with his wife and three-year-old son. His wife took communion as it was passed down the pew while her husband, who was not a Christian, let the emblems pass without partaking. As the trays were passed to the end of the pew, the three-year-old yelled out at the top of his voice, "My dad didn't get any of the refreshments!" The very next Sunday the father made a personal commitment to the Lord and was baptized, bearing out the statement in Isaiah 11:6, ". . . a little child shall lead them."

Lanis E. Kineman

A Miracle of Faith

If you gain, you gain all; if you lose, you lose nothing. Wager then, without hesitation, that He exists.

Blaise Pascal

It was a bitter March day and snowing heavily. I was visiting my cousin, Charlotte, in her new house in a still-uncompleted development on the water's edge. Afternoon visits were something new for me; I had worked as a registered nurse ever since I'd completed my training. Just a week before, I had put aside my white uniform to await the birth of my first baby in another three months.

Charlotte and I sipped our hot tea. I was watching the snowstorm through the dining room window when I saw the man. He was walking out of the icy bay, naked from the waist up, his skin reddened and raw. He was approaching my cousin's house, stumbling as he walked, looking as if he was about to collapse. I could see his teeth chattering.

"There's something wrong, Charlotte," I said to my cousin. "Let me have my coat. I think he needs help!"

Charlotte looked frightened. "What if he's drunk, or an escaped lunatic or something? There's nobody else around to hear us if we shout for help. Don't go out," she pleaded.

"I've handled worse than this in the emergency room," I told her. "The man is sick or something. I can't just *sit* here!"

Reluctantly she handed me my coat. "Don't forget that you're six months pregnant. Don't lift him or anything."

I ran toward the man and reached him just as he collapsed in the backyard. I shouted to Charlotte, who was shivering in the doorway. "Come out here and help me. If you don't, I'll drag him into your garage myself!" She realized that I meant business and hurried out. Somehow we managed to pull the now-unconscious man into the garage.

"He's probably in shock," I said. "Get some blankets and put some water up to boil. Bring some liquor, and your portable heater, too. And hurry!"

Charlotte ran into the house. The "head nurse" tone in my voice was stronger than her apprehension. I elevated the man's feet so that the blood could return to his head. His pulse was weak and his flesh was ice cold. But within five minutes I had wrapped him in three blankets, the garage was warming up and I had a conscious patient! He sipped slowly at the tea Charlotte had made. Finally, he spoke. "God bless you," he whispered.

I reassured him while we waited for the ambulance. In a weak voice, he told me his name was John Riley. He had been fishing, but the stormy winter sea was too strong for his rowboat. The small craft collapsed. He'd kicked off most of his clothes in an attempt to swim to shore. The lights in Charlotte's windows had shone through the storm and he prayed that there would be help for him. I lifted a glass of brandy to his lips.

The ambulance arrived soon after, but before leaving for the hospital, the driver took my name and address. After calming a very distressed Charlotte, I left for my own home.

That evening my telephone rang. A woman's voice, heavy with emotion, said, "I am John Riley's mother. Are you the person who saved his life this afternoon?"

"I did what I could," I replied. "How is he?"

"He has pneumonia, but the doctors think he'll live. God bless you, my dear, for being there and helping him."

"Why on Earth was he fishing on a day like this?" I asked.

"He has six children," his mother explained, "and there's never enough money for food. I told him it was foolish, but—"

My eyes filled with tears. *What if I hadn't been there?* I thought. Charlotte probably would have been too frightened to have done more than call the police. He might have been dead before the ambulance arrived.

"John told me you're expecting a baby," the woman went on. "I'm going to pray for you and your unborn baby—so that he'll be a healthy, strong child. You saved *my* son's life; the least I can do is pray for *your* child!"

I kept in touch with the nurses at the hospital and soon learned that John Riley made a speedy and complete recovery. But unfortunately, things didn't go as well for me. In my seventh month, I went into premature labor.

My child was born quickly—a three-pound boy closer in size to a mouse than a baby. The doctors weren't optimistic. My tiny son was moved to a specially equipped nursery for premature babies. I prayed fervently for his life.

John Riley's mother prayed, too. We had spoken to each other often while John was hospitalized. In addition to her constant prayers, she burned a candle in the church every morning for my little Michael. Somehow, Michael pulled through and slowly grew stronger.

The miracle of his survival never ceases to amaze me. There was every reason for him not to live: His lungs and heart were not fully developed. His body was not ready to leave mine—not ready to function on its own. As a nurse, I understand that. But I know, too, that a miracle of faith helped him survive. Perhaps God helped me because I had helped John Riley, who might have died had I not been there that snowy day in March.

Maxine Karpen

The Faith of Stanley Reimer

Look out fear! Here comes faith!

Anonymous

Every Sunday morning I see a very special person sitting about ten rows back on the right side of the auditorium. His name is Stanley Reimer, and he's an elder on our church board. I'll never forget the day when I received the tragic news that Stanley had a heart attack. Stan was a chemist with a large company, and the news was that he had a twenty-two-minute cardiac arrest. Twenty-two minutes! You know what that means. There was a considerable amount of time when oxygen did not reach the brain. And if Stan survived, he would probably be a vegetable all of his life. They managed to get him breathing again, but he was in a death coma. He was placed in the intensive care unit immediately, and his body was breathing on its own, but he was still in a coma. There was no sign of life other than the breathing that was going on. The neurosurgeon told Stan's wife that there was no hope. "If he keeps breathing, he'll be a vegetable all his life. He'll never close his eyes. They'll be open in a death stare as you see now. Totally, a vegetable."

I rushed to the hospital as soon as I could, praying the whole time. "God, what will I say? What will I say to his wife?" And then I remembered what I was taught in theological seminary: *Someday, as a pastor, you may be talking to someone in a death coma. When that happens, only think life! Only talk life! If you're ever at the bedside of a presumably dying patient, and he's in a coma so deep that no response is indicated, talk life! He may lack the power to move his lips or manifest a physical indication that he is hearing, but his subconscious may hear! And you must not place a negative thought in that mind!*

So I went into the intensive-care unit where he was lying, and there was Billie, his wife, standing at the bedside, tears streaming down her face. My once outgoing friend looked like a statue. He couldn't move—dead for all practical appearances—but he was breathing. His eyes were wide open. I put my arm around Billie and prayed with her. Then I took hold of his hand and softly said, "Stanley, I know you cannot talk. I know you cannot respond, but I know that deep down within you, you can hear me. I'm Bob Schuller. I've just come from church where everyone is praying for you. And Stanley, I've got news for you. You had a bad heart attack, but you are going to recover. You are going to live, and it's going to be a long battle. It's going to be hard, but you're going to make it!"

And at that point I had one of the most moving experiences of my life. A tear rolled out of my friend's eye. He understood! No smile, no quiver of a lip, but a tear rolled out of his eye. The doctors couldn't believe it! That was over a year ago and today Stanley is able to speak full sentences, he can hear and his faculties are becoming normalized.

A miracle? Remember: "If you have faith as a grain of mustard seed you can say to your mountain, 'Move' and nothing will be impossible."

Robert H. Schuller

7

THE MEANING
OF CHRISTMAS

*The human contribution is the essential
ingredient. It is only in the giving of oneself
to others that we truly live.*

Ethel Percy Andrus

Heart Sounds

One afternoon about a week before Christmas, my family of four piled into our minivan to run a short errand, and this question came from a small voice in the back seat: "Dad," began my five-year-old son, Patrick, "how come I've never seen you cry?"

Just like that. No preamble. No warning. One minute it's, "Mom, what's for supper?" The next it's, "Dad, how come . . ." My wife, Catherine, was as surprised by this as me. But she is one of those lucky souls for whom tears come naturally; are spilled spontaneously then quickly forgotten. Patrick has seen his mother cry dozens of times. So my wife was entitled to turn my way in the front passenger seat with a mischievous smile that said, "Explain this one, Dad." I couldn't, of course. I mumbled something in reply about crying when my son was not around, at sad movies and so forth. But I knew immediately that Patrick had put his young finger on the largest obstacle to my own peace and contentment, i.e., the dragon-filled moat separating me from the fullest human expression of joy, sadness, anger and disappointment. Simply put, I could not cry.

I know I am scarcely the only man for whom this is true. In fact I believe that tearless men are the rule in our society, not the exception. When, for instance, did John Wayne shed tears, or Kirk Douglas, or any of those other Hollywood archetypes of manliness? For instance, Wayne's best buddy has been slain on the battlefield and The Duke looks down to the body of his fallen friend with studied sobriety, but also with his typical calm. Then he moves on to the next battle with his typical bravado.

We men. We fathers and sons have been condemned to follow Wayne's lead. Passing centuries have conditioned us to believe that stoicism is the embodiment of strength, and unfettered emotion that of weakness. We have feigned imperviousness to the inevitable slings and arrows, traveling through life with stiff upper lips, calm on the outside, secretly dying within.

A recent television news report only confirmed what I have long suspected. According to the news, the number of men being diagnosed with depression today is sky-rocketing. But I submit that we men have always been depressed to one degree or another, though we tend to medicate it with alcohol, or work, or afternoons and evenings sitting mindlessly in front of one televised sports event or another.

Take me, for instance. For most of my adult life I have battled chronic depression, an awful and insidious disor-der that saps life of its color and meaning, and too often leads to self-destruction. Doctors have said much of my problem is physiological, an inherited chemical imbal-ance, something akin to diabetes. Those physicians have treated it as such with medication.

But I also know that much of my illness is attributable to years of swallowing my rage, my sadness, even my joy. Strange as it seems, in this world where macho is every-thing, drunkenness and depression are safer ways for men like me to deal with feelings than tears.

In my own battle, I had begun to see the folly of this long ago, well before my son's penetrating backseat query. I could only hope the same debilitating handicap would not be passed on to the generation that followed mine.

Hence our brief conversation on the sunny December afternoon after Patrick's question. He and I were back in the van after playing together at a park near our home. Before pulling out, I turned to my son and thanked him for his curiosity of the day before. Tears were a very good thing for boys and girls alike, I said. Crying is God's way of healing people when they are sad.

"I'm very glad you can cry whenever you're sad or whenever you're angry." I said. "Sometimes daddies have a harder time showing how they feel. You know, Patrick, I wish I were more like you in that way. Someday I hope I do better.

Patrick nodded. But in truth, I held out little hope. Lifelong habits are hard to break. I was sure it would take something on the order of a miracle for me to connect with the dusty core of my own emotions.

From the time he was an infant, my son has enjoyed an unusual passion and affinity for music. By age four, he could pound out several bars of Wagner's *Ride of the Valkyries* by ear on the piano. More recently, he has spent countless hours singing along with the soundtrack to the *Hunchback of Notre Dame*, happily directing the music during the most orchestral parts. But these were hidden pleasures for him, enjoyed in the privacy of his own room or with the small and forgiving audience of his mother, father and older sister, Melanie.

What the youth director of our church was suggesting was something different altogether.

"I was wondering if Patrick would sing a verse of 'Away

in the Manger' during the early service on Christmas Eve." Juli Bail, the youth director, asked on our telephone answering machine.

My son's first solo. My wife and I struggled to contain our own excitement and anxiety. Catherine delicately broached the possibility, gently prodding Patrick after Juli's call, reminding him how beautifully he sang, telling him how much fun it would be. Patrick himself seemed less convinced. His face crinkled into a frown.

"You know, Mom," he said. "Sometimes when I have to do something important. I get kind of scared."

Grown-ups feel that way, too, he was quickly assured, but the decision to sing on Christmas Eve was left to him. Should Patrick choose to postpone his singing debut, that would be fine with his parents. His deliberations took only a few minutes.

"Okay," Patrick said. "I'll do it."

For the next week, Patrick practiced his stanza several times with his mother. A formal rehearsal at the church had also gone exceedingly well, my wife reported. But I could only envision myself at age five, singing into a microphone before hundreds of people. When Christmas Eve arrived, my expectations of my son's performance were limited indeed.

My son's solo came late in the service. By then, the spirit of the evening, and many beautiful performances by young voices had served to thaw my inner reaches, like a Minnesota snow bank on a sunny day in March.

Then Patrick and his young choir took the stage. Catherine, Melanie and I sat with the congregation in darkness as a spotlight found my son, standing alone at the microphone. He was dressed in white and wore a pair of angel wings, and he sang that night as if he had done so forever.

Patrick hit every note, slowly, confidently, and for

those few moments, as his five-year-old voice washed over the people, he seemed transformed, a true angel, bestower of Christmas miracles. There was eternity in Patrick's voice that night, a penetrating beauty rich enough to dissolve centuries of manly reserve. At the sound of my son, heavy tears welled at the corners of my eyes, and spilled down my cheeks.

His song was soon over and the congregation applauded. Catherine brushed away tears. Melanie, my daughter, sobbed next to me. Others wept, too. After the service, I moved quickly to congratulate Patrick, but found he had more urgent priorities. "Mom," he said as his costume was stripped away. "I really have to go to the bathroom."

So Patrick disappeared. As he did, my friend and pastor, Dick Lord, wished me a Merry Christmas. But emotion choked off my reply as the two of us embraced. Outside the sanctuary in our crowded gathering place, I received congratulations from fellow church members. But I had no time to bask there in Patrick's reflected glory. I knew I had only a short window in which to act only a few minutes before my natural stoicism closed around my heart. I found my son as he emerged from the church bathroom.

"Patrick, I need to talk to you about something." I said, sniffling.

Alarm crossed his face. "Is it something bad?" he asked.

"No, it's not something bad." I answered.

"Is it something good?"

I took him by the hand and led him down a long hallway, into a darkened room where we could be alone. I knelt to his height and admired his young face in the shadows, the large blue eyes, the dusting of freckles on his nose and cheeks, the dimples on one side.

He looked at my moist eyes quizzically, with concern.

"Patrick, do you remember when you asked me why you had never seen me cry?" I began.

He nodded.

"Well, I'm crying now, aren't I?" I said.

He nodded again.

"Why are you crying, Dad?"

"Your singing was so pretty it made me cry."

Patrick smiled proudly and flew into my arms. I began to sob.

"Sometimes," my son said into my shoulder, "life is just so beautiful you have to cry."

Our moment together was over too soon, for it was Christmas Eve, and untold treasures awaited our five-year-old beneath the tree at home. But I wasn't ready for the traditional plunge into Christmas giving just yet. I handed my wife the keys to the van and set off alone for the mile-long hike from church to our home.

The night was cold and crisp. I crossed a small park and admired the full moon hanging low over a neighborhood brightly lit in the colors of the season. As I left the park and turned up a street toward home, I met a car moving slowly down the street, a family taking in the area's Christmas lights. Someone inside rolled down a backseat window.

"Merry Christmas," a child's voice yelled out to me.

"Merry Christmas," I yelled back, and the tears began to flow once again.

Tim Madigan

Our Christmas Tree Boy

A few days before Christmas in 1961, when I was driving home after a client's office Christmas party, I suddenly remembered my wife Joy Marie's parting words as I left for work that morning. "If somebody I know is not in possession of a fine, upright Christmas tree when he returns this evening, it will be somewhat difficult getting into this house where the climate will be a lot cooler than the climate outside." With this little warning ringing in my ears, I quickly made the rounds of a few tree lots and purchased a fine balsam, which I knew would serve as the fee for getting into the house.

I started right in with the chore of getting it into the stand and properly secured, as straight as possible. I had been working on the project only a short time when I saw what looked like a small roll of paper covered with black plastic, and tied to the trunk with black thread. I tore it off and tossed it to Joy Marie who was busily separating the decorations and lights.

"What's that?" she asked.

It is well-known in the Detroit area that a lot of our trees come from Canada, so I rather flippantly answered,

"Probably a note from some kid up in Canada, and he no doubt wants something for Christmas."

I was joking, but in fact I couldn't have made a more accurate statement. Joy Marie and I read the note we found, and it was indeed from a little Canadian boy asking for skates for Christmas.

The note was nicely written, but we couldn't be sure if the town was spelled Legere or Lagare, or if it was in New Brunswick or Nova Scotia. So now the great search began. I checked maps, asked friends and called all of the Canadian freight lines with whom I did business, but all to no avail, and Christmas was rapidly approaching.

In the meantime, Joy Marie had adopted a hands-off attitude about the whole thing. She is the kindest and most generous person I know, but she is a little suspicious about anyone who uses Christmas trees as a means of carrying correspondence regarding gifts. She and her friends discussed it thoroughly, and they decided a kid that age could not write that well, and probably had little knowledge of English, and that there was a large cartel in Canada dealing in ice skates and other toys from unsuspecting and gullible American folks.

God didn't make me a stubborn Irishman for nothing, so I immediately took the opposite position. I announced loudly and clearly to anyone who would listen, "I don't care if the whole thing is a fraud or a joke. If I can find a kid named Egbert McGraw somewhere in New Brunswick or Nova Scotia, Canada, he's going to get a pair of the finest skates I can find!"

On December 24th, I was having a cup of coffee at my local diner, talking to Sid, the owner, explaining my problem. He said, "Why don't you tell the guy at the end of the counter? He's been bugging me because he can't find someone he can help, and he says it's his job at Christmas time. Probably works for some charity. I don't know what he's talking about, but tell him your story and maybe he'll get off my back."

I needed no further urging. I noticed the young man was dressed in a gray suit, white shirt and tie. I introduced myself, and poured out my story. I finished with, "Sid said you might be able to give me some advice."

He said, "Thank you. I was beginning to think I wouldn't be able to do my job this year, but you present me with a very easy problem. Why don't you just contact the post office?"

I felt a little foolish as I heard myself saying, "Why didn't I think of that?" I thanked the man profusely, wished him a very Merry Christmas and said, "You're an angel." He did have a white feather with a gold tip stuck in his lapel.

I then hurried to the public phone and dialed the post office. I silently prayed that someone would answer who had enough time at this busy season to help me. A kindly sounding gentleman finally answered, listened to my tale, and put me on hold. I really didn't expect much, but after a few minutes waiting, I heard him say, "I find a Legere office in Tracadie, New Brunswick."

I wrote it down, thanked him, hung up and hurried back to tell my new friend. He was gone. The bartender said, "I didn't even see him leave. He just disappeared."

"Well," I said, "if he returns, tell him he did his job. He made my Christmas, and I hope I helped him with his." I had an enjoyable Christmas, but knew I'd be up early the next day shopping.

Now that I had the address situation straightened out, I ran smack into another problem. I hadn't realized how arduous it would be to buy a pair of ice skates for a little boy the day after Christmas. I tried every department store, toy store and sporting goods store, and could find nothing in a kid's size.

The next day I was once again telling my problem to Sid, when who should walk in, but my recent helper with the gold-tipped feather in his lapel. I said by way of starting the conversation, "I suppose that feather has something to do with your work."

He answered, "I guess you could say that, but what's your problem now? You have that same perplexed look on your face."

I filled him in on the lack of skates the day after Christmas and he asked, "Did you try Sears on the corner of Van Dyke and Gratiot?"

I told him I did, and he said, "Try them again, I'm sure you'll have better luck this time."

Sears was very busy with after-Christmas shoppers, but I caught a sales clerk in the sporting goods department and said, "A friend of mine said you might have a pair of skates for a small boy."

He said, "I doubt it very much, but I'll look. This morning we only had a few very large sizes left."

He returned a few minutes later with an expression of total confusion, carrying a pair of super hockey skates that looked like they would fit an eight-year-old boy just right. He said, "They weren't here this morning, and I don't know where they came from, but they're yours."

The next morning the skates were packaged, safely in the hands of the postal service, and on the way to Egbert in far-off New Brunswick.

We received a "thank you" note in a few weeks, and since my writing is illegible at best, I asked Joy Marie to drop Egbert a few lines. She still wasn't convinced that the boy even existed, but she agreed to write a note, and she also included some recent photographs of the two of us.

As the months flew into vacation time, Joy Marie continued her correspondence with Egbert. We had never visited the East Coast and the New England states, so that became our vacation destination. Some dear friends moved to Delaware, so we decided to visit them, and then extend our vacation by driving north to Maine. I mentioned to Joy Marie that when we got to Maine, if we still had enough vacation time left, we might head farther north to Tracadie. I also reminded her that in her last letter to Egbert, she told him that we might be in the Northeast on our vacation and would try to pay a visit if at all possible.

When we arrived in Bar Harbor, Maine on a Friday, that's exactly what we decided to do. We checked into a hotel on Saturday in Newcastle, New Brunswick, a short distance from Tracadie, and Joy Marie called Egbert's grandmother's house because she had learned he and his brother were living there. Grandmother answered with a decidedly French Canadian accent, and she and Joy Marie had a very enthusiastic conversation. Then came the moment of truth. Joy Marie asked, "May I talk to Egbert?"

After a moment of silence, while Joy Marie and I held our breath, grandmother answered, "I'm sorry, but Egbert does not speak English."

Grandma explained that she wrote the original note, and Egbert had climbed up on a railroad flat car and tied it to the trunk of one of the many trees scheduled for shipment to Detroit. She had written all of the other notes we'd received but always as if Egbert wrote them. It was good to now know the complete unusual story and we were even more eager to meet the entire McGraw family.

On the short trip to Tracadie the next day, Joy Marie asked, "How are we going to find the house?"

I said, "We'll probably stop at the only gas station in town, and the attendant will point to it," which is what happened.

When we pulled into the driveway at the grandparents'

house, we were astonished at the number of children and others who turned out to welcome us. One nice old neighbor gentleman in the crowd had gotten up early to go out and pick a basket of succulent wild berries for us. Apparently we were an event in the very modest but clean neighborhood.

When we entered the living room, we noticed a fine, old, upright piano. On the top, to one side, stood a picture of the Queen of England and Prince Philip. On the opposite side, a photo of Joy Marie and myself. In the middle, were the skates still in the carton. Grandma said it was the nicest present Egbert had ever received, and he just liked looking at them and told everyone, "Nobody touch the skates."

Egbert turned out to be a good-looking lad, who seemed like he could handle a pair of ice skates and maybe a hockey stick. Communication with him was difficult, but with lots of pointing, waving and help from Grandma, we managed. Further conversation would have to wait a few years.

The older children had some knowledge of English, learned in school, and Joy Marie has a limited knowledge of French, learned as a student of St. Mary's Academy in Windsor, Canada, across the river from Detroit, so they all enjoyed an afternoon of smoothing out the language barrier.

One of the children came into the house and whispered to Grandma, and she said, "The kids wondered if you could take them for a ride in your car with the top down." I had just purchased a new convertible, and I spent the best part of the afternoon driving up and down the highway with as many kids as I could safely pile into the car, with Egbert at my side on every trip. Convertibles are rare in that area where the economy is based solely on fishing and lumber.

Our stay was far too short, and although we could not

talk to Egbert, Joy Marie and I relied on kisses and hugs. As we drove off, we agreed that we had never met such a lovely group of people, and had never been treated so royally.

A few years ago our doorbell rang, and when Joy Marie answered it, there, on our front porch, were a man, a woman and a little boy. She didn't recognize them until the man said, "Hello, Mrs. Beckwell. I'm Egbert, and this is Nicole and Pierre Luc."

Joy Marie was flabbergasted. Egbert was attending an educational seminar in Windsor. We enjoyed a very nice visit.

As they were leaving, I said, "Egbert, you didn't seem to have any trouble finding our house. How did you do it?"

He said, "Oh, I'm sorry. I've had such a pleasant time that I almost forgot. I've read so many fine things about Father Solanus and the Capuchin Monastery in Detroit, and have become such a fan and devotee, that when we found out we'd be passing quite closely to the monastery on the way here, we decided to stop to visit his grave site. We knew that someone there could give us directions to your neighborhood. As we neared the heavy wooden and very impressive-looking front doors, they creaked open, and there stood a tall young man, who, without asking where we wanted to go, took us directly to Father Solanus's tomb and memorial.

"When we prepared to leave, I asked the stately young man for directions to St. Clair Shores. He smilingly gave us not only that, but also directions to your street and house. This did not really surprise me because he looked like a man who would be knowledgeable about almost anything. Then he handed me an envelope and said, 'Please give this to Mr. Beckwell. He'll know what it means.'"

Egbert handed me an envelope, which I eagerly tore

open and found a small, pure white feather with a gold tip. *From an angel's wing?* I wondered.

Then I smiled and quietly murmured, "God's angels certainly have beautiful calling cards."

Edward J. Beckwell

[EDITORS' NOTE: *Below is the actual note attached to the Christmas tree, which Edward and Joy Marie found a few days before Christmas in 1961.*]

I am a little boy 8 years the 4 of December I hope you think of me on christmas day send me somethink for my christmas I liked to have a pr of skate No 3. please tell santo to come here and dont forget me

Egbert Mc Graw
Legue office
N.D. '61

My Best Christmas

A bone to the dog is not charity. Charity is the bone shared with the dog when you are just as hungry as the dog.

Jack London

The holidays are heading my way this year with the usual frenetic rush. There's so much to celebrate that I can't help pausing every now and then and pinching myself to make sure it's all real.

I've been promoted in my job at a Portland, Oregon, apartment complex. My twin daughters, Deirdre and Caitlin, both have happy memories and challenging careers. And Caitlin and her husband, Matt, have settled close to my home, which is a joy. Combine this with the recent arrival of my first grandchild, and it's going to be an especially blissful Christmas.

Yet no matter how wonderful our holiday is, there's no way it can possibly top my best Christmas ever. Paradoxically, that came during the worst year of my life—a year that taught me some profound lessons about giving and receiving and realizing what I already had.

It happened in 1983, when I was struggling through the financial and emotional morass that follows a very difficult divorce. I had the girls, thank goodness. But I also had a car that wouldn't run, a house that was in danger of being repossessed, and a marginal job that wasn't keeping up with the bills. Because of the house and the car and my job, I was told I was ineligible for food stamps. We were in serious trouble.

By December of that year, we didn't have much money left, and the power company was threatening to shut off service. I had nothing to spend on the girls for the holidays. I do have a flair for handcrafting things, so I made a few whimsical gifts from scraps we had around the house. But there would be no new clothes or bicycles or any of the popular toys my children had seen advertised on TV appearing under our tree. There would certainly be no special treats, no holiday feast with all the trimmings. I found myself staring at the worst Christmas of our lives.

My large extended family had helped a little—and could have helped a lot more, if they'd known the extent of our plight. But the divorce had left me feeling like a failure, and I was too humiliated to let anyone know just how desperate things had become.

Soon, my bank account and credit completely dried up. With no food and no money, I swallowed my pride and asked the girls' elementary school principal for help. The kindly woman put Deirdre and Caitlin, then ten years old and in fourth grade, on the government-subsidized lunch program. She even arranged it so the children could go to the school's office each day to pick up their lunch tickets, which looked just like everyone else's. My daughters never knew.

I thought things couldn't get any worse, but about a week before Christmas, my employer, a painting contractor, stunned me by shutting down operations for the holidays and telling me I was laid off. The girls left for school, and I stayed home to battle my despair in the private gloom of a dark, snowy day.

That afternoon, a car pulled into the driveway. It was the school principal—the same woman who had helped me put Deirdre and Caitlin on the lunch program. In the car, she had a giant foil-wrapped gift box for us. She was so respectful of my feelings. "Now, Jill, I want you to know that every person who signs up for the lunch program automatically gets one of these around the holidays," she said. "It's just something the school district does."

As soon as she left, I set the box on my dining room table and discovered that it contained all we needed for a fine holiday meal. There were also two bright pink boxes, each containing a Barbie doll.

I was hiding the dolls in a closet when Deirdre and Caitlin came home from school. Through the window, they saw the big box on the table and came racing in the door squealing gleefully and jumping up and down.

Together, the excited girls went through the box, admiring everything. There was fresh fruit, canned vegetables, candies, nuts, cookies, chocolates, a large canned ham and much more. I felt so elated, as if all my burdens had been lifted—or at least the stress over how we were going to make it through the holidays had been. Then Deirdre asked where the box had come from.

As I gently explained that it had come from the school district, Deirdre's whole demeanor quickly changed. She stepped back and looked down. "Oh, Mom," she finally said after a prolonged silence. "This is so nice, but they've made a terrible mistake. They meant to give this to a poor family."

Rather awkwardly, I tried to tell her that the three of us, at least temporarily, were indeed poor. But Caitlin chimed in with Deirdre. "No, they must have meant this for someone who really needs it. Someone *needy*."

A sinking feeling swept over me as the girls began to ponder the dilemma of whom to give the box to. I didn't stand in their way, but a touch of despair came creeping back. Selfishly, I thought, *What am I going to do? I have almost nothing to give them for Christmas.*

The girls finally settled on giving the box to an elderly neighbor named Juanita, who worked in a nearby laundry and lived alone in a dilapidated old house down the street. Its wood-burning stove—her only source of heat—had broken down, and Juanita had been ill lately. Even her dog was sick.

Deirdre and Caitlin repacked the gift box and hefted it out to the garage. There, beside the broken-down Volvo, they put the cargo on Deirdre's red wagon.

I watched through the kitchen window as my two girls, clad in coats and scarves and smiles from earmuff to earmuff, pulled the heavy wagon toward Juanita's house. Suddenly, the snowy street began to sparkle, and a little sunlight broke through that dark sky. I stood there with goosebumps and began to realize the beauty and meaning of what was happening, and it changed everything.

I began to feel joy. Today, fifteen Christmases later, I still treasure the warm blessing the girls and I received in a note from Juanita. And now, as Deirdre and Caitlin— two college-educated, successful, grown women—start families of their own, I finally feel ready to share my story and tell them some things they didn't know about that year of the big gift box.

The truth is, it was a great Christmas. Thanks to them, it was the best of my life.

Jill Roberts

I'm Not Poor at All

For where your treasure is, there will your heart
be also.

Matthew 6:21

Dear Lord, I'm feeling down today,
The bills are stacked up high;
With Christmas just two weeks away,
Our bank account's run dry.

The kids have all presented lists
Of things they want to see;
I hope and pray there's nothing missed
Beneath our Christmas tree.

But I don't have the money for
Expensive clothes and toys;
My credit card can't take much more,
Lord, where's my Christmas joy?

Perhaps it's wrapped up in that hug
My daughter gave this morn;

Or stacked with wood my son did lug
To keep us nice and warm.

Perhaps it's in my oldest's eyes
When he comes home on break,
And sees I've baked those pumpkin pies
He wanted me to make.

Perhaps it's in the tired lines
Around my husband's eyes;
Perhaps in love that's grown with time
I've found the greater prize.

A friend who gives a hearty smile,
And cupboards that aren't bare;
And, even if they aren't in style,
I've got some clothes to wear.

A family who believes in me
In all things great and small;
Dear God, I think I finally see—
I am not poor at all!

Michele T. Huey

The Little Black Book

Many years ago I worked for a man whom today I call a great American funeral director. His lifelong motto was "Families first, no matter what," and he lived this with a consistency that few men ever achieve.

The funerals he conducted were flawless, and people genuinely admired and respected him. He was a grand person. However, one of the most interesting mysteries which accompanied this man was his "little black book." It was a small black book with a lock on the cover. It looked as if it was very old, and it was his constant companion.

If you went to his office, you would see it lying on his desk. At funerals, he would pull the black book out and scribble brief notations in it. If you picked up his suit coat, you could feel the black book in his coat pocket.

You can imagine the gossip by the staff and speculation around the funeral home coffee room as to precisely what was in the black book. I remember on the first day I worked, I very seriously asked the embalmer what the book was for, and he responded with a very mysterious glance, "What do you think is in the book?"

I was not the sharpest knife in the drawer and very innocently I said, "I have no idea."

"Oh, come on, farm boy," the embalmer replied. "He keeps his list of girlfriends in there." I was stunned!

Later I asked the receptionist about the black book. Her response was that it was where he kept the list of the horses he bet on at the race track. Again, I was stunned. My employer was a womanizing gambler! I could not believe it.

For nearly three years the mysterious saga of the little black book continued—all the time, the stories, gossip and intrigue getting more and more spectacular and ridiculous.

Then suddenly one day, while conducting a funeral, my boss, this great funeral director, had a massive heart attack and died.

Four days later, we had a grand funeral for him—he was laid out in a solid bronze casket, flowers were everywhere, and when we took him to the church, the place was packed and the governor was in the front row.

I was standing in the back of the church protecting the church truck (that was my job), sobbing as the minister went on about what a great man my boss was and how just knowing him made us all better people. I couldn't have agreed with the minister more.

Then the minister asked my boss's widow to come up and talk about her husband's character. I thought, *Now this will be beautiful,* as she rose to walk to the pulpit. It was then I saw she was carrying his little black book! My tears of grief instantaneously turned to sweats of terror.

She walked to the pulpit, stood with complete dignity, looked at the assembly and said, "Thank you all for being here today. I want to share with you a secret about my husband's character."

I thought, *Oh God, here it comes!*

She continued, "You see this small book. Most of you know he carried it with him constantly. I would like to read to you the first entry of the book dated April 17, 1920—Mary Flannery, she is all alone. The next entry August 8, 1920—Frederick W. Pritchard, he is all alone. The next entry November 15, 1920—Frieda M. Gale, she is all alone. You see when he made funeral arrangements or saw somebody at a funeral that he knew was all alone, he would write their names in this book. Then, every Christmas Eve, he would call each person and invite them to share a wonderful Christmas dinner at our house. I want you all to know that this was the true character of my husband; he was concerned, compassionate and caring. This is what the little black book is all about, and I also want you to know that this being 1971, he did this for fifty Christmases."

There was not a dry eye in the church.

Now almost a quarter of a century after his death, I look back at the inner spirit that motivated this funeral director to do what he did. May this spirit of warmth and compassion guide each of us in this great profession. Just think of the humanitarian possibilities if every member of the funeral profession developed our own little black books. The results of human kindness would be staggering.

Todd W. Van Beck

Santa in Disguise

I scratched my thumbnail across the thick white frost that covered the window. With my eye pressed against the cleared spot, I could see the outside thermometer hanging against the weather-beaten siding. It read a chilling twenty degrees below zero. Inside, it didn't feel much warmer. Frozen condensation creeping down the walls looked liked last night's leftover spaghetti noodles.

Because we couldn't yet afford a furnace, I had stuffed newspapers into the center of the old pot-bellied stove and piled them high with logs. The flick of the match was the beginning and also the end.

John gulped a half-cup of coffee, grabbed a slice of toast and hurried off to his job at the paper mill. Three-year-old Anne and two-year-old Michael sat huddled together, waiting patiently for a cup of hot cocoa.

I poked another log into the stove and felt the cozy warmth replace the cold that chilled every bone in my body. That's when I heard a strange noise. At first, it sounded like the rustling of crumbling newspapers, but it grew louder and began to roar.

I yanked open the door leading to the vacant upstairs

and shrieked as I saw huge yellow and blue flames devouring the walls.

Everything blurred. I heard frantic voices and then someone crashed through the front door.

"Your house is on fire. We have to get you and the kids out of here."

A neighbor wrapped the children in blankets and carried them to her car. I snatched the phone and called my father.

Functioning on automatic pilot, I carried out a drawer containing important papers. Ignoring the danger, I charged back inside. With Christmas just five days away, I was determined to rescue the suit I'd purchased for John. It had taken me fifty weeks at a dollar a week to pay for it. A stranger grabbed my arm and dragged me out of the house.

My dad notified the mill, and John returned home. In less than an hour, all that remained of our house was the chimney standing in the center of a pile of smoldering ashes.

The next few days were chaotic. We'd moved in temporarily with my parents. The phone and doorbell rang constantly. Everyone, friends and strangers alike, wanted to help. The donated clothes in one of the spare bedrooms eventually replenished the Red Cross inventory. My friends from the Home Bureau replaced my canned goods from their own shelves.

A day before Christmas, the owner of Carl's Auto Supply Store called, "I'd like to see you and your husband this afternoon at five o'clock. Can you come?"

I couldn't imagine what he wanted, but I told him we'd be there.

Mr. Carl was known around town as Mr. Scrooge. He sold auto parts for cash only. He sold seasonal items but never had a clearance sale at the end of the season. No credit and no deals. Rumors had it that he didn't believe in charity organizations and refused to donate to them. He wouldn't even buy Girl Scout cookies.

When we arrived, he acknowledged us with a nod and continued helping a customer. After everyone had left, he locked the door.

He then asked, "What ages are your children? Boy or girl?"

Without another word, he grabbed two large boxes and proceeded down the aisle. New toys of all descriptions were displayed on the shelves. He picked up two packages of building blocks and dropped one in each box. "Little girls like to build, too." His mouth almost smiled.

He stuffed the boxes. A dump truck in one, a baby doll in the other. When the boxes were nearly full, he topped them off with books to read and books to color.

Mr. Carl thrust the toy-filled boxes toward us. "Take these and give your children a nice Christmas." He looked directly at first one and then the other of us.

"There's one condition. You aren't to tell a soul. I don't want anyone else to know. Understood?"

Over the years, there's been another rumor circulating. A Santa-in-disguise has come to the rescue of many people in need.

We know for a fact that it's true.

Jeanne Converse

Christmas Love

Every year, I promised it would be different. Each December, I vowed to make Christmas a calm and peaceful experience. But, once again, in spite of my plans, chaos prevailed. I had cut back on what I deemed nonessential obligations: extensive card writing, endless baking, Martha Stewart decorating, and, yes, even the all-American pastime, overspending. Yet still I found myself exhausted, unable to appreciate the precious family moments, and, of course, the true meaning of Christmas.

My son, Nicholas, was in kindergarten that year. It was an exciting season for a six-year-old, filled with hopes, dreams and laughter. For weeks, he'd been memorizing songs for his school's upcoming Winter Pageant.

I didn't have the heart to tell him I'd be working the night of the production. Not willing to miss his shining moment, I spoke with his teacher. She assured me there'd be a dress rehearsal in the morning, and that all parents unable to attend the evening presentation were welcome to enjoy it then. Fortunately, Nicholas seemed happy with the compromise.

So, just as I promised, I filed in ten minutes early, found

a spot on the cafeteria floor and sat down. When I looked around the room, I saw a handful of parents quietly scampering to their seats. I began to wonder why they, too, were attending a dress rehearsal, but chalked it up to the chaotic schedules of modern family life.

As I waited, the students were led into the building. Each class, accompanied by their teacher, sat crossed-legged on the floor. The children would become members of the audience as each group, one by one, rose to perform their song. Because the public school system had long stopped referring to the holiday as "Christmas," I didn't expect anything other than fun, commercial entertainment. The Winter Pageant was filled with songs of reindeer, Santa Claus, snowflakes and good cheer. The melodies were fun, cute and lighthearted. But nowhere to be found was even the hint of an innocent babe, a manger, or Christ's precious, sacred gifts of life, hope and joy.

When my son's class rose to sing "Christmas Love," I was slightly taken aback by its bold title. However, within moments, I settled in to watch them proudly begin their number. Nicholas was aglow, as were all of his classmates, adorned in fuzzy mittens, red sweaters and bright snowcaps upon their heads. Those in the front row, center stage, held up large letters, one by one, to spell out the title of the song. As the class would sing "C is for Christmas," a child would hold up the letter C. Then, "H is for Happy," and on and on, until each child holding up his or her portion had presented the complete message, "Christmas Love."

The performance was going smoothly, until suddenly, we noticed her, a small, quiet girl in the front row holding the letter M, upside-down! She was entirely unaware that reversed, her letter M appeared as a W. She fidgeted from side to side, until she had moved away from her mark entirely. The audience of children snickered at this little one's mistakes. In her innocence, she had no idea they were laughing at her and stood tall, proudly holding her W.

You can only imagine the difficulty in calming an audience of young, giggling children. Although many teachers tried to shush them, the laughter continued. It continued, that is, until the moment the last letter was raised, and we all saw it together. A hush came over the audience and eyes began to widen. In that instant, we finally understood the reason we were there, why we celebrated in the first place, why even in the chaos, there was a purpose for our festivities. For, when the last letter was held high, the message read loud and clear, "CHRIST WAS LOVE." And, I believe, He still is.

Candy Chand

"We're gonna have REAL people at our Christmas play. Not just parents."

Reprinted with permission from Bil Keane.

My Appointment with Santa

As I pulled away from the hospital parking lot, I wasn't expecting something special to happen. The day seemed like all others. Every day I made a one-hour trip to the hospital for my three-year-old child to get his daily radiation treatment. Every day when we left the hospital, we passed the Santa in front of the flower shop on The Esplanade. And every day my son, Cameron, asked to see him.

Today was no exception.

As I pulled onto the street, the shops and businesses that I'd driven past daily for almost six weeks melted into a monotonous blur. I had memorized this road and barely had to concentrate on maneuvering my car. My mind was free to brood over my worries.

So much to do with only two days left until Christmas. I checked off my mental list: mail Aunt Ellen's package . . . shop for the boys . . . wrap Mom and Dad's presents. . . .

Cameron shouted from his car seat behind me, bringing my mind back to the present. "Mommy, I wanna see Santa!"

I glanced to the side of the road, and there sat the same Santa we'd driven past for weeks now, waving and smiling the same bearded smile.

"Cameron, I have to do some shopping. There's probably a Santa out there for you to see," I told him.

"I don't want that Santa Claus—I wanna see this Santa!" Cameron protested loudly.

"Okay, okay, I'll try to get over."

I tried to weave into the right lane to go around the block, but I couldn't get over. I tried for several blocks and still didn't manage it.

What is this? I thought. *The traffic is never this bad at this time of the day.* Finally, I gave up.

"Cameron, I couldn't get over," I said. "We'll have to see the Santa at the mall."

My son wailed all the way to the mall. I glanced at him in the rearview mirror.

Poor little guy, I thought. *He's as pale as a ghost, and looks a sight with his hair almost gone.*

I wondered about the results of our doctor's last effort to radiate away a second cancerous brain tumor in Cameron's small head. They didn't want to attempt another operation on someone so young—he was only eighteen months when he'd had the first surgery. Oh, how we had rejoiced when they said they'd "got it all." We'd hoped, held our breath, prayed and hoped some more for two long years. Then just six weeks before Christmas 1986, we'd been told the tumor had grown again.

Although my hopes dwindled, I knew we had to keep fighting it. When the doctors suggested radiation treatment, we agreed, even though I knew it would mean a two-hour daily drive to a larger city for six weeks up to Christmas Day. The drive, stress and worry were draining me, even as the radiation drained the life from Cameron's once-pink cheeks.

I entered the mall with a heavy heart. The sounds, sights and smells of Christmas were everywhere: Lights and colors flashing, the jingle of the Salvation Army bell, carols playing softly in the background, package-laden people rushing here and there, some tense, some laughing. A candy shop cooled chocolate fudge on its counter. . . .

Christmas everywhere but in my heart, I thought, as we stopped at the back of the line to see Santa.

The long line moved slowly. Children whined and mothers grew impatient. I clutched Cameron's cool, small hand and gazed at him wistfully, wishing away the whiteness of his skin. He was stretching his neck for a better view and had an expectant gleam in his eyes. We were almost up to Santa!

Finally, it was our turn. Cameron scrambled up into the ornate, red sleigh and looked up into Santa's face with anticipation. I stood off to the side and watched.

"Well, what do we have here?" Santa asked, noticing Cameron's balding head. "Are you going to have an operation, son?"

"No, he's having radiation for a brain tumor," I answered from where I stood.

"What's his name?"

"Cameron!" my son piped up.

"Come over here, Mom," Santa called. I stepped nearer to hear him. "You know that after the doctors have done all they can with their technology, that the ultimate healing is up to the Lord."

"Oh, absolutely!" I agreed.

"Would you sit up here with me, Mom?" I climbed up into the sleigh.

"Do you mind if I pray for this little guy?" I shook my head. Santa continued, "I had a serious problem in my brain at one time and the Lord healed me. I believe He will heal Cameron, too."

Santa pulled Cameron and me close, and I felt as if God had reached down and wrapped me up in a warm hug. I needed it so badly right at that moment.

Santa prayed, "Father, I ask you to touch this little fella from the top of his head to the bottom of his feet. Make him feel good for Christmas. Your word promises us, 'for nothing is impossible with God.' We thank you for healing this little child's body. Amen."

When I opened my eyes, about thirty people had gathered around the sleigh, some bewildered, others with knowing looks. I thanked Santa. With Cameron beaming, he and I left the mall.

On the ride home, I realized how easily I could have missed that special moment. But God had something much better planned.

He had steered me to a Santa whose fur-clad arms were used by God to touch me with his concern, and whose lips had offered a prayer of hope when I was too weak to pray. God had led my small son and me to a saintly Santa—the Santa he would use to put Christmas back into our hearts!

Sharon Lopez
As told to Cynthia Culp Allen

Seeing Love in the Eyes of Santa Claus

The call came early in the afternoon. Anxiously awaiting and dreading it, we were still somewhat relieved when it finally came.

Our neighbor Mary's pain and suffering had ended, but now her family was experiencing grief that is known only by those who have lost a loved one. The children were especially touched by the event, even though both parents had prepared them.

Of the children, I knew that Christine would accept her mother's death more easily. The memory of her visit with Santa Claus would soften her pain. I knew this firsthand because I played Santa Claus the year she shared her precious secret.

My husband was initially going to put on the Santa suit and visit the neighbors, but at the last moment had qualms about the trip to Mary's house. Mary was then terminally ill, and the children were trying to understand. What would he say if the children asked him to make their mother well again? I had recently read an article about "proper" Santa responses. It explained how to ward off children's requests for live animals and what to say if they wanted their illness cured, etc. So I felt knowledge-able enough to play Santa, even though I was a woman.

The beard and wig hid everything except my eyes, and, of course, the oversized suit took care of the rest. After practicing a few hearty "Ho Ho Ho's," I was ready to go.

The younger child, Katey, opened the door. Her eyes grew wide, her smile was small and crooked. Her older sister, Christine, was solemn and uninterested, barely aware that I had arrived. I was invited into the living room, and I encouraged the girls to come over and talk. Katey soon warmed up to me and excitedly told me about all the presents that she expected to see under the tree.

Christine edged closer to me, but she still seemed unsure. When she finally looked at me, she suddenly became excited and a wide grin spread across her face. Not saying a word, she continued to stare at me, speech-less. Everyone in the room kept asking her to tell Santa what she wanted for Christmas, but it was almost as if she didn't hear them, she just continued to stare at me and smile. Finally the adults drifted away.

"Christine," I said, "what do you want Santa to bring you?"

Her smile got smaller, and she said, "You know, Santa, my mom is really sick."

My stomach did a flip-flop, and I knew her next request would be to ask Santa to make her mommy well again.

"Well," Christine continued, "my mom told me that even though one day she would die, she would always be around for me. I told her I didn't understand that. So she told me a secret. She said whenever I wanted to know that she was near me, to look into faces of people who loved me, and I would be able to see her in their faces, and know she loved me.

"Santa, it didn't work! When I looked into my sister's face, I just saw my sister, and when I looked at my dad, I just saw my dad. And I was afraid to tell my mom that the secret wasn't working. I didn't want to make her sad.

"But, Santa, today it worked! When I looked into your eyes just now, they looked just like my mom's eyes, and now I know the secret will come true. My mom will never leave me, because I can find my mom in the faces of the people who love me."

Lorie McCrone

What Goes Around Comes Around

Eve Gordon had difficult duty on Christmas Eve, 1940. She was a special-duty nurse at a London hospital, and she had been assigned to care for a desperately ill German student from a nearby college. The young man had contracted pneumonia and was in critical condition. Staff physicians held out little hope for his survival. The student, aware of his perilous circumstances, pleaded with the nurse to keep him awake, saying, "If I go to sleep, I'll never wake up."

Throughout the long hours of the night, Gordon kept her patient from drifting off into sleep. With painstaking detail she told him the biblical Christmas story—the journey to Bethlehem, the birth in a stable, the adoration of the shepherds, the visit of the Magi, the flight into Egypt. When she had exhausted the story, she sang to him every Christmas carol she could recall from memory. And whenever her patient seemed on the verge of falling asleep, she gently shook him back to consciousness.

The dawn of that Christmas morning found the student still alive and able to celebrate the day. The crisis passed, and the young man gradually improved and was released from the hospital.

Several years passed. Britain and much of the rest of the world were engulfed in World War II. Gordon, now a medical doctor, had been conscripted into the service of her country. Because she was fluent in Norwegian and a skilled skier, she was placed undercover in Nazi-occupied Norway.

One morning German occupation troops arrested her along with scores of Norwegian civilians. Someone had tipped off the Germans that one of that group was a British secret agent. Knowing that her true identity and mission would be discovered, Gordon prayed that death would come quickly and that she would not be subjected to torture.

Gordon was brutally shoved into a small room, where she faced her interrogator, a Nazi soldier. The man reached for his side arm. *My prayer is answered,* she thought. Then their eyes met, and there was surprise at the mutual recognition. The German student and the English nurse were face to face again. Replacing his gun in its holster, the soldier pointed to the back door and said: "Go. I give you back your Christmas."

Victor Parachin

8

OVERCOMING OBSTACLES

*Whether you turn to the right or to the left,
your ears will hear a voice behind you,
saying "this is the way; walk in it."*

Isaiah 30:21

Just Two Tickets to Indy

We had talked about the possibility and its ramification for months as test after test failed to confirm or deny the diagnosis. But now we sat in my office crushed by the reality that it was true: John had ALS, Lou Gehrig's disease. The insidious affliction strikes the muscular system of its victim, eventually draining the body of all strength to support even breathing and a beating heart.

John had been my business partner, my friend, my mentor for many years. He was the kind of friend who pushed you beyond what you thought you could do. John always saw you not for what you are but for what he thought you could be, and then he never let you accept anything less. He told me one time, "I wouldn't really be much of a friend if I let you settle for what *you* think is your best."

We sat in the office crying and holding hands like two adolescent children, realizing that the crippling death sentence would not allow John to live for more than two years. I asked him to think about *the* one thing he had always dreamed of doing that he hadn't done. Was there some event he would like to see, the running of the bulls in Spain or would he prefer to take Bonnie, his beloved, to the Great Wall of China or the Wailing Wall?

His response was predictable. As a lifelong car-racing enthusiast, John had always wanted to go to the Indianapolis 500. Unfortunately, it seemed that the tickets for the event were tied up in corporate commitments or fans who handed their seats down through the family as a legacy.

However, I confidently told John it would be no problem. Many of my clients had connections to the automobile industry from tire makers to parts suppliers; someone was bound to have access to tickets. But my confidence was misplaced. Time after time I was told that even though the request was noble, the corporate allotment was predetermined for years in the future. The 1996 Indy came and went and I was unable to get the tickets for Bonnie and John.

I took advantage of my position for fifteen months as a speaker and asked over one hundred audiences for the tickets. My hopes were sagging as the months passed and the 1997 Memorial Day classic loomed nearer. While John's faith remained and his hopes drove him on to lead a normal life, his body declined and his strength weakened. He would often say, "This disease thinks it has me, well little does it know I got it and it ain't seen anything like me."

For all of his positive faith, I knew in my heart that 1997 would be John's last chance to see the event. By the time I became desperate enough to call them, even the scalpers were out of tickets. In a depression for weeks because I failed to act sooner, I could barely face John and Bonnie. I had failed to make his wish come true. John reassured me that he appreciated my efforts but said, "You are going to die worrying about this ticket thing before I die of ALS."

Then two weeks before the event, the telephone rang

and Peggy Zomack of Cooper Power in Pittsburgh asked the question that stopped my breathing.

"Rick," she asked, "are you still looking for those Indy 500 tickets?" Then she had to ask, "Rick are you still there?"

I couldn't say anything. My voice was paralyzed. Eventually, I got the words out and through tears assured her that she was heaven sent. She put the tickets in overnight mail, and I called Bonnie.

"Bonnie," I said. "Tomorrow, before 10:00 A.M. I will have in my hands tickets to the 1997 Indy 500 for you and John." She and I rejoiced for several minutes through bouts of more tears. Then a horrifying thought struck me, "Bonnie, I don't know if you will be able to find a room. The 500 is just a couple of weeks from now."

"Oh don't worry about that," she replied, "I paid for the room almost a year ago. I knew if I showed enough faith, God would provide the tickets somehow."

Rick Phillips

The Day Mother Cried

Coming home from school that dark winter's day so long ago, I was filled with anticipation. I had a new issue of my favorite sports magazine tucked under my arm and the house to myself. Dad was at work, my sister was away, and Mother wouldn't be home from her new job for an hour. I bounded up the steps, burst into the living room and flipped on a light.

I was shocked into stillness by what I saw. Mother, pulled into a tight ball, with her face in her hands, sat at the far end of the couch. She was crying. I had never seen her cry.

I approached cautiously and touched her shoulder. "Mother?" I asked. "What's happened?"

She took a long breath and managed a weak smile. "It's nothing, really. Nothing important. Just that I'm going to lose this new job. I can't type fast enough."

"But you've only been there three days," I said. "You'll catch on." I repeated a line she had spoken to me a hundred times when I was having trouble learning or doing something important to me.

"No," she said sadly. "There's no time for that. I can't

carry my end of the load. I'm making everyone in the office work twice as hard."

"They're just giving you too much work," I said, hoping to find injustice where she saw failure. She was too honest to accept that.

"I always said I could do anything I set my mind to," she said, "and I still think I can in most things. But I can't do this."

I felt helpless and out of place. At age sixteen I still assumed Mother could do anything. Some years before, when we sold our ranch and moved to town, Mother had decided to open a day nursery. She had no training, but that didn't stand in her way. She sent away for correspondence courses in child care, did the lessons and in six months formally qualified herself for the task. It wasn't long before she had a full enrollment and a waiting list. Parents praised her, and the children proved by their reluctance to leave in the afternoon that she had won their affection. I accepted all this as a perfectly normal instance of Mother's ability.

But neither the nursery nor the motel my parents bought later had provided enough income to send my sister and me to college. I was a high-school sophomore when we sold the motel. In two years, I would be ready for college. In three more, my sister would want to go. Time was running out, and Mother was frantic for ways to save money. It was clear that Dad could do no more than he was doing already—farming eighty acres in addition to holding a full-time job.

Looking back, I sometimes wonder how much help I deserved. Like many kids of sixteen, I wanted my parents' time and attention, but it never occurred to me that they might have needs and problems of their own. In fact, I understood nothing of their lives because I looked only at my own.

A few months after we'd sold the motel, Mother arrived home with a used typewriter. It skipped between certain letters and the keyboard was soft. At dinner that night I pronounced the machine a "piece of junk."

"That's all we can afford," Mother said. "It's good enough to learn on." And from that day on, as soon as the table was cleared and the dishes were done, Mother disappeared into her sewing room to practice. The slow *tap, tap, tap* went on some nights until midnight.

It was nearly Christmas when I heard her tell Dad one night that a good job was available at the radio station. "It would be such interesting work," she said. "But this typing isn't coming along very fast."

"If you want the job, go ask for it," Dad encouraged her.

I was not the least bit surprised, or impressed, when Mother got the job. But she was ecstatic.

Monday, after her first day at work, I could see that the excitement was gone. Mother looked tired and drawn. I responded by ignoring her.

Tuesday, Dad made dinner and cleaned the kitchen. Mother stayed in her sewing room, practicing. "Is Mother all right?" I asked Dad.

"She's having a little trouble with her typing," he said. "She needs to practice. I think she'd appreciate it if we all helped out a bit more."

"I already do," I said, immediately on guard.

"I know you do," Dad said evenly. "And you may have to do more. You might just remember that she is working primarily so you can go to college."

I honestly didn't care. In a pique, I called a friend and went out to get a soda. When I came home the house was dark, except for the band of light showing under Mother's door. It seemed to me that her typing had gotten even slower. I wished she would just forget the whole thing.

My shock and embarrassment at finding Mother in

tears on Wednesday was a perfect index of how little I understood the pressures on her. Sitting beside her on the couch, I began very slowly to understand.

"I guess we all have to fail sometime," Mother said quietly. I could sense her pain and the tension of holding back the strong emotions that were interrupted by my arrival. Suddenly, something inside me turned. I reached out and put my arms around her.

She broke then. She put her face against my shoulder and sobbed. I held her close and didn't try to talk. I knew I was doing what I should, what I could and that it was enough. In that moment, feeling Mother's back racked with emotion, I understood for the first time her vulnerability. She was still my mother, but she was something more: a person like me, capable of fear and hurt and failure. I could feel her pain as she must have felt mine on a thousand occasions when I had sought comfort in her arms.

Then it was over. Wiping away the tears, Mother stood and faced me. "Well, Son, I may be a slow typist, but I'm not a parasite and I won't keep a job I can't do. I'm going to ask tomorrow if I can finish out the week. Then I'll resign."

And that's what she did. Her boss apologized to her, saying that he had underestimated his workload as badly as she had overestimated her typing ability. They parted with mutual respect, he offering a week's pay and she refusing it. A week later Mother took a job selling dry goods at half the salary the radio station had offered. "It's a job I can do," she said simply. But the evening practice sessions on the old green typewriter continued. I had a very different feeling now when I passed her door at night and heard her tapping away. I knew there was something more going on in there than a woman learning to type.

When I left for college two years later, Mother had an

office job with better pay and more responsibility. I have
to believe that in some strange way she learned as much
from her moment of defeat as I did, because several years
later, when I finished school and proudly accepted a job
as a newspaper reporter, she had already been a reporter
with our hometown paper for six months.

Mother and I never spoke again about the afternoon
when she broke down. But more than once, when I failed
on a first attempt and was tempted by pride or frustration
to scrap something I truly wanted, I remember her selling
dresses while she learned to type. In seeing her weakness,
I had not only learned to appreciate her strengths, I had
discovered some of my own.

Not long ago, I helped Mother celebrate her sixty-
second birthday. I made dinner for my parents and
cleaned up the kitchen afterward. Mother came in to visit
while I worked, and I was reminded of the day years
before when she had come home with that terrible old
typewriter. "By the way," I said. "Whatever happened to
that monster typewriter?"

"Oh, I still have it," she said. "It's a memento, you know
. . . of the day you realized your mother was human.
Things are a lot easier when people know you're human."

I had never guessed that she saw what happened to me
that day. I laughed at myself. "Someday," I said, "I wish
you would give me that machine."

"I will," she said, "but on one condition."

"What's that?"

"That you never have it fixed. It is nearly impossible to
type on that machine, and that's the way it served this
family best."

I smiled at the thought. "And another thing," she said.
"Never put off hugging someone when you feel like it.
You may miss the chance forever."

I put my arms around her and hugged her and felt a

deep gratitude for that moment, for all the moments of joy she had given me over the years. "Happy birthday!" I said.

The old green typewriter sits in my office now, unrepaired. It is a memento, but what it recalls for me is not quite what it recalled for Mother. When I'm having trouble with a story and think about giving up, or when I start to feel sorry for myself and think things should be easier for me, I roll a piece of paper into that cranky old machine and type, word by painful word, just the way Mother did. What I remember then is not her failure, but her courage, the courage to go ahead.

It's the best memento anyone ever gave me.

Gerald Moore

Somebody in the Corner

Strangers are friends that you have yet to meet.

Roberta Lieberman

Every Christmas Eve the women of Renshaw, Nova Scotia, gather at nightfall on the railroad platform. Their children in bed, they come to wait for the fathers and husbands who, having shopped all afternoon in the county seat, are bringing home the Christmas playthings.

When I was a very young man, I knew a woman named Emily Sanders. Year after year on Christmas Eve she waited there in the frosty starlight, all in vain. This is the story of the man she was waiting for. And while I have changed names and altered facts, this is substantially a true account of what befell us there long ago.

It began on a June day when I was a divinity student filling a summer "practice pulpit" in that orchard land of Evangeline. Bumping along a back-hill road on my second-hand bicycle, I was caught in a sudden and furious thunderstorm. Ahead of me, through the downpour, I could see a barefoot little girl sloshing across a rickety wooden bridge.

"Shouldn't you stop crying?" I called to the red-haired moppet. "The bridge is wet enough already."

From behind the seat I unleashed a collapsible umbrella, and then, with the child straddling in front and the umbrella held shakily over us, I tried to guide the bike with one hand, on down the hill.

"Where do you live?" I shouted into her ear.

"Second house just at the bottom."

"What's your name?"

"Mary. My father is Frank Sanders. Does that mean I have to get off?"

There was no time to pursue the strangeness of her question; we had arrived. Standing at the doorway was a tall, gaunt woman, and the only well-kept part of her was the sleek hair wound up in tight golden braids. Already the flush of life was gone from this woman, and yet there was in her eyes the memory of happiness now gone.

"How was it you happened to have an umbrella when all day it's been sunny?" She asked me suspiciously. She pulled Mary inside with her three other children.

"I'm the summer preacher at the crossways church," I explained, smiling. "At prayer meeting the other night we asked God for rain, so I thought I had better pack an umbrella."

Motioning me inside, she fastened the door and began peeling off Mary's soaked clothing. On the wall I was noticing three faded photographs of the same man, a boxer in trunks, balled fists lifted in a John L. Sullivan guard.

"Who's the fighter?" I asked.

From all four children came a shrill chorus: "That's Pop!"

"He used to be a light heavyweight champ!" screamed the older boy.

"He still packs a terrific right!" yelled the other.

"Pop's strong," said Mary softly.

As the mother hushed her gossipy brood, I changed the subject.

"You might as well understand," the mother announced stiffly, "that your congregation don't want us. And we sure don't want them. No, there's no mistake. They all think my husband is no good. As long as I stick to Frank, they won't help us. So—"

There was a sudden violent blast of wind as the door was flung open and a man stamped in. He was a dripping wreck but still recognizable as the boxer on the walls.

"You that summer reverend?" he demanded.

"Yes, I'm John Bonnell—"

The light heavyweight pointed with backward thumb toward the storm outdoors; I had to wave good-bye to his silent wife and children, and ride off.

It was, therefore, a shock to me at the Sunday service to behold Frank Sanders, scrubbed and shaved, sitting all by himself in the back pew. *Why had the dilapidated slugger come to church?*

Since Sanders had turned me out of his house, I had been making inquiries. Emily, his wife, as a laundress spare helper, earned the family money, while he hunted rabbits and wild geese, and fished in the ponds. A lot of his time was spent with his lone friend, an atheist whom everybody called Doctor Tom. This broken-down professor kept Frank in whiskey and sent him on errands, fetching and delivering newspapers and mail to his reeking bachelor cabin on the other side of town. I had good reason to wonder about Frank's business in my congregation.

After the service, Frank remained in his pew until all the other parishioners stood waiting outside by the graveyard gate; they thought I was facing a fight.

"Mr. Sanders," I told him, "you're welcome here."

"Don't get any ideas, Reverend," he reported, rising

with a wink. "I don't believe in pious balderdash."

"Is that boxing lingo?" I asked. "Sounds more like your friend Doctor Tom. Frank, why did you come?"

"Reverend, you want to attract crowds to your meetings, don't you? Well, you're going to get 'em. Because I'm going to be here every time you have a service. That's bound to set people talking. They'll come in droves, hoping for the knockout—they want to see me plead to be saved from my sins. Hah! You realize I'm never going to do any such thing!"

"Then why," I demanded, quite bewildered, "do you want me to have crowds?"

"For the nice help you gave our Mary in the rain, Reverend. When I ordered you out of my house, I didn't realize—so I've got to square myself."

Chin up and whistling, he walked off toward the hills and his friend Doctor Tom.

Never before had our little gray church with the red steeple held such crowds; the splintery pine benches could not seat them all. And Frank, keeping his promise, was invariably there, in the last row, and at first alone. Later he brought in the whole family, starched and well-behaved. And later still I learned that he had taken a job in the planing mill; for more than a month he kept sober.

Then one morning I was stopped in front of the general store by a puffy, red-whiskered man who barred my path and held up a bottle.

"Look, Rev!" he panted. "If I fill this with water, can you change it into good hard liquor?"

Getting no answer from me, he turned to Frank Sanders, just coming out of the store.

"I suppose," he shouted, "he's got you to believe in the miracle of changing water into wine!"

"Doctor Tom, I can tell you a bigger miracle than that," Frank grinned. "He's turned rum into food and clothing, and my miserable home into a happy one."

"Balderdash!" tittered Doctor Tom, holding on to my lapel. "Listen, Rev! Suppose you think you're converting Frank. Well, let me prophesy what's going to happen. Immediately after you go back where you came from, good old Frank will quit his job. Immediately! He'll junk his family. Immediately! And he'll come back to my way of living. Immediately!"

"And you consider that a good thing?"

"At least he can have a little fun for himself out of this so-called life. You won't get him. I'll get him. You'll see."

Off he waddled toward the hill road, but over his shoulder he called back: "Ask Frank what he'll be doing next Christmas Eve."

There was deep worry in Frank's eyes.

"Whether I can stick it out after you've gone back to school, Reverend, I just ain't sure. This is a lot tougher fight for me than you might realize. What keeps me going is listening to you—you're like my trainer in the corner, my second; you keep up my nerve. Everybody needs somebody in his corner."

"Everybody has Somebody," I told him. "You can count on Him too."

He flashed me a blank look of doubt.

"You can't see Him, though," he muttered. "He ain't got skin on. I won't be able to see Him next Christmas Eve."

That was the crux of his fear. For the past five years Frank had gone into Earlton with money for Christmas toys and then drunk himself into a stupor.

"That's what Doctor Tom is counting on now," he finished miserably.

"Frank," I said impulsively, "if you can keep going steady right up to the morning of December 24, I'll come back up here to see you through Christmas Eve."

"Reverend," cried my friend, "that's a deal!"

After the first week in September, when I went back to Halifax, the church at Renshaw was shut up until spring. A letter from Emily Sanders told me how Frank was sticking to his job and even talking about building some fine new pews for the church. But the hardwood he wanted was scarce, except for a big stock in Doctor Tom's backyard, and the professor refused to sell unless Frank Sanders would take a drink with him.

"So far," wrote Emily, "Frank hasn't taken it, but he will do almost anything for the church now."

Doesn't it seem strange that by the time the holidays came around, I had forgotten my Christmas Eve appointment? I don't know why I did, except that schoolwork had been completely absorbing all that autumn, and now my folks were planning a jolly time over the fortnight; they had even invited as their houseguest a young woman in whom I had become deeply interested. I was even considering a romantic Christmas morning proposal beside the yule tree. What reminded me, just in time, was a run-through of my diary; I was making some notes for Christmas greetings and suddenly came upon the name Frank Sanders.

By telephone calls I made my excuses, then grabbed the first train for the Grand Pre' country. At noon I was once more at the Sanders' home in Renshaw, but I was too late.

"Frank's gone to the county seat with all the other men," Emily told me. "He took the money for the toys. But when you didn't arrive on the morning train, the heart seemed to go right out of him."

"I'll drive after him," I exclaimed. "I'll hire an automobile." But in those innocent days Renshaw had no cars for hire. I was marooned in town.

That night when the return train from town was due, I stood with Emily on the platform. What would we see when the train arrived—Frank Sanders drunk or sober?

We were afraid to look at each other, afraid of the answers already in our eyes. Presently, in fur cap and jacket and smoking a cigar, Doctor Tom accosted us.

"Well!" he exclaimed with a snort that would have done credit to a bull moose. Raising his voice so that everyone could hear, he added: "What are you keeping this poor woman waiting here for? Emily Sanders knows as well as I do what's coming home to her on that train. Immediately!"

"Pray, Reverend," murmured Emily. "The train ride home is the worst part. Everybody has a bottle to pass around. Pray hard!"

"Pray, hah!" shouted Doctor Tom. "That shows you're not sure. Well, I'm sure! Enough to bet good hard cash! Who'll take me up? Who has five bucks that says Frankie Sanders gets off that train sober—who? What? Nobody? Three dollars? Two, then. Surely for two measly bucks somebody in this crowd will bet on good old Frank. Think, neighbors—you're betting on a human soul. How about you, Rev? Will you bet a buck?"

"Don't believe in gambling," I told him.

"You mean you don't believe in Frank Sanders—not even a buck's worth!"

Was it righteous wrath or just plain temper? To this day I am not sure. Then, as now, I detested gambling. Yet I said: "I'll take your bet. If Frank Sanders comes home a sober man, you will give the hardwood stored in your back shed to be made into new pews for the church. Otherwise, I pay you the price of the wood."

"It's a bet?"

"It is," I concurred shakily, "a bet!"

No one would ever have expected Doctor Tom and me to shake hands. Yet we did, and none too soon, for already on the snowy night we heard the far-off whistle of the train. Shamelessly holding the hand of another man's wife, I prayed to Almighty God that I would win this, my

first and last wager. I remember the confusion in my feelings; in those last waiting minutes it seemed to me that
here at this crossroads was all the trouble of the world,
the struggle of good and evil making the windswept platform an everywhere—and the result very much in doubt.

Now, we could hear the bell, loud and strong, and we
all stood in the yellow flame of the headlight gleaming on
the walls of snow as the engine, hauling two dimly lit
coaches, came snuffling to a stop.

Farmers and breeders and orchard men streamed off
the train, but there was no sign of Frank. Doctor Tom
looked around him with a toothy smile. I climbed aboard
and marched through the cars, peering under seats and in
the washrooms, like a woodsman looking for a wounded
animal. As I came out on the back steps, I shouted: "Has
anybody seen Frank Sanders?"

The engineer, bending far out of the window cab, called
hoarsely: "Sure, I seen him. About two hours before train
time. He was going into the Blue Nose Tavern."

That was all we needed to know. There was an audible
sigh from the crowd as they turned and surged on toward
the bridge over the tracks. As I took Emily by the arm and
we started off together, I came as near to weeping as is
good for a senior student.

Beyond the bridge loomed a wagon drawn by two
white horses. The driver stood up and waved his hat:
"Merry Christmas, everybody!"

And then suddenly I saw—and all the others saw with
me—a familiar figure clambering from behind the load of
barrels and casks. It was Frank Sanders jumping to the
snow-packed highway, and the driver was handing down
to him a doll and a drum, a ship and a toy cradle—a whole
Santa Claus cargo of Christmas toys!

"Hey, Emily!" Frank was yelling. "Don't get scared. Ain't
had a drop! Thought it was safer not to come home on the

train. Too much temptation, with bottles being passed and all. So I hopped a ride home on the Blue Tavern's truck."

Emily ran toward him and then for the first time he saw me.

"Rev!" he yelled. "You did come! Well, thanks. But you were right. There was Somebody in my corner all the time—even among the beer kegs! Knowing that fixes everything. Come on home and help trim the tree."

"First," I told him, "I've got to see Doctor Tom—and make sure the church collects my winnings. Immediately!"

John Sutherland Bonnell

A Rainbow's Promise

"MaiLy! Wake up, little one!" the nun said in a frantic whisper.

MaiLy rubbed her sleepy eyes with the back of her hand. "Wake! Hurry!" Sister Katrine grasped her arm and pulled her to a sitting position. "It's time!"

Time for what? Mai wondered as she obediently stood beside her cot and watched Sister wake the other nine-year-olds in the same way. She nudged them toward Mai, then to the door and into the black night. Explosions sounded in the distance. Whimpering children from other cottages rushed past them down the dirt path. Mai ran with them to the main gate of the orphanage where they shivered in silence. They heard the familiar rumble of Vietnamese army vehicles, then gunfire blasts nearby. Huddling closer, they wrapped their arms around each other as tanks thundered past the gate. The vibration shook through their bones. Repeated gunfire blazed sudden bursts of light against a pitch-black curtain of night as the explosions grew nearer. The trembling children cried softly. Sister Katrine opened the gate a few inches.

"The war is here, my children. Do not be afraid. God will

save us but we must run for safety now." One by one she coaxed the frightened children out the gate and commanded them to run to the convent at the top of the hill. "Run!" she yelled as she shoved Mai through the gate.

Run! Run! Run! Mai commanded herself as her bare feet pounded the earth. Bombs exploded like fireworks, providing the only light as she stumbled along the rocky path. The sky became brighter as the bombing increased, but smoke clouded her way. She tried to suppress the sobs that spent her diminishing breath.

Run! Run! Run! she repeated to herself. Her tears tasted like dirt as she wiped them with her grimy hand. When she reached the convent, she ascended the stairs two at a time, then crouched in the corner and waited for the other children.

Soon an army truck pulled up. "Come! Hurry!" the nun commanded. A Vietnamese soldier pulled back the canvas canopy and boosted the children into the back of the truck two and three at a time. When the bench seats were full, the remaining children crowded together on the floor. The truck lunged forward and their treacherous journey to freedom began. Mai cuddled closer to her friends and wondered if she would see the orphanage, or the American who had promised to come back for her, ever again.

The truck snaked its way through the chaos of war and eventually to a coastal city. There the nuns and children sought refuge in a church. Hesitantly, Sister Katrine approached Mother Superior and told her of her plan to leave with MaiLy.

"Absolutely not!" the older nun hissed.

But Sister Katrine insisted. "I must try to get her to Saigon, then to the American GI who has waited for seven years to adopt her." Looking into her superior's eyes she repeated firmly, "With or without your consent, I am taking MaiLy."

With the sun setting to her back, Sister Katrine gripped Mai's hand and raced eastward toward the shore. Her habit hiked to her knees, Sister Katrine assisted in building a tiny raft, then a dozen frantic people crowded on. As their rig pushed off at sunset and drifted into the South China Sea, they looked back at a city on fire.

Sister placed MaiLy in a cardboard box, but it was flimsy protection against the tempestuous sea. Wind and mountainous waves lashed at the raft, threatening to consume it and the refugees on board. The deafening roar drowned out hollered commands and prayers. For hours the ruthless waves battered their bodies relentlessly and they fought to keep from being devoured by the monstrous sea. The sun's slow descent on the horizon seemed to steal the power from the storm. Then a vibrant rainbow appeared. "That's a sign of God's promise," Sister whispered to MaiLy. "He will protect you from life's storms."

Days later, the raft docked in Saigon. Sister Katrine and MaiLy joined the throngs of panicking people in overloaded carts, and on oxen and scooters racing for their freedom. Miraculously, Sister Katrine found the agency that had wanted to facilitate Mai's adoption. There, Sister squatted to Mai's level. "Do you remember the special American GI who came to visit you many times at the orphanage?" Mai nodded. "He lives far away. If I leave you here they will take you to him."

"But I don't want you to leave me," Mai whimpered, stepping closer to her.

Sister took a handkerchief from her sleeve and wiped her eyes. "Haven't I always taken good care of you, MaiLy?"

Mai nodded again.

"Now I can take the best care of you by letting you go."

Mai wrapped her arms around Sister Katrine's neck.

Sister whispered, "Remember, God will take care of you—and will give you rainbows after the storms." Then she took Mai's hand and led her to the steps of the orphan evacuation center. Mai waved good-bye to the only family she had ever known.

The next day, she was loaded on board a gutted cargo jet with one hundred other children. Babies were placed two and three to a cardboard box with toddlers and older children sitting on the side bench seats. As the plane lifted off the ground, Mai pressed her face against the window. Her tears trickled down the glass.

Babies gently bumped against each other when the plane landed in the Philippines. All the children were escorted in open-air buses to Clark Air Force Base. Mai leaned her head against the window and gazed solemnly at the scenery. The palm trees seemed to wave a tranquility unknown in Vietnam.

There was no congestion of carts, scooters or oxen.

No thunderous bombings.

No hordes of frightened people.

But also no orphanage.

No Sister Katrine.

No American GI.

Mai spent most of the next two days curled up on her mattress at Operation Babylift headquarters. Hundreds of children ran merrily and joined in games as they waited for a larger, safer plane to complete their journey. Mai lay curled, ignoring the kind acts of her volunteer caregivers. Feeling betrayed and abandoned, she wondered if she would ever see her friends, her homeland or the American GI again. She recalled the day, when she was three, that she saw him the first time. It was then she had chosen him. Clinging to his leg, she sat on his foot for a "ride" as he diapered and fed the babies. She closed her eyes and remembered swinging on his lap on the old rope swing in the dusty playground. She could almost feel his whiskers on her face as she did when she pressed her cheek to his in their usual hug. A smile crossed her lips as she relived the day he brought dozens of balloons and kazoos to the orphanage. He had handed a kazoo to each child and motioned for them to watch him as he hummed into his. They all followed suit, spraying spit and slobber without song. Laughing, he showed them again and again until the room vibrated with the sounds of joyful children blasting their tunes. Mai rolled over on her mattress and sighed, wondering why he hadn't come back for her as he promised. *Where was he now? Who would take care of her? Where was she going?*

Over and over again Mai asked that question. The answer, "America," was meaningless to her.

The next day she and the three hundred children were loaded onto a mammoth plane with dozens of volunteers. Again she asked the question. Again they answered, "America."

After several more plane flights and bus rides, the answer was, "Denver." Mai stepped off the bus with the other children and ascended a flight of stairs to yet another gathering place for the war orphans. She sulked into the room and heard a man call out breathlessly, "MaiLy!"

And there he was.

The American GI she had chosen in Vietnam ran to her, swooping her into his arms. He twirled her as she pressed her cheek to his in their familiar hug. He took her home that same evening, where she was welcomed by his wife, his two little girls, sugared Cheerios and Mickey Mouse sheets.

As she cuddled with her daddy on an overstuffed sofa, multicolored snowflakes glistened in the moonlight on the window pane. Sister Katrine was right: There are rainbows at the end of the storms.

LeAnn Thieman

A Refugee Camp Birthday

My eleventh birthday was just a week away when we arrived in the refugee camp on that bleak and cold November day in 1947. My grandparents, who were raising me, and I had successfully fled our Soviet-occupied, communist country, Hungary, with only the clothes we were wearing. The refugee camp, called a Displaced Persons Camp, was in Spittal, Austria.

To frightened, cold and hungry people like us, the refugee camp was a blessing. We were given our own little cardboard-enclosed space in a barrack, fed hot cabbage-and-potato soup, and given warm clothes. We had much to be grateful for. But as for my upcoming birthday, I didn't even want to think about it. After all, we had left our country devoid of possessions or money. And even if Apa (my grandfather) had managed to flee with a few *pengos* (Hungarian small currency) in his pocket, it wouldn't have done us any good in Austria. So I had decided to forget about birthday presents from then on.

My grandmother, who was the only mother I had known, had taken over my care when I was only a few weeks old, because her only child, my mother, had died suddenly. Before the war intensified, my birthdays had been grand celebrations with many cousins in attendance, and lots of gifts of toys, books and clothes. The cake had always been a dobosh torte, which Anya (my grandmother) prepared herself.

My eighth birthday had been the last time I received a bought gift. Times were already hard, money was scarce and survival the utmost goal. But my grandparents had managed to hock something so they could buy me a book. It was a wonderful book, too, full of humor and adventure, and I loved it. In fact, *Cilike's Adventures* had transported me many times from the harshness of the real world to a world of laughter and fun. After that, birthday presents, thanks to Anya's deft fingers, were usually crocheted or knitted items, but there was always a present. However, in the refugee camp, I was resigned to the inevitable.

On November 25, 1947, when I woke in our cardboard cubicle, I laid there on my little cot beneath the horsehair blanket and thought about being eleven now. Why, I was practically a grown-up, I told myself, and I would act accordingly when Anya and Apa awoke. I didn't want them to feel bad because they couldn't give me a present. So I dressed quickly and tiptoed out as quietly as possible. Outside, I ran across the frosty dirt road to the barrack marked Women's Bathroom and Shower, washed, combed my hair and took my time, even though it was chilly in there, before returning to our cubicle. But finally, return I did.

"Good morning, Sweetheart. Happy birthday," Apa greeted as soon as I walked in.

"Thank you. But I'd just as soon forget about birthdays from now on," I replied, squirming in his generous hug.

"You are too young to forget about birthdays," Anya said, taking me in her arms. "Besides, who would I give this present to if birthdays are to be forgotten?"

"Present?" I looked at her dumbfounded, as she reached into her pocket and pulled something out.

"Happy birthday, Honey. It's not much of a present, but I thought you might enjoy having Cilike back on your eleventh birthday," she said, tears welling up in her eyes.

"My old *Cilike's Adventures* book! But I thought it was left behind with all our other things," I said, hugging the book to my chest, tears of joy welling up in my own eyes.

"Well, it almost was. But when we had to leave so quickly in the middle of the night, I grabbed it, along with my prayer book, and stuck it in my pocket. I knew how much you loved that book, and I couldn't bear to leave it behind. Happy birthday, again, Honey. I'm sorry it's not a new book, but I hope you like having it back," Anya said.

"Oh, thank you, Anya. Having Cilike back means so much to me. So very much," I said, hugging her again, tears streaming down my cheeks. "It's the best birthday present I ever received!" And it truly was, because I realized that day that God had blessed me with a wonderful grandmother/mother, whose love would always see me through.

Renie Burghardt

It Is Well with My Soul

If you have anything against anyone, forgive him.

Mark 11:25

In 1984, every parent's worst nightmare came true for my husband and me; our youngest daughter, Jonelle, was abducted from our home and has never been found.

The nightmare began on December 20. I intended to surprise my ailing parents, who lived in California and whom I hadn't seen for years, with a holiday visit. I left on the twentieth and was to return on the twenty-sixth. My trip was my Christmas present to my parents. But, Jonelle, twelve years old and still attached to family traditions, had objected at first to my plan. "What about celebrating Christmas on the twenty-fifth?" she protested.

"We only have to wait one extra day," I told her, "then we'll celebrate Christmas as a family on the twenty-sixth." Reluctantly, she agreed.

We spent that evening together—Jim and I, our two daughters, Jennifer and Jonelle—drinking hot cider while waiting for my ride to the airport. After I left at about

5:45 P.M., life resumed its regular, hectic pace for Jim and the girls: Jennifer dashed off to her varsity basketball game while Jim took Jonelle to McDonald's for a quick bite to eat before dropping her off at school. Her choir was performing a Christmas concert at a local bank. Jim remembers waiting as Jonelle boarded the school bus. Then he left to watch Jennifer's game.

When he came home later that evening at around 9:30, he expected Jonelle to be home. "Hi, Jonelle!" he called out. When there was no response, he looked around for a note, thinking perhaps she had gone to a friend's instead.

Downstairs, the TV was on, as was the quartz heater and Jonelle's nylon stockings were strewn about. She had been there. Beginning to worry, Jim called our pastor and dear friend, James Christy, and asked him what he should do. Pastor Christy advised Jim to call the police, then check with Jonelle's friends, which he did. Jim learned that Jonelle had indeed been dropped off after choir by her best friend's dad at 8:20 that evening.

Whenever we travel, we have a habit of calling and letting each other know we're okay. A little after midnight that night, after arriving in California, I called to let Jim know that my plane had arrived safely.

"Gloria," Jim began, "I don't know how to tell you this, but Jonelle isn't home. She's nowhere to be found."

It was immediate: the cold, hard knot in the pit of my stomach. It didn't occur to me to dismiss her absence matter-of-factly. ("She's probably at a movie or something. Nothing to be alarmed over.") Something was wrong, and I knew it instantly. After I hung up, I dropped to my knees and prayed. Later I tried to sleep, but sleep wouldn't come. I spent the whole night crying and praying.

The next day I made arrangements to fly home, hoping that before night came it would be fixed—Jonelle would be found, I could stay in California, the nightmare would end, everything would be fine.

But everything was not fine. I arrived home to unmistakable evidence: On the night of December 20, 1984, between the time Jonelle had been dropped off from choir at 8:20 and the time my husband came home a little over an hour later, someone had entered our home.

Nothing in the daily routine of life prepares you for something like this. Yet somehow, I was prepared. Maybe it has something to do with simply believing that God is sovereign. It's like that hymn, "It Is Well with My Soul." The writer of that song lost his children and his wife in a tragedy at sea. Yet he had peace with God, and he could still say, after all his losses, *It is well with my soul.*

People have asked me, "How could you live day to day with a child missing?" All I can say is we clung to hope. I left lights on at night. I set a place for Jonelle at the table on Christmas Eve so she wouldn't feel left out if she returned unexpectedly. Even as weeks turned into months, we truly believed Jonelle would be found, certain that at any minute she would walk through the door.

We tried everything in our efforts to locate her. Bloodhounds sniffed the property while helicopters scoured the surrounding area. Jonelle's picture was plastered everywhere. Friends formed a Rescue Jonelle committee. We networked with truckers. A video of Jonelle singing with her school choir that night was aired by Peter Jennings. We even went on *Geraldo* to tell our story. You'll do anything—anything—to find your child. And, of course, we prayed. Thousands of people locally, nationally, even internationally, prayed for Jonelle. Certainly, with all this prayer, God wouldn't leave us hanging.

But I discovered that God's ways aren't always our ways. Six months after Jonelle disappeared, I was driving to work. I was praying as I drove, and my prayer that day concluded with these words: "Lord, you know we'll give you the honor and glory through all this. Just give us some answers." That day, sitting at a signal, I seemed to hear God say, "Gloria, will you ever give me the honor and glory if you *never* learn what happened to Jonelle?"

This wasn't what I wanted to hear. I wanted to know what happened to Jonelle. *I needed to know!* Surely God could show us something. Was this too much to ask? For the first time since my daughter disappeared, it dawned on me that I might never know what happened. I sat in my car at the signal and wept.

I didn't realize it at the time, and to be honest, it took years before I really understood it, but this was, in fact, God's way of answering our prayers. It's so easy to think, *Why isn't God answering? Why won't he at least give us some answers?* But I began to see that it doesn't matter whether God is going to answer prayers the way I think he should answer. What matters is that God will give me the strength to endure any ordeal without being completely destroyed by it. And when the senselessness of my loss was too much to bear, I found comfort in the scripture: "The Lord is . . . my God, my rock, in whom I take refuge." (Psalm 18:2)

To this day, there's no answer to the mystery about Jonelle's disappearance. But I've stopped asking God to tell me what happened to her. Maybe he has a reason for not giving me the answers I want. What if what happened to Jonelle is worse than what I can imagine? Maybe not knowing is better. . . .

On December 20, 1994, we had a memorial service for Jonelle. It was our way, not only of saying good-bye to our daughter, but of also saying to God, "We're letting her go now. She's yours." The next day, it felt as if a huge burden was lifted from us. I knew I could do nothing else for Jonelle. As a mother, you never really want to let go of that sense that there's more you could have done. But that night, I finally let go.

Yes, sometimes I wish I knew what happened to Jonelle. But I've finally surrendered myself to the fact that we may never know. The day will come when everything will be explained. But by then, Jonelle will be welcoming us to heaven, showing us around, and telling us where to go and what to do. That's the way she is. She loves to tell you what to do. . . .

Gloria Matthews
As told to Elaine Minamide

The Girl with the Golden Hair

As twilight painted the room lavender, Sandy Moreno whisked a dust rag across knick-knacks. Reaching an angel figurine with a flaxen halo, she paused—and a train whistled in the distance.

You're still here, Tina, aren't you? Sandy thought as goose-bumps danced across her skin. *Still working your miracle. . . .*

Three years previous, the forty-nine-year-old insurance agent was sitting beside her husband's bed in the ICU of Baylor Medical Center in Dallas. Mike had built their Honolulu cottage with his own hands, and even after he contracted hepatitis, you could find him surfing. But five years after Mike's diagnosis, he had deteriorated into complete liver failure.

"He needs a transplant," the doctors explained.

He will make it! Sandy felt in her heart. And Mike was in disbelief as he was placed on an organ waiting list.

"For me to get a new liver," he said, "someone must die." So they made a vow that after waiting the year required by the donor organization, they'd write and thank the donor family.

Finally, one stormy night five months later, doctors said: "We have an organ!"

Here's my chance, Mike thought as Sandy raced alongside his gurney.

For the next six hours, Sandy paced the waiting room. As morning broke, she bought a newspaper. *I'm too nervous to read,* she decided. *But I'll save it for Mike as a souvenir marking his re-birthday!*

Finally, the surgeon emerged. "That was the healthiest organ I've ever seen," he smiled.

Sandy felt excited, but at the same time sad: Someone had died for Mike to live. Yet that evening, Mike still lay in a coma.

"Why won't he wake up?" Sandy demanded.

"We don't know," doctors confessed.

Unable to sleep, sitting in a chair beside Mike's bed, Sandy picked up the *Dallas Morning News.* Her hands trembled as she flipped to an article about an eighteen-year-old girl who'd died when a train crashed into her car. There was a picture of Tina, her golden hair cascading over her shoulders.

Sandy bolted upright. She'd seen Mike's chart: His donor was a young woman. *This must be her,* Sandy thought. She glanced at the girl's youthful smile. Then she took her husband's hand. "You'll pull through!" she said.

After ten days and nights, Mike awoke—but he was babbling incoherently. Soon, an MRI revealed that Mike had central pontine mylenisis, a rare brain disorder.

"Maybe, with rehabilitation, he can have a normal life," the doctors said. "But there's only a 2 percent chance. . . ."

For the next two weeks, Mike struggled. His right side was paralyzed. "You can do this!" Sandy urged him.

But after a month, Mike was still in pain. "I can't . . . take . . . any more!" he blurted. He looked at his wife. *I've put her through enough suffering,* he despaired. *Maybe I should give up.* Then he fell into a deep sleep.

Everything turned murky. *This is the end,* Mike realized. But then he felt a breeze—and saw a pinpoint of brightness. The light grew and grew. And from the illumination appeared . . . a girl.

"Come on, Mike," she encouraged. "God wants you to live!"

Stunned, Mike peered into her face, at her twinkling eyes framed by short hair the color of honey.

"Who are you?" he stammered.

But the girl was already disappearing. "You can do it!" she sang.

She sounds like a cheerleader! Mike almost laughed, and he felt encompassed by a radiant warmth. Suddenly, he realized: *I can do it!*

The next morning, Mike said to Sandy, "I had a vision!" His eyes blazed as he continued. "I saw a light, and this blond girl. . . ."

Sandy instantly recalled the photo in the newspaper, and she swallowed hard. *Could it be the same girl?* she thought.

"I want to get better," Mike stated with determination. Smiling, Sandy kissed his forehead. *Let him believe whatever gives him hope,* she decided. But she also resolved not to say anything about the girl in the train accident. *It may upset him,* she thought.

That day, Mike got into his wheelchair. Soon he was storming down hallways. The doctors were amazed. "There's no explanation for why Mike recovered," they marveled.

Sure there is, Mike thought. *I met an angel.*

Only a month and a half later, Mike went home 70 percent recovered, his new liver working well. A year later, he felt strong enough to surf again. Sandy told Mike, "It's time to write the letter."

You gave me a second chance, Mike penned. *Thank you.* Then he sent the letter to a national transplant organization, which sent it to his donor's family.

One month later, Mike received a letter postmarked Argyle, Texas. *We're the parents of your donor,* it read. *And we'd love to meet you. Signed Donna and Terry Minke.*

So Sandy and Mike flew to Texas. There, Donna presented Mike with a picture of long-haired Tina—and Mike gasped. It was the girl in his vision!

"I've already met your daughter," he began, trembling as he told them about his vision. "But she had shorter hair."

Donna's hand flew to her mouth. "Tina cut her hair after that picture was taken," she choked. "Before she . . . died in a train accident."

Sandy and Mike exchanged glances. The girl in the newspaper was Mike's donor!

"She was the youngest registered nurse's aide in Texas," Donna began. "And the day she got her driver's license, she said she'd checked off the boxes to be an organ donor."

"Tina was one heck of a third baseman, too," her dad chimed. "She even lobbied to get a softball diamond built. Her nickname was 'the cheerleader.'"

She was my cheerleader too, Mike realized. Then, placing his hands on his body, he said, "She's still doing wonderful things." Tina's parents fell into Sandy and Mike's arms.

Today, Mike is back to his old self, and the Minkes plan to visit him in Hawaii. In the meantime, they keep in touch. *How're ya feeling?* Terry writes.

Your little girl lives on, Mike writes back. And Sandy agrees. *Thank you, Tina, for your wonderful final gift,* she thinks. *You truly earned your wings.*

Eva Unga
Excerpted from Woman's World *magazine*

We Almost Lost Her

New York City, April 20, 1996. It is Parents' Day at Columbia University's College of Physicians and Surgeons. About three hundred professors, medical school students, and proud parents gather in Bard Hall, waiting for the luncheon speaker. We've spent the morning touring the facility. We're delighted that our children are learning at a school so obviously dedicated to excellence.

It is hard for me to believe today that more than twenty-four years have slipped by since our daughter came into the world. I remember her first year of life so vividly. How could I not? We almost lost her. . . .

My mind quickly skips backward across the years. It is 5:00 A.M. on April 8, 1972. Gordon and I suddenly awaken in the pre-dawn hours to a sharp cry coming from the crib in the corner of our bedroom. It is uncharacteristic of our six-month-old daughter to announce her needs with such urgency, so I jump out of bed. As I approach her, Valerie throws up and begins to cry.

"Now don't you worry, Mrs. Jones," comes the calm voice of Valerie's pediatrician over the telephone line. "Little babies often throw up very hard when they have the stomach flu. It's going around, you know, but it's nothing to be concerned about.

So I cradle Valerie in my arms, trying my best to emulate the attitude of her thoroughly unalarmed pediatrician. But her face, usually relaxed and smiling, reflects a mixture of anxiety and discomfort.

By lunchtime, I'm even more alarmed. "The baby is throwing up blood!" I exclaim in a second phone call.

"That's perfectly normal," says the unruffled physician. Just keep giving her fluids."

"But she doesn't want to nurse anymore."

"Well, that's all right. After all, when we have the flu, we're not usually very hungry, are we?"

My heart continues to sink when, a few hours later, I put Valerie on the changing table and see traces of blood in her diaper. As a first-time mother, am I overreacting?

And so it goes throughout the day, with me calling the doctor, then waiting for the doctor to return my calls. Valerie finally is admitted to our neighborhood hospital late that afternoon when the pediatrician decides she will improve quicker with the help of intravenous fluids. When we arrive, emergency-room personnel cut deep gashes in her chubby little ankles to insert needles when they can't find her veins. Valerie reacts with admirable stoicism to these painful procedures, refusing to cry in spite of the obvious miseries.

By 9:00 P.M. that night, Gordon shares my concern. "She's not doing very well at all," he frowns. Turning to the pediatrician, who remains unruffled, he underscores my observations. "My wife says she's been throwing up ever since she got here."

"And I still see blood!" I add.

"The capillaries are still acting up, are they?" the doctor says. "When the spasms stop, the capillaries will heal."

"Now go home and get a good night's sleep," he adds

stepping aside to let us pass. "There's nothing you can do sitting here. Valerie needs her mom and dad to be fresh and rested when she checks out tomorrow!"

Early the next morning, I am shocked into consciousness by a ringing phone.

"I don't want to alarm you, Mrs. Jones," says the pediatrician, "but I thought it best for me to talk to you first. Valerie had a little setback during the night."

"A setback?" I echo, bolting up in bed.

"It's nothing serious, I assure you," he continues. "She had a seizure, but it's completely under control now, and she's resting peacefully."

"A *seizure?*" I exclaim, feeling the blood rise to my face. "Why?"

"Well, it's easy to explain, really. The IV caused a slight imbalance in her blood chemistry. It's not at all unusual."

"I want to be with her," I tell him. "I'm coming right away."

I arrive to find Valerie drowsy. I am told it's because of the heavy dose of medication prescribed to prevent further seizures.

After Gordon leaves for work, I spend the day hounding the nurses. Are they still taking blood tests to determine the level of her electrolytes? Why is she so restless? Why does she seem so much sicker than the other babies in the flu ward? How long had the seizure lasted? What is wrong with my baby?

By nighttime, Valerie cannot get comfortable. No matter how much she twists and turns, she cannot find a position that satisfies her.

"Can't I hold her on my lap?" I ask one of the nurses. The tolerant nurse decides that the easiest thing is to let me have my way.

But after about an hour helping Valerie find a comfortable position, I realize her abdomen has distended noticeably. Though I want to go to the nurses' station to report my findings, Valerie is hooked to two separate IVs, and there is no way I can get her back to bed without help. I sit there, trapped and horrified, watching her abdomen continue to grow, until a nurse materializes.

"Look!" I cry. "Look at the size of my baby's abdomen! And how could it distend so *quickly*? I don't understand!"

"The doctor will answer your questions in the morning, Mrs. Jones."

"But I want to know right *now!*" I insist.

"The doctor can't be disturbed," says the nurse. "He's at *home.*"

"*I'll* call him," I say. "He can't fire *me!* What's his number?"

"I'm sorry, Mrs. Jones, but we can't give out that information."

"Then *you* call him!" I plead. "If he gets mad at you, just blame me. Tell him I threatened to report him to the chief of pediatrics!"

"Mrs. Jones, he *is* the chief of pediatrics," the nurse replies, smiling pleasantly, turning and walking briskly away.

I sit there for an hour, frustrated and scared. Suddenly, the door bursts open.

"I decided to call the doctor after all," says the nurse. "He told me to get Valerie to X-ray *immediately!*"

As Valerie is moved straight to X-ray, a group of doctors, including the pediatrician, gathers and examines the results. Gordon slips his hand into mine as we listen to the doctors.

"How could you have missed it?" says one, looking angrily at the chief of pediatrics. "Haven't you heard of an intussusception?"

"It never occurred to me!" he replies. "She didn't fit the statistics! She's a girl, for one thing. This usually happens to boys! She's only six months old, and that puts her on the low end, age-wise. And besides, I did not know she was in pain! She never even cried!

Suddenly, the doctors turn and see us. The chief of pediatrics turns pale.

"Mr. and Mrs. Jones," he says in a trembling voice, "there's no time to waste. Valerie's life is in the balance. She must have an operation *right now*. It's up to you to decide whether you want my colleague to do it here, or whether you want to risk sending her to Columbia Presbyterian in New York, an hour away. I can't guarantee that she'll live for another hour, but they have the best pediatric surgeons in the world there."

"He's absolutely right," says one of the other doctors, a general surgeon. "The physicians at Columbia Presbyterian are highly trained specialists. I've never operated on a baby before, but I'll do the best I can if you want me to go ahead. It's your call. You have to decide right now, though."

"We want the best for our baby," says Gordon. "Send her to Columbia. She's a fighter. She'll make it there."

"What exactly is wrong?" I ask.

"It's called telescoped bowel," explains the pediatrician. "By some fluke, the large intestine managed to catch a piece of the small intestine at the valve where they meet, and began sucking it down."

"Why is her abdomen so distended?" I ask, fearing his answer.

"Her abdomen," the doctor replies, "is swollen with gangrene."

There is no time for grief, panic or tears. The surgeon and the pediatrician, feeling there is nothing more they can do, go home. Gordon and I wait anxiously for the ambulance. We hound a kind resident who repeatedly picks up the phone and checks on the ambulance; it's a good thing. The driver gets lost, and the resident directs him the rest of the way via telephone.

Thirty minutes later, the paramedics come running down the corridor.

"What do you think you're doing?" says one of the paramedics as I climb inside the ambulance.

"I'm going with you!"

"No, you're not," he shouts, pulling my arm. "It's against regulations!"

But I protest, digging in my heels and holding on to a bar on the wall. "Let's go," I tell them. "We don't have time for this!"

"All right," he says finally, "but if the baby starts to fail, we may have to resuscitate. So I'm warning you, lady, if you interfere in any way *I'll knock you out!*"

"It's a deal," I say. "Let's go!"

Once we arrived at the hospital, Gordon and I say good-bye to Valerie as we are ushered to a waiting room.

We anxiously wait there for the pediatrician. Finally, a young blond man enters the room and moves toward us, a clipboard clutched in his left hand. *This can't be the surgeon,* I think. *They must have sent a medical student.*

"Mr. and Mrs. Jones?" says the fair-haired youth, extending his right hand. "I'm Dr. John Schullinger. We don't have much time, so forgive me if I come straight to the point. The prognosis for your baby is extremely poor. The truth is, she is moribund. It would be unfair of me to give you any real hope that she'll survive. If she does live, she may very well suffer serious brain damage, and she'll almost certainly have intestinal problems for the rest of her life. I'm deeply sorry to have to be the one to bring you this news, but you have every right to know the facts. And now, if you'll excuse me, every minute counts."

I've given my baby into the care of a boy, I think with sudden alarm.

Now, there is nothing to do but sit on the couch in the waiting room and cry. I sob until I hear Gordon.

"Stop," he is saying in a pleading voice. "I can't stand it! You *must* stop crying."

Grief is a feeling that is hard to share, even with loved ones. Gordon seems in another world, far away and out of reach. I feel walled in by a cocoon of pain, hollow silence and unbearable loneliness. We are completely alone together. The only thing I can do for him now, the only gift I can give him, is to stop crying.

I pray to God for the first time. Like many other supposedly self-sufficient people, I have waited until I am overcome with grief and helplessness before it occurs to me to turn to God for comfort. I have often heard it said that God is merciful and is, in fact, love itself. Indeed, those words come to life for me in the barren, silent waiting room at the Babies' Hospital, a room that surely witnessed the bitter tears of countless other parents.

I peek out the door of the waiting room several times during the night, wishing there were someone I could ask how the operation is going, but the halls are dark and the nurses' station is empty. Then I hear the squeak of crêpe soles coming down the corridor. I open the door and see a nurse putting her shoulder bag on the desk.

"Could you please call the operating room and find out how my baby is?" I cry breathlessly.

"Okay!" she says wearily, picking up the phone. "What's the name of the patient?"

"Valerie Jones."

"And the surgeon?"

"Dr. John Schullinger."

"Dr. John Schullinger?" she repeats. "You have no worries. He's the best there is. I'm sure your baby is just fine."

"No, you don't understand! He doesn't think she'll make it! She is *moribund*!"

The nurse holds up her hand to silence me as she speaks to someone on the line.

"She's doing just fine," says the nurse in a matter-of-fact tone as she replaces the receiver. "She's in intensive care now. I told you that we don't lose babies here!"

New York City, April 20, 1996: The voice of the Parents' Day program coordinator brings me back to the present. Gordon and I, meanwhile, look with astonishment as Dr. John Schullinger rises from his chair at the head table. As he makes his way to the podium, I quietly approach a professor and ask if I might make a short speech after Dr. Schullinger's address. When I explain what I want to say, she agrees.

When the doctor takes his seat after speaking, I keep my words brief. I say to the smiling audience, after recounting that unforgettable night twenty-four years ago, "I am delighted to have this opportunity to thank Dr. Schullinger publicly. I now know that God was guiding his hand that night. Who could have predicted our daughter would end up being mentored by the very man who saved her life?

"In retrospect, it is obvious that you save babies here at Columbia Presbyterian so you can train them to become doctors who will save *other* babies in turn. Isn't this, after all, what medicine is all about?"

I take my seat as the audience erupts with the applause Dr. Schullinger so richly deserves.

Valerie Jones has completed her second year of medical studies at Columbia. She continues to enjoy life free from symptoms or complications.

Dr. Schullinger is no longer "the boy" I first met, but he seems perenially young.

And God? He's the same yesterday, today and tomorrow.

Sonia Jones

Prayer of Thoughts

Thanks for the hardship and pain I experienced as a child; the sickness and death I survived. They were only lessons I learned in becoming a man, and not punishment and guilt for things I had only thought in my mind.

Thanks for the painful need for acceptance I had as I tried to replace the loves I had lost. The need gave me an understanding and empathy for others with even a greater need for love and understanding than myself. It gave me the way to gain my acceptance by giving my love to other even more barren hearts.

Thanks for the loss of a parent, so needed, so loved. It taught me by example of my mother's equal loss and how strong a human can be in the face of tragedy. Her dignity and strength were beyond my comprehension and yet, through her example, I learned.

Thanks for the strength and hope through each stage of life to continue to improve and understand not only my own life but also all my brothers and sisters of the world. It is only through loving ourselves that we can understand the meaning and true beauty in the greatest gift of love.

Thanks above all for being a caring and loving God who resides within each of us to remind us that impossible is possible and that forgiveness is not only possible but necessary.

And most importantly of all, thank you for reminding us that love is the key to all the questions, fears and desires in our small but beautiful world of yesterdays, todays and tomorrows.

John W. Doll

2

INSIGHTS
AND LESSONS

*With a holy relationship, one never looks for
what one can get, but only what one can
joyfully share. It is here that one learns the
truth that giving and receiving are the
same.*

Christine Smith

Andy

It was a Wednesday night. A half-dozen kids mingled inside the youth room as I tuned my guitar atop a stool in front of a few scattered bean bag chairs. The room was alive with budding youth, blossoming and fragrant with sweet fellowship. Everyone mingled and maneuvered themselves amid the Christian camaraderie.

Everyone, except for Andy.

He entered the room unnoticed and, like always, took his position in the back corner. His pock-marked face appeared timid, almost frightened beneath a head full of fuzzy, unkempt hair. Andy kept his eyes on the carpet, and yet he was keenly aware of everything going on around him.

"Okay, everybody, let's come together," I admonished above the strum of a familiar worship chorus. "Let's worship the Lord, shall we?"

Within seconds the group burst forth in robust, heartfelt singing.

Characteristically, Andy wouldn't sing. He looked around the room with his hands tucked away inside a denim jacket. At first, his reluctance to worship didn't bother me. I figured once he made a few Christian friends, the Lord would touch his heart. But friends didn't come easily for this kid.

Andy had a history of involuntary seclusion.

I first laid eyes on Andy while moonlighting as a water polo coach at a local high school. His scrawny frame shuffled out of the locker room to join a group of brawny swimmers. He was the shortest high schooler on the pool deck, but there he stood, shivering with an invisible sign around his neck that read: "I want to fit in . . . maybe."

As veteran swimmers torpedoed through the water, Andy thrashed across the pool in the slow-traffic lane. The harder he tried, the larger the sign grew, and I made it a point to let Andy know I could read.

"Hey, Andy," I said as he took a breather. "Ever been to church?"

"Yeah," he panted. "Couple times."

"Wanna come with me sometime?"

"Sure."

"Great. Tell your parents, and I'll pick you up next Wednesday night."

That's all it took. Within a week, Andy occupied the corner of the youth room.

Within a month, his mother joined our adult service. She was a divorced, single parent who worked two jobs: A grocery checker by day and full-time mom at night. After Andy figured out he was no Mark Spitz, he quit the water polo team. His mother caught me between services and pleaded, "Please, Pastor Tom, would you encourage the youth to reach out to my boy? All he needs is someone to pay attention to him." Slumped shoulders and the tone in her voice told me she was a desperate, overworked mother who had no clue how to deal with a socially dysfunctional son.

"Of course, I will," I reassured her, but that was easier said than done.

I came up with a plan. First, I sicced a couple of social kids on him, but like a cornered possum, he played dead until they left. Peer-led small group brought little response, and a personal invitation to a movie night never materialized. Once, I got him to be part of a skit, but he refused to play anything more than a rock. After the strategic blitzes failed, I found myself growing dangerously indifferent. I needed to find the right button to push in Andy's life, but searching for it took the time I was reluctant to give.

However, this particular Wednesday night, things would be different. The right button was about to be pushed by Andy himself.

After a few more worship choruses, I looked up and asked for testimonies. Marcie, the cheerleader, talked about the group's outing to an upcoming concert. Connor, the football jock, gave the blow-by-blow details of Friday night's big game. I was careful to give everyone an opportunity to share the latest sagas surrounding their lives. After several more testimonies, I looked around the room to make sure I hadn't missed anyone, and then it happened.

Andy reluctantly raised his hand. I quickly acknowledged it.

"Andy, you have something to share?"

"I got a bike," he mumbled.

"Say again?"

"I got a bike," he repeated. "A moped."

"A motor bike?" I smiled at the sound of his voice. "Great! We'll have to take a look at it after Bible study."

The room turned absolutely still. The slightest growl from an empty stomach would have been heard. The reaction to Andy's testimony told me the youth group not only noticed Andy's boldness, but a few saw it as a break-through. A gratifying smile came from a youth leader, and a concealed two-thumbs-up came from a boy up front. When Andy spoke, people listened. But no one knew exactly what to do about it.

Andy acknowledged my answer, then immediately took his usual posture. I couldn't believe he spoke! For this insecure boy to open his mouth in front of thirty-five peers was nothing short of a miracle. After the meeting I made a beeline toward the door and caught Andy just as he tried to leave.

"I want to see your bike," I said.

He was obviously pleased and pointed toward the parking lot. Something seemed different about Andy. Instead of a nervous demeanor, Andy was aflame with his new toy.

I followed Andy outside, but unfortunately, I was alone. The other youths were preoccupied or clueless of the golden opportunity to woo Andy from his shell. I kept looking back, hoping that others would join us, but the more I looked, the more frustrated I became.

There, sitting in the church parking lot, was Andy's shiny, red moped. I looked it over thoroughly, sat on it and asked him if I could take it for a spin. After a couple of laps around the parking lot, I dismounted and had the pleasure of listening to Andy rattle on about the finer points of being a moped owner. Winning his trust gave me an even greater pleasure. During those few short min-utes, we talked more than all the other moments com-bined. I not only learned about mopeds, but I learned details about Andy's life at school, his family and his faith in Jesus.

When it was all over, we both smiled.

"See ya Sunday?" I asked as he mounted his moped.

"I'll be there," he waved and rode away.

That was the last time I'd ever talk to Andy. Two days later, on his way home from school, Andy ran headlong into the back of an eighteen-wheeler. Stuck beneath the axle with his jacket tightly wrapped around his neck, Andy was asphyxiated. Without oxygen for over fifteen minutes, he was left comatose in the hospital.

The news left me weakened and speechless. For two days, I wandered around in prayer and reflection about the kid who sat in the corner.

For six months Andy hung on to life. During that time, his absence was more than noticed. Weekly, Andy's peers sent flowers and cards and visited him in the hospital. Amid tears and frequent prayers, the youth group mentioned Andy's name in heaven and talked among themselves about missed opportunities and life's priorities. The chance to touch Andy's brief life had passed, and they suddenly realized it.

Marcie and Connor accompanied another pastor to the hospital to hand-deliver a large get-well card with peer-written, personal messages covering the inside pages. Connor sat in the back seat and began reading some of the messages out loud.

"Check it out," he said. "'Dear Andy, we love you and we'll be praying for you.'

"'Dear Andy, wish you were here. Hurry back.'

"'Andy, you're a real cool guy, and we're all here for ya, man.'"

Connor stopped reading, and it became obvious to all three occupants what needed to be said. Then Connor said it. "Woulda been kinda nice to say all this before the accident, huh?"

No one answered. No one needed to.

Strange how one little fuzzy-haired boy can touch so many lives. Without a word, Andy taught my youth group the value of human life, the uncertainty of tomorrow and the importance of each individual.

At his funeral, church members, school administrators and over a hundred teenagers from his neighborhood, school and church turned out to say good-bye to a young man who blended into the back wall. Perhaps they were also saying good-bye to a spirit of complacency and indifference toward those whom we often take for granted.

From that day on, something wonderful happened inside the youth group. Oh, sure, the teenagers still plowed inside the youth room late, teased and harassed each other for their slightest flaws, but miraculously, no one had to be reminded to greet the newcomers. They were immediately included, and given personalized greeting cards without the ink and paper.

Of course, "Andy" still comes to our youth group, but he usually goes by another name. Never again will Andy be allowed to blend into the back wall.

All of us will see to that.

Tom C. Long

Susan's Magic Carpet

Wrinkles of confusion rippled across Holly's forehead as she unwrapped the gift from her best friend, Susan.

"I . . . I thought you could use it for something." Susan's stammered explanation did nothing to help us understand why a twelve-by-eighteen-inch dark blue carpet remnant was being presented as a birthday gift.

My heart went out to our daughter. Starting out at a new school during her freshman year had been a difficult adjustment. Until she met Susan, Holly had experienced little success making new friends.

The murmured "thanks" was barely audible as Holly tried valiantly not to allow her disappointment to show. She laid the piece of carpet on the kitchen counter, and the two girls headed outside to play with the family dogs.

The extent of Holly's disappointment over the incident didn't become evident until the following evening when she came downstairs to say good night. "Well, I guess we know how much my best friend thinks of me, huh, Mom?" Her attempt at a breezy tone failed miserably.

Still bewildered by the situation myself, I didn't have

much to offer in the way of enlightenment. "I'm so sorry, honey," was all I could manage to say.

The next morning, I carried a bulging kitchen sack outside. My heart wrenched as I lifted the lid of the trash can and saw Susan's carpet lying among the other discarded items. Hesitating only a moment, I reached in and plucked it from amid the debris. After giving it a light brushing, I brought it into the house and tucked it away in the hall closet. Overshadowed by the business of daily living, the carpet was soon forgotten.

Prior to Holly's birthday, Susan had been a regular visitor in our home. On several occasions, she rode the bus home with Holly and was one of the few friends ever permitted to stay over on a school night. The girls did their homework together and went to bed at a reasonable hour.

Now as I slid the evening meal into the oven, I realized it had been nearly three weeks since we'd even heard mention of Susan's name. I missed her warm smile and eager-to-please ways.

A rustle at the front door told me Holly had arrived home from school. "Susan invited me to come over to her house after school tomorrow," she announced as she plunked her books down on the kitchen table. Although her voice carried a so-what attitude, I sensed she was pleased by the invitation.

In spite of the number of times Susan had visited with us, our invitations were never returned. "She wants you to come, too, so you can meet her foster mom." The words "foster mom" dangled in the air like a spent birthday balloon. Susan never talked about her home life, and we didn't find it necessary to pry.

Arrangements were made, and the girls rode home together on the school bus the following day. As I negotiated the winding country road that led to her house, Susan babbled nervously about her foster mom and the seventeen cats she had taken in and cared for with Susan's help. Several of these foster kitties scattered as we pulled into the rutted gravel driveway.

A tall angular woman wearing a shapeless tan sweater over navy blue pants stood in the screened doorway to greet us as we approached the small farmhouse. "Excuse the mess," she apologized, holding the door open while we threaded our way through stuff that seemed to be everywhere. Knowing my reputation for neatness, Holly's eyes darted in my direction to quickly assess my reaction to such chaos. Susan's foster mom waved a hand toward the kitchen counter, which was barely visible through the assortment of cat medicines. "This is my medicine cabinet," she explained.

Susan ushered us through the house. It seemed to be alive with four-legged fur balls roaming underfoot and sprawling across the backs of the dingy sofa and chairs. She proudly showed us her room, which was sparsely but neatly decorated with used furnishings. A tarnished picture frame sitting on a crate beside the bed contained pictures of Susan's parents and siblings from whom, we later learned, she had long since been separated.

As the girls flopped down on the grayish-white bedspread to compare notes about the school day, I followed Susan's foster mom—who introduced herself as Glenda— into the kitchen. After clearing a small area, Glenda placed a couple of mugs on the table. Her hand trembled slightly as she poured us each a cup of steaming black coffee. The tightness of her features began to relax as we sipped our coffee and chatted about her cats.

A warm glow shone in her eyes as she revealed to me her fondness for Susan. But her expression turned pensive when she referred briefly to the girl's past. In a short time, I came to respect this generous-hearted woman who had opened her home to a young girl and attempted to make a difference in her life.

As daylight began to fade, we offered our thanks for the visit and said good-bye.

Holly sat quietly in the car on the way home. Stealing a glance, I noticed her back was ramrod-straight. Her head and shoulders were thrust forward as if willing the car to move faster. No sooner had we come to a stop in the driveway than she flung open the car door and walked purposefully toward the side gate. Curious, I shifted into park and followed. A lump caught in my throat as I observed my daughter standing next to the trash can peering inside. Her shoulders slumped as she replaced the lid and shuffled into the house.

After pulling the car into the garage, I went inside and headed for the hall closet. By this time, Holly was sitting at the kitchen table staring out the window.

"Is this what you were looking for?" I placed the piece of carpet on the table in front of her.

"Thanks, Mom." A tear or two slipped from her eye and splashed onto the dark blue remnant that, as if by magic, had become the most precious birthday present in the whole world.

Karen Taylor

Son for a Season

The last Friday in September was supposed to have been Jeremy's "Special Day" at nursery school. That's when he would have brought a favorite toy for show-and-tell and picked the book his teacher would read to the class. His mom would have supplied snacks for all the kids.

"Special Day" came differently for Jeremy. He didn't go to school with his toy and book and snacks. Instead, his day began at 7 A.M. when a man he didn't know arrived in a car he didn't recognize. Imprinted on the car were the words STATE OF NEW JERSEY. Jeremy was still rubbing the sleep from his eyes when the man carried the single bag that contained Jeremy's entire wardrobe to the car and tossed it into the trunk. He returned for two boxes of Jeremy's stuffed animals, miniature cars and other cherished items. Then it was Jeremy's turn.

I will never forget the look on his face as he was taken away. We'd tried to prepare him, telling him he was going to live with his Grandma and Grandpa in Pennsylvania. But he didn't understand. To three-year-old Jeremy, I was "Mommy." My husband was "Daddy." His "sister" and "brother" were our children, Catherine and Michael.

All Jeremy understood was that he was going somewhere in a strange car with a strange person. "I want Daddy," he cried, tears stinging his soft cheeks and hazel eyes. "Where's Catherine?" he wailed as the state worker strapped him into his car seat. "No, no, no!" he screamed. We waved good-bye as the car pulled away and disappeared from sight.

Both my husband and I had tears in our eyes. Finally I was able to comment, "That's more than Jeremy could say when he got here," referring to Jeremy's departing words. And it was true. When he came to live with us, he could barely talk.

Jeremy was our foster son. He stayed with us from June 20 to September 30, 1994. We would have kept him longer—forever, if possible—but the state of New Jersey felt it was better for him if relatives, in this case grandparents in their seventies, raised him. Who are we to judge?

He came into foster care for many reasons, but I'll just generalize and say he was neglected. When he arrived, his vocabulary numbered no more than twenty-five words. He couldn't dress or feed himself, and he wasn't pottytrained. At night, despite all our efforts to calm him, he screamed for hours, unable to sleep without the lights on and someone near him.

By summer's end Jeremy was a different child. He had grown two inches and gained two pounds. We gave him vitamins and a diet of healthful foods, and sent him to nursery school and speech therapy. His vocabulary increased, and he began forming sentences. He was no longer afraid of the dark and went to bed willingly by 8:30 P.M., sometimes earlier, after learning to announce, "I'm tired."

And then, he was gone.

People ask us why we became foster parents. "You have your own children," they say. "Why do you want other people's problems? How can you bear to let these kids go, wondering what will happen to them? Doesn't it break your hearts?"

Yes, it does. But not doing something would make our hearts ache even more.

When Jeremy first came to us, I cried a lot, wondering how we could cope with his many problems while caring for our own children. I asked my husband then, "Why are we doing this?" He didn't reply because neither of us truly knew why.

Months after I posed that desperate question, Mike and I attended church together. We listened to the scripture reading: "He then took a little child whom he set among them and embraced, and he said to them, 'Anyone who welcomes a little child such as this in my name, welcomes me; and anyone who welcomes me, welcomes not me but the one who sent me.'"

Mike nudged me and whispered, "That's why we do this." I suddenly remembered my question—and I'll never forget my husband's answer. And that's why we'll be foster parents for years to come.

Jo Ann C. Nahirny

The Day Healing Began

Every gift, though it be small, is in reality great if given with affection.

Pindar

Snow crunched angrily under my tires, and my car's headlights made only feeble streaks through the driving snow. My eyes ached from trying to find my way through an unfamiliar neighborhood.

As a certified medical assistant, I was making a house call to administer a flu shot to an elderly, bedridden patient. When the request had come into the doctor's office, there had been so much red tape concerning the vaccination that I finally volunteered to do it myself. I was frustrated then at all the fuss and bother; now I was angry at myself for getting involved.

I know all about frustration. One week earlier, the trial of my sixteen-year-old daughter's attacker finally ended. She had been kidnapped and raped by a stranger. He had been sentenced to five and a half years. *Not long enough,* I thought bitterly.

Later that day, as I relayed the judge's ruling to my

mother, she asked what I thought would have been fair. I
didn't know. I only knew I wanted to sleep through the
night without nightmares. I wanted the tension between
my husband Joe and me to be over. I didn't want to be
afraid to let my children walk to school.

I glanced at the clock on the dashboard. Seven P.M.
Usually by this time, I would be in pajamas and on my
second glass of wine. Without the alcohol to deaden my
senses, scenes from the courtroom would come, unbid-
den, to mind. Erica's lawyer questioning the rapist,
"Which part of 'No!' didn't you understand?" And then
Erica on the witness stand being asked to "describe in
detail what he did to you." The windshield wipers
reminded me of Erica swiping at tears as she recalled the
atrocities.

I pulled up in front of the house and took a deep breath
to release my tension and anger. Would I ever feel normal
again? Just then, the house's front door opened and a
little girl in the doorway yelled back over her shoulder.
"She's here!"

Dogs barked in the background. I didn't feel like dealing with yowling dogs and a little girl in addition to an
elderly patient. I wanted to give the shot and go home. A
woman appeared and pushed the two dogs back so I
could enter.

"Hi, Marilyn," she greeted me. "I'm Judy, and this is my
granddaughter, Gwynney. Thanks for coming! Can I get
you something to eat or drink?"

"No, thanks. I've got to get home and make dinner for
my family," I lied. I knew Joe would have fed the children
by now.

Then Gwynney peeked from behind her grandmother's
legs. She was a chubby little thing with a mop of blond hair.
When I looked at her closely, I shivered. Gwynney was
almost my daughter's double when Erica was the same age.

"We just made macaroni and cheese," the child volunteered. "You can take it home to your 'fambly' if you want."

The telephone rang. "Gwynney," Judy instructed, "show Marilyn to Great-Grandma's room while I get the phone."

Gwynney nodded, taking her responsibility seriously. "I'm five years old," she informed me.

"No, you're not!" Judy called from the kitchen. "She's only three, Marilyn."

Gwynney smiled sheepishly then pointed to the bigger dog, a dignified yellow Labrador with a graying muzzle. "This is Barney," she said. Barney thumped his tail politely. Pointing to the other dog, a mixed German shepherd with intelligent eyes, she said, "And this is Susie." Susie woofed. "Okay," Gwynney concluded, "now I will take you to Great-Grandma's room."

I put my coat on the living room couch and fell in behind Gwynney and the dogs. Judy reappeared just as we entered the old woman's bedroom. "Mom," she yelled in her mother's ear, "the nurse is going to give you a shot!" When there was no response, Judy pushed back her mother's hair and kissed her gently on the forehead.

"I'll be in the other room if you need me," she said and quietly left the room.

I loaded the syringe and was about to give the injection when I looked over my shoulder. Gwynney, Barney and Susie were lined up in order of size against the wall. Each was watching my every move.

I stopped and explained what I was doing. "Don't worry," I reassured them, "this won't hurt your great-grandma."

Gwynney nodded. As I turned, I heard her reassuring the dogs, "This won't hurt Great-Grandma, so don't worry."

Six months before, I would have smiled. Now I just swabbed the woman's arm with alcohol and administered the shot.

The moment I withdrew the needle, Gwynney was at my side with a wastebasket to collect my disposable gloves. "Boy, you really have the program down, don't you?" I said, laughing in spite of myself.

Gwynney looked at me seriously. "Are you sad?" she asked.

"What makes you ask?" I stammered, taken aback.

"Well, your laugh sounds kind of sad."

I knelt and gave her a hug. "You sure are smart for a three-year-old," I said, tousling her fine golden hair. "You could pass for a five-year-old any day."

Gwynney bolted for the kitchen. There, I heard her telling her grandmother, "She says I could pass for a five-year-old!"

After Judy thanked me profusely for coming, Gwynney and the dogs walked me to the door. "I hope you feel happy soon," she said and squeezed my hand.

"Thank you," I answered. "Me, too."

Gwynney waved, and the dogs wagged their tails as I left. Outside, the storm had passed. It had turned colder, and snow squeaked under my feet as I made my way to the car. The dark sky was full of stars. I started the car but didn't go half a block before I had to pull over to the curb.

Tears flooded out of me, as I cried out, "God, why didn't you protect Erica?" All the feelings I had squelched over the past six months poured out. I let God have it with both barrels.

First, tears of bitterness. And then sadness, the sadness that was so obvious to Gwynney. I grieved for my daughter's stolen innocence. I was sad that with all Joe and I were able to provide, we weren't able to keep her safe.

Then a stillness enveloped my car, and I fell silent. I

thought of all the things that had happened to us in the past six months. I remembered the faces of the homeless that we passed each day driving to court, and the battered women and children who lined the corridors as we made our way into the courtroom. Until six months before, I had known only the safe haven that had been our world. Our family had been so richly blessed.

Suddenly, I was thanking God for all the goodness in our lives. "Lord," I said, "I need to move beyond this and start living again. You've given me so much. Help me to focus on those who really need your help."

Tomorrow, I vowed, I would not retreat into pajamas and wine. Instead, I would go home and make my "fambly" macaroni and cheese. I would smile more and offer words of encouragement. I would brighten the world around me.

Peace washed over me. I forgave myself for not being there to shield Erica from harm.

I looked back at Gwynney's house, where the porch light still glowed warmly into the night. I smiled.

"Lord, thank you for Gwynney," I prayed. "Her resemblance to Erica and her wise words melted my heart."

Marilyn K. Strube

No Fishing Allowed

'Twas a thief said the last kind word to Christ.
Christ took the kindness and forgave the theft.

Robert Browning

A legend is told of a priest in a small Midwestern parish who as a young man had committed what he felt was a terrible sin. Although he had asked God's forgiveness, all his life he carried around the burden of this sin. Although he was a priest, he could not be completely sure God had forgiven him.

But he heard about an elderly woman in his congregation who sometimes had visions. During these visions, she would often have conversations with the Lord. One day the priest got up enough courage to visit this woman.

She invited him in and offered him a cup of tea. Toward the end of his visit, he set his cup down on the table and looked into the old woman's eyes.

"Is it true that sometimes you have visions?" he asked her. "Yes," she replied.

"Is it also true that, during these visions, you often speak with the Lord?"

"Yes," she said again.

"Well . . . the next time you have a vision and speak with the Lord, would you ask Him a question for me?"

The woman looked at the priest a little curiously. She had never been asked this before. "Yes, I would be happy to," she answered. "What do you want me to ask Him?"

"Well," the priest began, "would you please ask Him what sin it was that your priest committed as a young man?"

The woman, quite curious now, readily agreed.

A few weeks passed, and the priest again went to visit this woman. After another cup of tea he cautiously, timidly asked, "Have you had any visions lately?"

"Why yes, I have," replied the woman.

"Did you speak with the Lord?"

"Yes."

"Did you ask Him what sin I committed as a young man?"

"Yes," the woman replied, "I did."

The priest, nervous and afraid, hesitated a moment and then asked, "Well, what did the Lord say?"

The woman looked up into the face of her priest and replied gently, "The Lord told me He could not remember."

God not only forgives sins, He chooses to forget them. The Bible tells us He takes them and buries them in the deepest sea. And then as Corrie ten Boom used to say, "He puts up a sign that says, 'No fishing allowed.'"

If God forgives us, can we do less?

Gigi Graham Tchividjian

Brief Encounter

Several Saturdays ago I was cleaning my car at a do-it-yourself car wash. As I vacuumed, I noticed a few wisps of yellow dog fur.

I stopped my cleaning. I picked up the fur, placed it in an envelope and put the envelope in the glove compartment. The fur belonged to Buddy. As I went about the rest of the day, I couldn't help but think of the brief encounter with Buddy and his "family" just a couple of days before.

It was a Wednesday afternoon. I had just gotten off work. As I passed a truck stop, I noticed a man with a large backpack. There beside him was a dog on a leash sitting in the grass strip that separates the entrance and exit to the interstate. It was about 4:30 in the afternoon and quite hot.

I stopped a few feet away and walked up to the man. "You and the dog okay?" I asked.

I guess he was a little startled. "I'm not breakin' no law sittin' here, am I?" he asked.

"No," I replied, "I just wanted to make sure you and the dog were okay."

"We're okay, just a little hot."

I noticed a handwritten cardboard sign beside him saying something about working for food. My guess was that
he hadn't had a good meal in some time.

"Look," I said, "here's a twenty—make sure you and the
dog get a good meal tonight."

"God bless you, sir," he said as he accepted the money.

I walked back to my car. As I turned around, the pair
were headed under an overpass to the westbound side of
the I-78 ramp. Somehow I felt I should have done a little
more. I went into the truck stop, bought a large hoagie
and soda for the man and a couple of hot dogs and water
for the dog.

As I approached the ramp, they were gone. I figured
someone had picked them up. I got back on the freeway
intending to get off at the next exit. There were my two
"friends." I pulled over. As we spoke, I gave pieces of the
hot dogs to the dog along with a few sips of cool water.
The stranger wolfed down the sandwich in two minutes.

I asked the dog's name. It was Buddy.

I don't usually give strangers a ride, but I just couldn't
let them walk down the busy freeway at night. I offered to
give them a ride, and they accepted. He instructed Buddy
to get in the back seat, but I told him it was okay if Buddy
rode in the front. Buddy put his head on my lap as though
we had been friends for years. I knew he enjoyed the cool-
ing breeze of the air conditioner. He very quickly fell
asleep, as I occasionally petted him on his head.

Buddy was a beautiful, noble dog, some kind of mixed
breed although the man said he was a sheltie. His fur was
soft and surprisingly well kept. The man was a drifter.

He told me bits and pieces about his life. He said he
didn't have any sort of identification. He told me he had
lost his wallet a few weeks back. My guess was he was
about forty. He was tall and lean, with a beard. His piercing blue eyes seemed to hold pain, but he was a gentle

person. He was born in Oregon and traveled around always looking for work, he said.

I asked him about Buddy. He told me he found him in Alabama as a puppy about a year and a half before. From that day to this, they had always been together.

There was a pause in the conversation and I asked him whether the dog was ever a burden to him, with all the traveling around. I would have gladly offered a great home to Buddy. There was a long silence. From the corner of my eye I could see tears rolling down the man's cheeks.

"Sir," he said to me, barely above a whisper, "old Buddy is the only family I got. Some days, when food is scarce, I'd gladly go without, so long as Buddy has somethin'."

There was no doubt he spoke the truth. I felt embarrassed that I would even think of offering to take the man's only worthwhile possession.

The ride was all too short. I pulled over and the man got his backpack out of the back seat. Then Buddy hopped out. The man began to slowly close the door. Buddy turned, looked up at me and wagged his tail a couple of times. I'm certain it was his way of saying "thanks."

I turned around and headed east. I had one last look at Buddy and his "family." As I drove off I was disappointed in myself; I didn't even ask the man his name.

That night I was out late watering the flowers. I looked up at the heavens. I wondered why it is that sometimes these brief encounters make such profound impressions on my life. I said a little prayer asking God to please watch over them in their travels, and to say thanks for just the few brief moments I was able to share with them.

Without their knowledge, the two "world travelers" had enriched my life, touched my soul and heart. The wisps of fur will always be a reminder to me of the summer afternoon that I encountered Buddy and his companion.

Joseph J. Gurneak

Blessed

A friend and I were standing in line at the grocery store the other day, and I was telling her how lazy my children were. I had come in from work that morning, and like most times, my house was wrecked.

"I believe children nowadays are just out for what they can get. I bend over backwards for them, and they can't even help keep our house clean. It wouldn't bother me so, but it's the woman who looks bad if the house is a mess."

"Do you know how blessed you are?" a woman behind us asked. "I would love to go home and find my house a mess. I wouldn't mind my carpet being ruined or the dishes left everywhere. I wouldn't mind the dirty clothes being piled high or the many socks to match. I wouldn't even mind anyone talking about my dirty home. Matter of fact, I would love it. I would dearly love to kick my way through the house just to get to my kids and be able to hug them, kiss them and tell them how much I love them. You see, my two children were killed in an auto accident and now it's just my husband and me. My house stays clean, my clothes stay put up, the dishes are done. There are no fingerprints on my walls, no mysterious spots on my carpets. There are no sounds of arguing, no slamming doors, no laughter, no 'I love you Mom.' So you see, you are very blessed. What I would give to be going through what you are right now. How I would love to be able to hold my kids, wipe away their tears, share their dreams. Just to watch them play. If I had my children, I wouldn't care how my house looked. I would be happy just to have them."

Now if you come into my house and see a big old mess, you can think bad thoughts if you want, but I feel greatly blessed.

Tammy Laws Lawson

The Supper

After receiving an ivory carving of the Last Supper, my friend Pat displayed it in a prominent place. When her six-year-old grandson came to visit, he noticed it and wanted to know what it was. So she told him a little bit about what the artist had portrayed.

Not long after, the boy visited again, this time with some cousins who hadn't seen the carving. One of them asked what it was.

Before Grandma could reply, the six-year-old said. "Oh, that's Jesus and the boys out to supper."

Margaret Wiedyke

A Child's Blessing

A couple invited some people to dinner. At the table, the mother turned to her six-year-old daughter and asked her to say the blessing. "I wouldn't know what to say," she replied. "Just say what you hear Mommy say," the mother said. The little girl bowed her head and prayed, "Dear Lord, why on Earth did I invite all these people to dinner?"

Richard Lederer

Change Comes to Maxwell Street

A man of many companions may come to ruin, but there is a friend who sticks closer than a brother.

Proverbs 18:24

Though no one could take the place of Bloke as my best friend, Jack Caldwell was a welcome addition to my young life. We lived on the same floor of the same derelict tenement. We often sat out on the rickety back porch listening to baseball games on the radio after it had gotten too late to be traipsing around the neighborhood.

When Jack moved in with the O'Tooles across the landing from our door, I assumed his parents were dead, but I never did ask. I was more interested in gaining a new playmate and buddy, so where he came from was of minor importance.

"He's come to live with his aunt and uncle," Mama told us the afternoon we'd noticed the stocky, red-haired boy carrying a suitcase up the three flights of stairs to our floor. "Keep your noses to yourselves!"

When I realized Jack was my age and seemed to be a

likable sort, I immediately invited him to join the tight-knit group that Bloke, Regan, Ritchie and I had formed. He fit in very easily, displaying a pleasant disposition and more than a bit of talent at stickball and other sports. In a very short time, it was as if he had always been a part of our Maxwell Street world.

The next spring, however, the friendship we had taken for granted seemed to crumble when I learned that Jack was leaving, most likely for good. I had just begun thinking of things to keep us busy during the lazy summer ahead.

"Goin' to live in Oregon," he said somberly, "with my Uncle Henry."

I was stunned.

"His uncle and aunt in Oregon have no children," Mama later explained, "and they felt it would be nice to have Jack there."

Though Mama had barely mentioned anything about the O'Tooles before then, I also learned that Jack had been summarily left at the O'Toole's with no further contact from his parents. Mr. and Mrs. O'Toole, up in years, were pleasant enough, but apparently they felt Jack would fare better with a younger set of substitute parents. Besides, everyone reasoned, Oregon was a beautiful place, a healthy and peaceful environment for raising a child.

Jack, though, seemed torn between his friends and the prospect of venturing farther west than any of us had dreamed. Looking after Jack's best interests, Mama solemnly declared it would help greatly for us to *support* him in the move rather than add to his troubles by moping about his leaving.

"But it isn't fair!" I moaned. "It just isn't *fair!*"

"Have you told him you'll miss him, Sean?" Mama asked seriously.

I shook my head. *She, the mother of six sons,* I thought,

should realize that boys don't talk about things like that. Still, Mama had some reason for encouraging me. She knew that even my eleven-year-old heart had feelings and that I could cope better with missing my new friend if I talked about it.

A few days before Jack was to leave, after early Mass, I mouthed my displeasure about the situation to Father O'Toole, an assistant at St. Columbkille. I suppose I felt that a priest who bore the same last name as Jack's aunt and uncle might be sympathetic to my cause.

And while Father O'Toole did listen with polite attention and tell me that he understood my feelings, he also suggested that I prepare myself for the inevitable. In reply, I muttered a few choice comments about things not being "fair" and stalked off to be miserable by myself.

The day before Jack's scheduled departure, Mama added to her earlier suggestion. "I would think you might be helpin' your friend to pack," she said. "I imagine it's a chore for him to do it alone."

I nodded and walked down the hall to the O'Tooles'. Mrs. O'Toole let me in and told me that I was welcome to join Jack in his room.

I found my soon-to-be-lost friend sitting on his bed staring out the window at the sycamore tree that grew out of our tenement's cement backyard.

"I suppose Oregon is a nice place. . . ." His voice trailed off. It was then I realized the parting must be even harder on him than on me. I was losing a friend. He was losing everything he knew.

We packed his clothes slowly and tucked small treasures between the folds of shirts or wrapped them in socks so they would survive the long train ride he was about to endure. What's more, I'd finally decided to tell Jack how much I would miss him. But just then, Danny appeared in the doorway and said that Mama wanted to see us in our apartment.

We hurried across the hall to find Father O'Toole sitting in the stuffed chair in our living room, talking to Mama.

He had dropped by to see how we were doing with Jack's impending departure.

Jack and I both frowned. In response, Father O'Toole handed each of us a paper bag and told us to look inside.

I opened the slim, flat bag to find a package of writing paper, twelve envelopes and twelve three-cent postage stamps. The priest had written the name of a month on the bottom of each envelope, and there were enough for one full year. Jack had an identical package.

We looked at Father O'Toole and smiled.

"It's only for one year," the priest grinned. "After that, you'll have to fend for yourself!"

Mama brought out her teapot, steeping with a rich Irish brew, for herself and Father O'Toole, while Danny mixed a pitcher of Kool-Aid for the boys. A plate of cookies had appeared, and we settled in for a small, unexpected treat.

The impromptu festivities, however, lasted only a short time. After Father O'Toole departed, I took my bag with its paper, stamps and envelopes to my bedroom and walked Jack back to his apartment.

"I'm really hatin' to see you go, Jack," I said, struggling to find the right words. "I'll miss you a lot."

We stopped just outside the door and faced each other for the last time.

"We'll keep in touch, Sean-o!" Jack promised. I happily agreed.

Jack and I were faithful to our words. Writing was not difficult, especially considering Father O'Toole's wonderful gift. Eventually, too, I became certain that, just as night followed day, when I posted my letter to Jack for a certain month, I would receive one from my friend in a few short days.

Years after Father O'Toole's stationery had been used up, I remember Mama looking over my shoulder as I wrote to Jack about the happenings in our lives.

"You've kept up with your friend!" Mama smiled.

"It brings him closer . . . like he's just around the corner," I grinned, remembering how I'd moped and complained before he left. Though he'd been gone a long, long time, our friendship had grown instead of dying.

Mama put her hand on my shoulder, "Maybe," she said, "things did not change as much as you feared."

I leaned back. I was still a teenager, but some adult wisdom was perhaps setting in. "Place is all that changed, Mama," I replied a moment later. "Jack is still my friend, and that's what counts!"

Jack and I keep in touch even today. Not as often as when we were younger, but we still do write and sometimes even talk on the phone. Mama had been correct—we did not have to lose each other. In fact, if anything, our friendship had been cemented firmly by the move. With the loving help, of course, of a young priest who knew the true meaning of friendship—as well as the value of a few postage stamps, some envelopes and a stack of paper.

Sean Patrick

Sleeping Through the Sermon

I was the pastor of a small church in a rural community. Wilbur and his wife, Leah, attended every Sunday morning. Wilbur was a farmer, and whenever he came into the house from the field and sat down, he would fall asleep. It was such a habit that when he came into church and sat in the pew he would also soon fall asleep. I discovered that some of the members of the church were taking bets to see how long I could keep Wilbur awake on Sunday mornings.

Wilbur's wife was embarrassed by his behavior, especially when he began to snore. She tried everything to keep her sleepy spouse awake. She complained to him that she was getting calluses on her elbow from poking him in the ribs in a futile attempt to keep him alert. One day while shopping in the grocery store, she saw a small bottle of Limburger cheese. Leah bought it and dropped it in her purse.

The next Sunday morning I had just started the sermon when Wilbur began to nod. When I finished the first point in my three-point sermon, I could see I was losing him. As I started the third point, Wilbur began to snore. Quietly,

Leah opened her purse, took out the bottle of Limburger cheese and held it under her husband's nose. It worked. Wilbur sat up straight and, in a voice that could be heard all over the church, said, "Leah, will you please keep your feet on your own side of the bed!"

William Webber

Waiting for the Bus

To understand how I became acquainted with Minnie, you need to know about The Bus.

The Bus, as they call it, is the main source of public transportation around Oahu, the island on which Honolulu is located.

There are two kinds of buses on the line. The first is the early bus. It usually arrives a minute or two ahead of schedule, and no matter how fast you run, you can never catch up with it. The second kind is the late bus. It's a good idea to bring a book so you can read while you wait.

The ten-thirty bus that travels through Hawaii Kai, where I once lived, is a late bus. Fortunately, a stone bench provides a place to rest and relax while you wait. That's where I met Minnie. Twice each week I rode The Bus into downtown Honolulu. Minnie was a tiny, wrinkled Oriental woman in her late sixties or early seventies. Her hair was knotted at the back, and she always wore a muumuu, usually a dark color faded from years of wear. She carried an umbrella, not to protect her from rain, but to keep the sun away. Most days her umbrella was open when I arrived at the bench.

Minnie stored her valuables in one of those plastic bags you get at the supermarket. She must have done a lot of shopping because she had a different bag every day, or so it seemed. What she stored in those bags was a mystery, but the contents seemed important because she hugged the plastic bags close to her as we waited for The Bus.

The first day I encountered Minnie, she pretended I did not exist. It wasn't until the third or fourth time we shared a bench that she nodded when I arrived. By the seventh or eighth day, we had reached the "hello" stage. Once the ice was broken, small talk took over.

Minnie's conversational style was definitely local in flavor, a combination of the various types of pidgin English spoken in Hawaii. At first, it was difficult to follow. But once I became accustomed to the rhythm of her words, I could understand what she was saying.

Once we boarded The Bus, Minnie and I went our separate ways. It was as though we didn't know each other. She got off in the Kaimuki section, and I continued my trip downtown.

While waiting for The Bus, Minnie and I learned a lot about each other. She cleaned several condos in a nearby high-rise, which explained her presence in Hawaii Kai on a regular basis. I also discovered that she was a widow who lived alone in a small flat in Kaimuki.

"You're a Christian," she said one morning. "I saw you outside Holy Trinity Church when I went by the other day."

I nodded.

Her next words took me by surprise. "I used to be a Christian," Minnie said matter-of-factly. "I was baptized. Wish I still was, but I lost track of being one."

Much to my regret, The Bus showed up just then.

A couple of days later while we again waited on the stone bench, I asked her, "How come you quit going to church?"

"I didn't really quit," Minnie disclosed. "Things went against me, and I lost track of what it meant. My oldest sister lives over on the Big Island, and she says I should return to church. She gives me a lot of trouble every time I visit her."

Bit by bit and piece by piece, Minnie told me her story. Occasionally we discussed the weather, sports, politics and a variety of other subjects, but the conversation always came back to Minnie and the church. I will relate as best I can what she told me.

I had assumed that Minnie was Chinese. She was not. She was born in a small town somewhere near Seoul, Korea.

"My family," she said proudly, "was a good Christian family. All my sisters and brothers were raised in the faith. They grew up and married in the faith. I was the youngest, and I was preparing for my confirmation when the Japanese came. They took over my country. Most Americans do not remember that.

"There were soldiers in our town, and we lived in fear. We dared not go out at night, and when we did, we had to sneak down side streets and keep clear of the lights. Everything was locked up at night. You could not get into the church. The priest lived in fear of his life. The Japanese were watching him, and he had to hold his services in secret.

"I hated the Japanese. The soldiers were cruel and made life difficult for all of us. They didn't beat us, but they filled us with fear and ordered us around, shoving us if we did not hurry. I still shiver when I think of those soldiers.

"One night I went to the church and asked the priest about my confirmation. He warned me to be careful and said that he would let me know when confirmation would be held for the children in our town. That was the last time I saw him. Some said that he had fled to the hills when the

Japanese came to arrest him one night. Others said that he was dragged away to a prison camp. Our priest never came back. The years went by, and the war ended. The Japanese went away, but I was never confirmed.

"By then I wasn't young anymore. I had grown up. I married a man who didn't share my faith. I lost track of my religion.

"My first husband died, and I came here to Hawaii. I married again, but we lost our only child in a fire. Later, my second husband died. I have been alone for several years.

"I hate the Japanese," Minnie concluded. "If they had not been so cruel, I might have grown up in the religion of my family. I'm an old woman now. I'm too old to go back."

I explained to Minnie that age had nothing to do with it. I think I was beginning to get the message across to her that day when The Bus came along.

On another day I arrived at the stone bench to find Minnie hugging two plastic bags. "Things I use for cleaning," she explained. "I won't be coming back to the condos anymore."

"Did you lose your job?" I asked.

"Not me," said Minnie with pride. "I quit. I'm moving to the Big Island. My older sister's husband has died, and I'm moving there to be with her. My sister's a Big Boss. She'll make me jump. Goes to church every day. Wait and see, she'll make me do the same thing."

A warm glow filled Minnie's eyes, and a look of contentment settled on her face. For the first time since I had met her, Minnie looked beautiful.

The Bus came then, and we climbed aboard. I never expected to see her again.

Several months later I spotted a sweet little lady, all spruced up, sitting on the stone bench waiting for The Bus. It was Minnie—without her plastic bags.

"I figured you'd be along," she greeted me. "It's Tuesday. You always take The Bus on Tuesday."

Minnie had been visiting one of her former employees in the high-rise. "I came to Honolulu to see my eye doctor," she informed me. "Need new glasses. Came to see old friends, too. You're one of them."

I was pleased. For the first time since we'd met, Minnie and I let The Bus go by that morning.

"I got big news," she said. "Big, big news!"

"What is it?" I asked quickly, figuring she had remarried.

"I'm a Christian now," she said. "God has welcomed me home again."

"That's wonderful, Minnie!" I exclaimed.

"There's something else," she said.

"What?" I wanted to know.

"To join our church," she said, "I had to go to classes. I don't read or write well. A little woman about my age helped me."

"Yes?" I said, a bit puzzled.

"She was a little Japanese woman who came to Hawaii about the same time I did," Minnie went on. "She was so kind, so good. I don't believe I would have made it if she had not been my friend."

Minnie paused to let what she had said sink in, and then she asked, "Know what?"

"What, Minnie?"

My friend did not hesitate. "Maybe I don't hate the Japanese anymore," she said, and she was smiling. "Maybe I'm beginning to like them. Maybe that was why God made me wait so long before he welcomed me home again."

Minnie and I took The Bus downtown together that day. Letting go of her hatred had transformed her.

Richard W. O'Donnell

The Card Player

One sweet-scented Carolina evening when I was six years old, Ransom shuffled into my world. I heard the rearranging of pebbles down the magnolia-skirted driveway long before I saw the holes in his gray knit cap, the tin cup, and the smile decorating his face like a new moon reflected in the dark depths of the sea. Scrape-shuffle-scrape-slide. Ransom moved closer. No taller than I, this curious little man wore a patched jacket that dragged on the ground, partially concealing two giant-sized shoes that looked like burlap pontoons stuffed with rags and laced with baling twine beneath him. They rocked, it seemed, in rhythm with some unseen force propelling him forward between two stubby canes. I can still feel my hands fly to my face, small fingers pressing my lips to stifle a cry. Ransom had no legs.

Today, I forget about the legs. What I remember is the smile shining angel-bright from his soul. Ransom was proud. He could walk. And before long I would learn that in spite of his physical suffering and loneliness, he supported himself and lightened the hearts of all whose lives he touched with his only possession—a deck of cards.

I knew it was wrong to stare, but from my hiding place behind lofty columns draped in purple wisteria, I watched him, unseen, as he labored up the hill toward the house. Without missing a beat, he rocked toward the back door, pulled the gray cap from his head and pressed it over his heart. "Mr. Lars," he called. "It's yo' friend out heah—yo' friend, Ransom."

The screen door swung open and Lars, my grandfather's Swedish butler, appeared. Lars had lost his wife, Anna, several months before. From Anna I had learned about angels. "Keep your eyes open," she used to tell me. "You'll know when you see one." Now, since her death, her once jovial husband had been shrouded in grief and grumbles.

"I haven't seen you in a while, Ransom," Lars growled slipping the usual offering of oranges, apples and a candy bar into the beggar's voluminous pockets. But Ransom seemed to pay no attention to the irritation in his voice. Instead he said, "Thank yo', thank yo', suh," then motioned to Lars to sit down a while on the bottom step so they could talk—"face to face." That's when I saw the deck of cards.

I was too little to understand the magic of kings, queens, jacks and the ace of spades, but suddenly there they were lined up in rows over the red-brick stoop like tiny bright windows of warmth against a black New York skyline. It wasn't long before I saw Lars' cheeks bunch into a forgotten grin. Soon I heard both men laughing. Voices rising and falling. Coins plinking into the tin cup.

An hour passed. It was time for Ransom to leave. Lars looked him straight in the eye. "I counted more than a dollar in the bottom of that cup before we even started to play," he said. "Wouldn't it be better to hide what you have so folks will give you more?"

"Oh no, suh." He smiled. "I wants them to know I works

hard." With that he turned and rocked across the snowy pebbles to the red-dirt road that led to his shanty on the other side of town. Packard tires crunched up the driveway and I dashed down the steps to greet my grandfather.

"What happened to his legs?" I cried, as Ransom rolled away.

"It's been said he fell under a train."

I thought about the agony. I wondered, *Did he cry?* I asked, "Did someone push him?"

"No, child." Grandfather took my hand and the voice of silence told me, *You're too young to understand.* "But I've heard," he said, "that even though he's a single soul with no one to care for him, he spends time each day at the hospital doing card tricks for little children just your age, and cheering the very ill in the men's wards with his crafty game of black-jack." But I couldn't stop wondering how this pitifully injured man could be so cheerful when he hurt all the time and had no one to love him. "Grandfather," I said, "Can't we do something to help?"

Although Ransom appeared at our house only once in a while, one day I saw Grandfather give Lars some money. "Buy the poor fella a wagon to ride in and a goat to pull him around," he said.

"I only wish there was something more we could do to ease the pain."

After that, Ransom didn't come to the house any more. Instead he rode around town in a little red wagon with brass fittings and patent leather mud guards, pulled by a gray goat with a white beard. Someone even gave him a silk top hat. People laughed and pointed when they saw him. They didn't call him "poor Old Ransom" any more. He'd become "The Little Squire of Aiken."

One day, Grandfather and I were leaving the post office when we spied Ransom out by the curb. I ran over to him

eager to pat the goat, and say, "Hello." But the face looking down at me from the plush suede seat wasn't the
same as the face that had come to the kitchen door.
Something had stolen the smile.

Several months passed. One evening, I was busy catch-
ing lightning bugs flashing among the wisteria when I
heard the unmistakable scrape-shuffle-scrape-slide.
Instead of riding in his goat-drawn carriage, Ransom
rocked slowly toward the kitchen door. Moments later,
Lars was beaming at the old man, laughing and talking as
he filled the empty pockets once more with oranges,
apples and candy bars. "Where have you been, you old
scoundrel?" he asked, tears of joy crowding his eyes.

"Talkin' with the Lord, suh."

Lars' eyes widened. "And what did He say?"

"He say, 'Ransom. Yo' is one lazy bum. Git rid o' dat
contraption and get back to work!'"

"And I tells Him, 'But it hurts! Lord.' Then the Lord
whispers soft and sweet in my ear. *It doesn't hurt nearly so
much as the pain of losing your soul.*"

Then Ransom's smile burst forth and reaching into his
pocket he brought out a brand new deck of cards. "I got
me these in trade," he murmured. "Wanna play?"

And in one glorious moment of childhood insight, I
realized that no matter how much Ransom hurt or how
alone he may have felt at times, his life was only worth
living when he could share what little he had to bring joy
to others. *Is that the way it is for everybody?* I wondered. Deep
down inside, I felt something else—a gladness that I had
"kept my eyes open" because later that night I knew I had
seen my first angel, one with holes in his gray knit cap
and coins jingling in a tin cup, shuffling down my grandfather's ivory-pebbled driveway.

Penny Porter

It's Only Stuff

On July 18, 1989, I received a frantic call from my sister: Our parents' home was on fire. Fortunately, I learned, no one was home—Mother was at her sister's cabin and Father was "out and about." This meant, however, that no one was able to retrieve irreplaceable family mementos.

During the twenty-mile drive to my parents' house, tears rolled down my cheeks as I thought about the destruction of the only tangible evidence of my youth. Then I heard a voice: *It's only stuff, you know.* It was not spoken out loud, but it was clear and distinct, and comforting.

When my mother arrived from her sister's cabin, we surrounded her and gently led her to the charred remains of her home. Though she knew she was returning to a disaster, seeing the remains of her home was still a shock.

Fortunately, the firefighters had arrived in time to save the room containing many of our photo albums. When mother saw the albums, she was grateful that she had reacted a few weeks earlier to an inexplicable urge to move them from one room, now completely destroyed, to the only room left untouched by the blaze.

But we had lost many sentimental items, such as our Christmas decorations. Mother had saved the homemade ornaments we children had made throughout grade school, and I had loved showing them to my own children each year.

Among the most treasured possessions were ten Christmas stockings, one for each of us, handmade by our now-deceased grandmother. Each stocking was among the first gifts she would give her newest grandchild. Because I was the oldest in my family and one of the oldest grandchildren, I had often stood next to her, mesmerized, as she carefully stitched each stocking by hand. She decorated them with felt shapes of trains, angels and—my favorite—Christmas trees, which were covered with brightly covered ornaments.

One of my brothers was convinced, against all reason, that these special remembrances of Gram had survived the fiery blaze. He therefore sifted through mound after mound of ashes and burned-out blobs. Finally he found them—in a box under what remained of the basement stairwell. In the box was another treasure, remarkably unscathed: our nativity set. The family rejoiced at this discovery and said a prayer of gratitude.

None of this, though, was a match for what occurred on September 15, my parents' wedding anniversary. After church, they went out to the homesite for a last look at the remains of their home. By now, it had been bulldozed, and a crew was coming soon to clear away the last traces of the building.

As my parents approached the site, which was still wet from a heavy rain the night before, both spotted something white on the sidewalk. My mother gasped as she bent to pick up the object. It was the prayer book she had carried down the aisle thirty-eight years ago, to the day. And it was bone-dry. My father says an angel placed it there.

The fire had destroyed nearly all of the other material possessions my parents had ever owned. But as we reflected on the significance of the items that did survive the fire, we realized each one was symbolic. The wedding prayer book, for example, is tangible proof of my parents' spirituality and religious beliefs, which we, their children, now try to pass on to our children. And every Christmas, as we hang those ten stockings, now lightly browned around the edges, we are reminded of the grandmother who made them. Finally, the photographs help us all recall our youth and remember the importance of family.

The love and happiness contained within the walls of the old house have expanded into ten more households. Those good feelings emerge often, whenever we gather as a clan that now numbers over fifty.

I can still hear my mother's voice calling me as a teenager, as I would back out of the driveway with a carful of my siblings: "Be careful, Honey!" she'd say. "You have my most precious possessions in that car!"

We still are her most precious possessions. The rest, after all, is just "stuff."

Mary Treacy O'Keefe

Annie Mae's Honor

Can it really be thirty years since I received the last of the payments from Annie Mae? I find myself thinking about them more often as I approach my sixtieth birthday. Something about closing the chapters on six decades and opening the pages of a new one makes one reflect.

Annie Mae's life has deeply touched mine. I first met her at the home of my in-laws in 1959. I had moved with my husband and our one-year-old child to Tuscaloosa, Alabama, so my husband could complete his undergraduate work at the University of Alabama. My father-in-law was a professor of finance at the university, and my mother-in-law was active in university and community affairs. I vividly recall entering their driveway and being overwhelmed by the size of their home, the beauty of the furnishings, the manicured grounds and the pecan orchard.

Annie Mae was my in-laws' maid. She prepared and served meals in her quiet, gentle way and then retired to the kitchen to read her Bible while we ate. She was a dedicated and devoted Christian. To me, she reflected the fruit of the Holy Spirit as found in Galatians 5:22–23. I found this increasingly true even though I came to know her more by observation than by conversation.

My husband and I visited his parents frequently, and I became increasingly taken with this gentle, remarkable lady. Often when I saw her eating alone, reading her Bible, I wanted to sit down with her and just talk. However, whites did not do that with African Americans in the South in those days, and I conformed to the local practice—though it conflicted with my Christian beliefs. I watched my son, Jimmy, play with her daughter, Jennifer Ann, who on occasion came to my in-laws' place with her mother. The two children laughed and frolicked amid the trees in the pecan orchard. It was so easy for them.

In 1965, my world was suddenly uprooted. I found myself alone with two young sons when my husband wanted a divorce. I was fortunate to receive a full scholarship to the University of Connecticut in the field of special education. I decided to sell the furniture and household items and return to my home state with just our clothes.

Annie Mae asked if she could buy the boys' beds. When I answered yes, she asked the price. "Thirty-five dollars," I replied. Then, in her quiet way, she asked if I would sell them to her and trust her to send a little money each month. I admired her and knew her to be a woman of God, trustworthy and honest. The words of Proverbs 11 came to mind: "A good man [person] is guided . . . and directed by honesty. . . . Be sure you know a person well before you vouch for his [or her] credit."

Annie Mae was honest, and I knew her well. So I said, "Annie Mae, take them, they are yours."

I returned to Connecticut with my two sons and found a chicken coop that had been converted into four apartments. My neighbors and I all became family as we struggled to earn our degrees. Faithfully each month, while my boys and I lived there, an envelope arrived from

Annie Mae—two dollars, three dollars, five dollars, always in cash. That became the surprise money for my boys; I used it to get them something special—an ice cream, cookies, an outing. My sons were thrilled when Annie Mae's money came, for they knew that a surprise would be coming their way.

A year passed. I earned my master of arts degree in special education and accepted a position as a special education teacher for the state of Connecticut. I had learned my lessons well. However, I was about to learn an even greater lesson, and Annie Mae would be the teacher.

Annie Mae's last payment arrived about the time I completed my studies. Along with it came the following note:

Dear Mrs. Holladay,

I am sending you my last payment of three dollars to pay for the beds in full. I told my two sons that they could now go to the storage shed and put the beds together and sleep in them, for they are now paid for and rightfully ours. Thank you for your trust.

Love in Jesus,
Annie Mae

I could not believe my eyes. I read the note two or three times, my eyes filling with tears. Had I only known earlier, I would have said, "Use them now. Don't wait until you pay for them."

Those would have been my thoughts, yet Annie Mae had other thoughts—thoughts the world could truly use. She sacrificed. She struggled. And finally, when the beds were truly hers, she let her sons, Paul and John, sleep in them. She was a living example of absolute honesty, the honesty that should characterize all who claim to be Christian.

This story has a postscript. After thirty years, I called directory assistance and found that Annie Mae still lived in Tuscaloosa. I called her, and later my second husband and I visited her, and I had that chat I never had thirty years ago. What a joy it was! Annie Mae had become a family and children's worker for the state of Alabama and retired in May of 1996.

Romans 13:8 says, "Pay all your debts except the debt of love for others, never finish paying that!" How Annie Mae reflects those words! Truly she is a remarkable woman, one whose life has been shaped by Bible principles.

Carol Holladay Treiber

More Chicken Soup?

Many of the stories and poems you have read in this book were submitted by readers like you who had read earlier *Chicken Soup for the Soul* books. We are planning to publish five or six *Chicken Soup for the Soul* books every year. We invite you to contribute a story to one of these future volumes.

Stories may be up to 1,200 words and must uplift or inspire. You may submit an original piece or something you clip out of the local newspaper, a magazine, a church bulletin or a company newsletter. It could also be your favorite quotation you've put on your refrigerator door or a personal experience that has touched you deeply.

To obtain a copy of our submission guidelines and a listing of upcoming *Chicken Soup* books, please write, fax or check one of our Web sites.

Chicken Soup for the *(Specify Which Edition)* **Soul**
P.O. Box 30880 • Santa Barbara, CA 93130
fax: 805-563-2945
To e-mail or visit our Web site:
www.chickensoup.com

You can also visit the *Chicken Soup for the Soul* site on America Online at keyword: chickensoup.

Just send a copy of your stories and other pieces, indicating which edition they are for, to any of the above addresses.

We will be sure that both you and the author are credited for your submission.

Passing It On!

Out of our commitment to tithing both personally and organizationally, it has become a tradition to donate a portion of the net profits of every *Chicken Soup for the Soul* book to one or more charities related to the theme of the book. Past recipients have included The American Red Cross, The Wellness Community, The Breast Cancer Research Foundation, The American Society for the Prevention of Cruelty to Animals, Covenant House, The Union Rescue Mission, Literacy Volunteers of America, Save the Children, Feed the Children and Habitat for Humanity, just to name a few.

We have also supported a project called Soup Kitchens for the Soul, which donates *Chicken Soup for the Soul* books to individuals and organizations that cannot afford to purchase them. More than fifteen thousand copies of *Chicken Soup for the Soul* books have been given to men and women in prisons, halfway hospitals, churches and other organizations that serve adults and teenagers in need.

"For I was hungry and you gave me something to eat, I was thirsty and you gave me something to drink, I was a stranger and you invited me in, I needed clothes and you clothed me, I was sick and you looked after me, **I was in prison and you came to visit me.**"

—Matthew 25:35–36

Due to the amazing personal and spiritual transformations that have occurred for many inmates as a result of reading *Chicken Soup* books while in prison, Jack and Mark—along with prison volunteer Tom Lagana—undertook the compilation of a *Chicken Soup for the Prisoner's Soul* book, which we intend to distribute free to all 1.3 million people currently incarcerated in America's prisons and jails. A portion of the proceeds from *Chicken Soup for the Christian Family Soul* will be used to underwrite the printing and distribution of these books beginning in July, 2000. It is our hope and dream that we can use this tool that God has given us to change lives, one story at a time, of those who so desperately need to change.

Who Is Jack Canfield?

Jack Canfield is one of America's leading experts in the development of human potential and personal effectiveness. He is both a dynamic, entertaining speaker and a highly sought-after trainer. Jack has a wonderful ability to inform and inspire audiences toward increased levels of self-esteem and peak performance.

He is the author and narrator of several bestselling audio- and videocassette programs, including *Self-Esteem and Peak Performance, How to Build High Self-Esteem, Self-Esteem in the Classroom* and *Chicken Soup for the Soul—Live.* He is regularly seen on television shows such as *Good Morning America, 20/20* and *NBC Nightly News.* Jack has coauthored numerous books, including the *Chicken Soup for the Soul* series, *Dare to Win* and *The Aladdin Factor* (all with Mark Victor Hansen), *100 Ways to Build Self-Concept in the Classroom* (with Harold C. Wells) and *Heart at Work* (with Jacqueline Miller).

Jack is a regularly featured speaker for professional associations, school districts, government agencies, churches, hospitals, sales organizations and corporations. His clients have included the American Dental Association, the American Management Association, AT&T, Campbell Soup, Clairol, Domino's Pizza, GE, ITT, Hartford Insurance, Johnson & Johnson, the Million Dollar Roundtable, NCR, New England Telephone, Re/Max, Scott Paper, TRW and Virgin Records. Jack is also on the faculty of Income Builders International, a school for entrepreneurs.

Jack conducts an annual eight-day Training of Trainers program in the areas of self-esteem and peak performance. It attracts educators, counselors, parenting trainers, corporate trainers, professional speakers, ministers and others interested in developing their speaking and seminar-leading skills.

For further information about Jack's books, tapes and training programs, or to schedule him for a presentation, please contact:

The Canfield Training Group
P.O. Box 30880 • Santa Barbara, CA 93130
phone: 805-563-2935 • fax: 805-563-2945
To e-mail or visit our Web site: *www.chickensoup.com*

Who Is Mark Victor Hansen?

Mark Victor Hansen is a professional speaker who, in the last 20 years, has made over 4,000 presentations to more than 2 million people in 32 countries. His presentations cover sales excellence and strategies; personal empowerment and development; and how to triple your income and double your time off.

Mark has spent a lifetime dedicated to his mission to make a profound and positive difference in people's lives. Throughout his career, he has inspired hundreds of thousands of people to create a more powerful and purposeful future for themselves while stimulating the sale of billions of dollars worth of goods and services.

Mark is a prolific writer and has authored *Future Diary*, *How to Achieve Total Prosperity* and *The Miracle of Tithing*. He is coauthor of the *Chicken Soup for the Soul* series, *Dare to Win* and *The Aladdin Factor* (all with Jack Canfield) and *The Master Motivator* (with Joe Batten).

Mark has also produced a complete library of personal empowerment audio- and videocassette programs that have enabled his listeners to recognize and use their innate abilities in their business and personal lives. His message has made him a popular television and radio personality, with appearances on ABC, NBC, CBS, HBO, PBS and CNN. He has also appeared on the cover of numerous magazines, including *Success*, *Entrepreneur* and *Changes*.

Mark is a big man with a heart and spirit to match—an inspiration to all who seek to better themselves.

For further information about Mark write:

P.O. Box 7665
Newport Beach, CA 92658
phone: 949-759-9304 or 800-433-2314
fax: 949-722-6912
Web site: *www.chickensoup.com*

Who Is Patty Aubery?

Patty Aubery is the vice president of The Canfield Training Group and Self-Esteem Seminars, Inc. and president of Chicken Soup for the Soul Enterprises, Inc. Patty has been working with Jack and Mark since the birth of *Chicken Soup for the Soul*.

Patty is the coauthor of *Chicken Soup for the Surviving Soul: 101 Stories of Courage and Inspiration from Those Who Have Survived Cancer, Chicken Soup for the Christian Soul* and future coauthor of *Chicken Soup for the Expectant Mother's Soul*. She has been a guest on over 150 local and nationally syndicated radio shows.

Patty is married to Jeff Aubery, and together they have two wonderful children, J.T. and Chandler. Patty and her family reside in Santa Barbara, California, and can be reached at The Canfield Training Group, P.O. Box 30880, Santa Barbara, CA 93130, by calling 1-805-563-2935, or faxing 805-563-2945.

Who Is Nancy Mitchell Autio?

Nancy Mitchell Autio is the director of all copyrights and permissions for the *Chicken Soup for the Soul* series. She graduated from Arizona State University in May of 1994 with a B.S. in nursing. After graduation, Nancy worked at Good Samaritan Regional Medical Center in Phoenix, Arizona, in the Cardiovascular Intensive Care Unit. Four months later, she moved back to the Los Angeles area and became involved with the *Chicken Soup* series. Nancy's intentions were to help finish *A 2nd Helping of Chicken Soup for the Soul* and then return to nursing. However, in December of that year, Nancy continued on full time with Chicken Soup for the Soul Enterprises, Inc., working closely with Jack and Mark on all of the *Chicken Soup for the Soul* projects.

Nancy says that what she is most thankful for is her move back to Los Angeles. "If I hadn't moved back to California, I wouldn't have had the chance to be there for my mom during her bout with breast cancer." Out of that struggle, Nancy coauthored *Chicken Soup for the Surviving Soul: 101 Stories of Courage and Inspiration from Those Who Have Survived Cancer*. Little did she know that the book would become her own guide of inspiration when her dad was diagnosed with prostate cancer in 1999. Nancy says, "After reading and compiling thousands of stories, I feel very fortunate to be where I am in my life right now. I have my health and I married Kirk Autio in 1998: my lifelong partner to whom I personally dedicate this book. He has taught me the true meaning of love: the giving and the receiving of it."

Nancy also coauthored *Chicken Soup for the Christian Soul* and will be coauthor of *Chicken Soup for the Expectant Mother's Soul*, which she hopes to be sometime in the near future!

Kirk and Nancy reside in Santa Barbara with their golden retriever, Kona, their "little mix" Piggy, and cats, Stoli and Squirt. You may contact Nancy at P.O. Box 30880, Santa Barbara, CA 93130 or by calling 805-563-2935 ext. 21.

Contributors

Many of the stories in this book were taken from books we have read. These sources are acknowledged in the Permissions section. Some of the stories and poems were contributed by friends of ours, who, like us, are professional speakers. If you would like to contact them for information on their books, tapes and seminars, you can reach them at the addresses and phone numbers provided below.

Many of the stories were also contributed by readers like yourself, who, after reading other volumes of *Chicken Soup for the Soul*, were inspired to submit a story out of their life's experience. We have included information about them as well.

Cynthia Culp Allen has published 400 articles in newspapers and magazines such as *Focus on Family, Decision, Guideposts* and others. She is a frequent speaker at churches, conferences and women's retreats across the country. Cynthia has been married for twenty-five years and has five children.

Steve Baal is an award-winning freelance writer with numerous national, regional and local credits for articles on a wide variety of subjects.

Robert F. Baldwin was a laborer, machine operator, hobo, banjo picker, newspaper reporter, editor of a weekly newspaper, and a freelance journalist before he began writing children's books. He is the author of three religious books for adults and three for children. His most recent title is *This Is the Sea That Feeds Us.* He resides in Newcastle, Maine.

Richard Bauman has been a freelance writer for over twenty-five years. His articles about spirituality, history, travel, and self-help have appeared in numerous national publications. Richard and Donna, his wife of thirty-eight years, reside in West Covina, California. They have two adult children and three grandsons.

L. Maggie Baxter is a single mother of four grown children and seven precious grandchildren. She is a teacher during the school months and loves to garden, camp, hike and canoe in her spare time.

Aubrey Beauchamp has been the USA coordinator for Hospital Christian Fellowship since 1972. She is also the editor/publisher of *A New Heart* magazine and has written several books. She can be contacted at P.O. Box 4004, San Clemente, CA 92674. E-mail *HCFUSA@Juno.com*

Edward J. Beckwell is a seventy-four-year-old cancer survivor and retired trucking executive. He writes short stories and, along with his brother, he co-authored a book *Hi-Goodbye, Detroit*. He can be reached at 22837 Doremus, St. Clair Shores, MI 48080.

Graciela Beecher is currently a Spanish correspondent of *Today's Catholic Newspaper* at the Diocese of Fort Wayne-South Bend, in Indiana. His work has appeared in numerous publications, such as *The Holy Rosary* and *Notable Hispanic-American Women*. He can be reached at 2904 Shawnee Dr., Fort Wayne, IN.

Dawn Billings, a licensed professional counselor, is the author of two books, *Greatness and Children: Learn the Rules*, and *ABC's of Becoming Great*. She travels nationally, speaking on leadership and greatness, violence prevention, and character education. She can be reached toll free at 877-UR GREAT, or e-mail *dawnlawray@aol.com*.

Arthur Bowler is a writer, speaker and co-pastor of the largest Protestant church in Zurich, Switzerland. A native of Massachusetts, he relocated to Switzerland after graduating from Harvard Divinity School and now lives with his Swiss wife and two daughters. He can be reached at *bowler@bluwin.ch* or by writing to Rautistrasse 114, 8048 Zurich, Switzerland.

J. Douglas Burford lives in Mission, Kansas, with his wife, daughter and two sons. They have the privilege of living near his mother and stepfather, as well as his wife's parents. Perhaps because of losing his father, Doug makes it a priority to spend time with his children. Doug is pastor of the Ward Parkway Presbyterian Church.

Renie Burghardt of rural Doniphan, Missouri, was born in Hungary. She immigrated to the United States at the age of fifteen with her grandparents. A freelance writer, Renie also enjoys reading, gardening, raising Silkieu chickens, observing nature, and most of all, spending time with her granddaughter. You can reach her at *renie@clnet.net*.

Candy Chand is a freelance writer living in Antelope, California. She is a wife and the mother of Tiffany and Nicholas, her constant reminders that miracles are everywhere, if we only open our hearts to embrace them.

Jim Comstock was an author, lecturer, humorist, editor and publisher. He passed on May 22, 1996. Jim was one of West Virginia's most well-known writers. After returning from Guam in 1946, he and Bronson McClung began the *Nicholas County News Leader*. Ten years later he began the *West Virginia Hillbilly*. During his fifty-year newspaper career, Jim was awarded six honorary doctorate degrees. He and his wife, the former Ola Stowers, are the parents of three children, Jay Comstock, Sandra Comstock Ferguson and Elaine Comstock Nagy.

Jeanne Converse lives in upstate New York with her husband of forty-nine years. They have seven children, twenty-one grandchildren and one great-grandchild. Her articles have been published in farm publications and newspapers. Jeanne is currently working on a young adult novel.

Kathleen Dixon is a present-day disciple of Jesus Christ, her mission field is a rehabilitation hospital in Chico, California. "The right attitude is everything," she says, "if you want to be in the right place at the right time, to be part of the blessings and miracles of God."

Mia Watkins Dockter survived cancer four times, a serious brain tumor and multiple sclerosis with no permanent aftereffects. She taught school for seventeen years and has a master's degree in administration. Mia lives with her husband, Darin, in Southern California. She can be contacted by e-mail at *dolfynent2aol.com*.

John W. Doll has been writing nostalgia and memories since his retirement from the *Los Angeles Times*. He lives in a 100-year-old home in the middle of an orange/avocado grove. With the *Times* he did international marketing and recently completed a chartbook titled, *Autumn Leaves Around the World*. The short stories and poems were each written in different countries and designated accordingly. The book can be purchased by writing John at 2377 Grand Ave., Fillmore, CA 93015 or by faxing 805-524-3821.

Kathryn Fanning, from Oklahoma City, teaches aspiring writers how to get published. A freelancer and former national magazine editor, her main interests are her four grandchildren and finding the truth about her husband Major Hugh Fanning, missing in action after his A6 Intruder was downed over North Vietnam in 1967.

Arthur Gordon was born in Savannah, Georgia. He has been managing editor for *Good Housekeeping* magazine, editor-in-chief for *Cosmopolitan* and editorial director for *Guideposts* and *Airforce Magazine*. He has written two books, *Reprisal* and *A Touch of Wonder*.

Lini R. Grol is a Canadian citizen from the Netherlands, who has written poetry, stories, plays and illustrations in books and periodicals in The Netherlands, the United Kingdom, Belgium, South Africa, the United States and Canada. She received the Canadian Authors Award from the Canadian Club of Hamilton Ontario.

Philip Gulley is a Quaker minister, writer, husband, and father. He is the author of *Front Porch Tales* and *Home Town Tales*. A bona fide homebody, Phil watches only one television program—reruns of *The Andy Griffith Show*. He and his wife, Joan, live in the town where Phil grew up—Danville, Indiana—with their sons, Spencer and Sam.

John Edmund Haggai has spent a lifetime studying and teaching leadership. He is the founder and CEO of Haggai Institute, a unique provider of advanced leadership training to credential leaders in over 150 developing nations. His vision for world evangelism has taken him around the globe more than eighty times.

Jeanne Hill is an author, inspirational speaker and contributing editor to *Guideposts* magazine. She has published hundreds of short stories and magazine articles, several of which have won Best Published Article awards in national competition. She has also published two inspirational books: *Daily Breath, Word Books* and *Secrets of Prayer-Joy*. She resides in Scottsdale, Arizona.

Michele T. Huey is a feature writer and photographer for her local newspaper, where she writes a weekly feature column, *People Who Make a Difference*, and a weekly devotional column, *Minute Meditations*. Michele was the winner of the Jean Berg Memorial Award, given to identify and encourage a talented writer, at the 1997 St. David's Christian Writers Conference. The founder and former leader of the Punxsutawney Area Christian Writers Fellowship, Michele taught English for twelve years, and has taught journalism and creative writing classes. A wife, mother of three, and grandmother, Michele lives in the country with her husband and youngest son.

Vicki Huffman is a freelance editor/writer who has worked for Cook Communications and Thomas Nelson Publishers. Vicki has won several EPA awards for her outstanding column and interview/profile articles. Vicki lives in a suburb of Nashville, Tennessee, with her husband Richard, who is fairly well behaved, and two dogs who aren't. The Huffmans have two grown children and three (remarkably beautiful) grandchildren. Vicki is available for editing, speaking engagements or writing assignments. She can be contacted at 118 Sun Valley Dr., Mt. Juliet, TN 37122, phone: 615-754-4880 or by fax at 615-754-4807.

Sonia Jones was born and raised in London, England, and later spent her teenage years in Greenwich, Connecticut. She received a Ph.D. in romance languages from Harvard and then accepted a position as chairperson of the Spanish department, where she taught for twenty years.

Maxine Karpen, a registered professional nurse, made a mid-life career switch to writing in 1981. She has authored a romance novel, a nursing textbook, a chapter in a health guide, and has had over 400 articles published and reprinted worldwide. An award-winning writer, she also lectures at writers' conferences. Maxine can be reached at *maxinekarpen@juno.com*.

Kimberly White Kerl lives in Greenville, South Carolina, with her husband, Marvin, daughter, Erin, and son, Nicholas. She allows the rich flavor of life's experiences to permeate and inspire her architectural career and freelance writing projects. She writes poems, short stories, essays, and critiques. She can be contacted by e-mail at *kwkerl@aol.com*.

Cheryl Kirking, "a Ripplemaker," is a popular conference speaker who encourages others nationwide through splashes of insights, humor and original songs. A songwriter, she has recorded six CDs. She is the author of *A Hundred*

Ripples. Contact her at P.O. Box 525, Lake Mills, WI 53551. Phone: 920-648-8959; e-mail *ckirking@gdinet.com.*

Vicki L. Kitchner has taught physically and mentally disabled children for sixteen years. She is the co-founder of Sky's the Limit, which produces educational and therapeutic materials and has developed a children's musical CD entitled: *It's Circle Time!* She has had several articles published in magazines and has just completed her first novel entitled *Shades of Rage.* Ms. Kitchner has been married for nine years and she and her husband enjoy backpacking, travel and reading.

Tammy Laws Lawson's hobbies include writing and reading. Tammy's favorite books are the *Chicken Soup* books. Tammy is married and has six children, three grandsons and one son-in-law.

Patricia S. Laye, author of romance-suspense and six regency novels, teaches at writers' conferences and colleges throughout the South. She resides with her husband on a farm where she is currently working on a mainstream novel and a mystery. She travels worldwide exploring new settings for her novels.

Richard Lederer is the author of more than 2,000 books and articles about laughing and humor including his bestselling *Anguished English* and his current book, *Sleeping Dogs Don't Lay.* He has been elected International Punster of the Year.

Tom C. Long has been in ministry for over thirty years, twenty of which were spent in the youth room. He currently lives in Southern California with his wife and two daughters and is the senior pastor at Heritage Christian Fellowship. Pastor Tom's passion is to preach the word of God and lead people to Jesus Christ.

Patricia Lorenz is an internationally known inspirational, art-of-living writer whose true stories have been featured in a number of *Chicken Soup for the Soul* books. She's the author of *Stuff That Matters for Single Parents* and *A Hug a Day for Single Parents* and has had over 400 articles published in numerous magazines. As an inspirational speaker, Patricia packs a wallop with her take-away messages. You may write to her at 7457 S. Pennsylvania Ave., Oak Creek, WI 53154. For speaking engagements contact Associated Speakers, Inc., at 800-437-7577.

Tim Madigan is a senior feature writer for the *Fort Worth Star-Telegram* newspaper in Fort Worth, Texas. He lives with his wife, Catherine, and children Patrick and Melanie in Arlington, Texas. His e-mail address is *tmadigan@star-telegram.com.*

Mayo Mathers is a columnist for *Virtue* magazine, contributing editor for *Today's Christian Women,* and a freelance writer who has contributed to nine books and coauthored *Like a Pebble Tossed* and *The Legacy of a Prayer.*

Lorie McCrone has been married for twenty-five years to Joe, a most wonderful husband. Lorie and Joe share their home with two dalmatians, Storm and Danny, and a twenty-one-year-old cat named Sheba. Her hobbies revolve around her dogs; she trains and shows them in obedience, agility and road-trip competitions. Lorie is currently writing a book that tells the stories of the many dogs, and their owners, who have touched her life. She's worked at the IBM Corporation in Endicott, New York, for twenty years, and is currently an accountant in the relocation department.

Robert J. McMullen Jr. is a retired Presbyterian minister. After duty as a pilot in World War II with missions over Germany, he served churches in West Virginia, suburban Washington, D.C., Atlanta and Charlotte. He and his wife have three children, one with cerebral palsy.

Cynthia Mercati is a playwright with over thirty scripts published and produced. She is also a professional actress and performs with a children's theater company, often appearing in her own shows. She was recently awarded The Bonderman Youth Playwriting Award. She's also written several children's books, and frequently contributes commentaries to national newspapers. One of her essays appeared in *A Second Chicken Soup for the Woman's Soul*. Cynthia has two children, one dachshund, and loves movies, the Chicago White Sox, and doing workshops for all ages on playwriting.

Roberta L. Messner, is a quality-management specialist, author and inspirational speaker. She has written over 100 articles, which have appeared in over 100 different publications, as well as two books. Her work has appeared in other *Chicken Soup* books and she is a regular contributor to *Guideposts* and *Daily Guideposts*. She is also a field editor and photo stylist for a number of home-decorating publications.

J. Michael Miller is a retired United Methodist Minister living in Roswell, Georgia. He entered the ministry in 1964 and earned degrees from Boston University's School of Theology and Graduate School. He served as pastor of United Methodist churches in Massachusetts and Illinois and was associate professor of Old Testament at Oral Roberts University School of Theology in Tulsa, Oklahoma, for seven years. Dr. Miller has written several Sunday school curricula for the United Methodist Church. He and his wife, Dolores, are the parents of two married daughters and they have eight grandchildren.

Nancy Miller is a freelance writer who specializes in short stories about her children and grandchildren. "The Smell of Rain" is a true story about her granddaughter, Danae Blessing. Nancy hopes others will embrace the emotion of the story, and realize that they, too, are one of God's greatest masterpieces.

Elaine Minamide has been married for fifteen yeas and has three children. Elaine is a junior high English teacher at her children's school who writes freelance from home. She has a BA and MA in English. She writes for newspapers, family and parenting magazines and has also had children's fiction books published.

Gerald Moore, whose written work ranges from short stories to political speeches, is the author of numerous magazine articles. Born in Albuquerque, New Mexico, he has been a reporter and magazine editor. He worked as an environmental technical writer in New York City where he lives with his wife, Joyce Nereaux.

Susan Morin resides in Passadumkeag, Maine, with her husband Victor, six cats and two dogs. She is the mother of a blended family of five children, ages twenty-one to thirty-four. At United Baptist Church in Old Town, Maine, she serves as women's ministry coordinator and teaches adult and women's Bible study classes.

Carla Muir is a freelance writer of poetry and stories that have been published in *More Stories for the Heart*, and *Keepsakes for the Heart*, with Multnomah; *Glimpses of Heaven*, and *Do Not Lose Heart*, with Zondervan and *A Second Chicken Soup for the Woman's Soul*. She can be reached through her agent, Susan Yates, at Yates & Yates, LLP 714-835-3742.

Jo Ann Nahirny, a New Jersey native now living in Florida, is the mother of two, and has served as a foster mother for eight neglected and abused children between the ages of one and seven. She and her husband, Michael, became foster parents in 1994. She is a graduate of St. Peter's College and holds a graduate degree in journalism from Columbia University.

John Neilsen is a professor at Western Michigan University and speaks frequently on simplifying life, staying in tune with values and managing professional stress. John can be reached at *john.nielsen@wmich.edu.*

Richard O'Donnell has had articles appear in a number of anthologies, most notably those published by Yankee, Inc., and Smithsonian. He currently is working as a freelance writer and enjoys collecting old-time radio shows. Richard considers himself a short story and movie buff.

Mary Treacy O'Keefe, a mother of four teenagers, plans to become a certified spiritual director after completing her master's degree in theology. A hospice volunteer, she loves to hear about the many ways God is present in peoples' lives. You can e-mail her at *mtokeefel@aol.com.*

Sharon M. Palmer is currently employed by the American Red Cross in the Finger Lakes as the coordinator for the Meals on Wheels program in North Seneca County, New York. Sherry credits her mentor, M. Kay Miller, and the Hazel Green Writers for instilling in her the desire to write, "for the fun of it," and for helping her see the potential in her work. When she isn't writing she enjoys spending time with her nine-year-old son, Charley, who has Down's syndrome. He is the blessing of her life and the inspiration for most of her writings. She is eternally grateful for her husband's unwavering support.

Victor Parachin is an ordained minister in the Christian church. He has served churches in Chicago, Washington, D.C., and the Los Angles area. He is a freelance writer and author of several books. He lives in Tulsa, Oklahoma, with his wife and three children.

Sean Patrick has published his family-oriented series in *Catholic Digest* since 1987. His stories about his Irish-American family have been published in a book, *Patrick's Corner*. A former deputy sheriff, he now lives in rural retirement in the heavily Amish area of northeast Ohio.

Dawn Philips lives near Rocky Mountain House, Alberta. She attended the University of Alberta, taught in one-room schools, and developed programs to integrate special needs children into regular school systems. She is married with four children, eight grandchildren and one great-grandchild.

Rick Phillips is an internationally recognized speaker focusing on highly customized sales and customer service systems. The author of several *Chicken Soup* stories, Rick speaks to thousands each year on developing the skills necessary to be successful in the millennium. You can reach Rick at *pssd@web-net.com*.

Penny Porter is one of the most successful freelancers ever to hit *Reader's Digest*. She has published stories in a wide range of national circulation magazines, including *Arizona Highways, Catholic Digest, Guideposts,* and *Honda,* and her work has appeared in several *Chicken Soup for the Soul* books. Penny often writes non-fiction accounts of her experiences and adventures with her husband and six children while cattle ranching in their remote ranch in Arizona. She has compiled her first illustrated collection of true stories, *Heartstrings and Tail-Tuggers,* (Ravenhawk Books).

Ellen Ingersoll Plum was born and raised in the Atlantic City area. Ellen became interested in the scholarship program for the Miss America pageant. After serving for ten years as chairman of the National Hostess Committee, she became the first women president. Her husband, Neil, was owner of the Plum Funeral Homes.

Cathy L. Seehuetter is a proud mother of four children (one who is now her own special guardian angel) and two adorable grandsons. She has been an on-again off-again student for thirty-plus years, hoping to return to college to become a grief counselor. She is a regular contributor to *The Bulletin Board,* and the chapter co-leader and newsletter editor of the St. Paul, Minnesota, chapter of The Compassionate Friends, a support group for bereaved parents. Her desire is to give back by helping newly bereaved see that there is hope at the end of their long and difficult journey down the grief road.

Michael Jordan Segal currently works as a psychotherapist. Shawn Elyse Segal is a happy and healthy eight-year-old, and Sharon is working part time as a speech pathologist and full time at her #1 job of being a mother. Mike has written an autobiography entitled, *Never Say Quit* and is currently looking for a publisher. He is also available for public speaking engagements.

Cheryl Walterman Stewart is a freelance writer and harpist living in the

Dallas-Fort Worth area with her husband, Jim. She is a graduate of CLASS, a training course for speakers and enjoys teaching on relationships and communication skills.

Marilyn K. Strube has been married for twenty-seven years and has five daughters. Marilyn works part time as a clerk at a nearby community hospital and does freelance writing for *Guideposts* the rest of the time.

Alan Struthers Jr. is a business and financial writer. Alan has written for major corporations and for government officials. Articles based on his speeches have appeared in the *Washington Post, New York Times* and other newspapers. He has a successful Christian financial planning practice in northern New Jersey. He is also a musician who has recorded two CDs playing the bluegrass banjo.

LeAnn Thieman is a nationally acclaimed speaker and author and a member of the National Speakers Association. LeAnn inspires audiences to truly live their priorities and balance their lives physically, mentally, and spiritually while making a difference in the world. She coauthored "This Must Be My Brother." You can contact her at *LeAnnThieman.com*.

Nanette Thorsen-Snipes has published over 350 articles, columns, devotions and reprints in over thirty-five publications including *Honor Books, Christian Reader* and others. She has also won many awards including Writer of the Year. She can be contacted by e-mail at *jsnipes212@aol.com*.

Carol Holladay Treiber was born in 1935 in New London, Connecticut. She is married to Harry Treiber and has two sons and one grandson. Carol is a retired teacher and spends her time volunteering at churches, hospitals and fairs as Bubbles, the Christian Clown. She has won numerous awards for her writing including the Higher Goals in Christian Journalism Award in 1998 for *Annie Mae's Honor*.

Eva Unga writes for the *Woman's World* magazine.

Todd W. Van Beck is the school director of the New England Institute of Funeral Service education at Mount Ida College in Newton Center, Massachusetts. Mr. Van Beck is in demand as a motivational speaker and seminar leader on a wide range of human service topics. Mr. Van Beck can be reached at *ToddVanBeck@aol.com*.

Charlotte "Charlie" Volnek has been married to her beloved Michael for twenty years and together they have three wonderful blessings for the Lord above: Christopher, Alex and Keri. As a Christian mother, Charlie focuses on raising her family in the glory of God and writing to inspire and encourage youth of today to follow the life of Jesus.

William Webber is an American Baptist pastor, public speaker and author. For a copy of his bestselling, award-winning book *A Rustle of Angels, Stories About Angels in Real Life and Scripture*, please send $15.00 to William

Webber, 275 Celeste Dr., Riverside, CA 92507. You may reach him also by fax at 909-784-6864.

Richard Whetstone has tried to follow the words of Helen Keller, "life is an adventure, or it's nothing." He has been a lawman, cowboy, nurse's assistant, salesman and whatever else it took to pay the bills. He's traveled to every state in the Union except Hawaii. Richard is fifty-three years old and has been happily married for the past fourteen years. He has two children and seven grandchildren.

Margaret Wiedyke is a former English teacher, mother of two married daughters and the grandmother of eight-year-old Derek. With her retired husband, Margaret enjoys traveling and baby-sitting her grandson. She also likes to read, write and cook.

Carol Wimmer has devoted her life to ministry through the arts. In addition to poetry, she writes musicals, plays and scripture memory songs for children of all ages published by Sheep School Press. Married for thirty years and the mother of two grown children, Carol currently teaches music, art and drama at Clovis Christian School in Clovis, California. She may be reached at *CCCWimmer@aol.com*.

Communion Blooper. Reprinted by permission of Lanis E. Kineman. ©1999 Lanis E. Kineman.

A Miracle of Faith. Reprinted by permission of Maxine Karpen. ©1999 Maxine Karpen.

The Faith of Stanley Reimer. Reprinted by permission of Robert H. Schuller. ©1999 Robert H. Schuller.

Heart Sounds. Reprinted by permission of Tim Madigan. Originally appeared in the *Fort Worth Star-Telegram,* January 12, 1997. ©1997 Tim Madigan.

Our Christmas Tree Boy. Reprinted by permission of Edward J. Beckwell. ©1999 Edward J. Beckwell.

My Best Christmas. Reprinted by permission of Jill Roberts. ©1998 Jill Roberts.

I'm Not Poor at All. Reprinted by permission of Michele T. Huey. ©1999 Michele T. Huey.

The Little Black Book. Reprinted by permission of Todd W. Van Beck. ©1999 Todd W. Van Beck.

Santa in Disguise. Reprinted by permission of Jeanne Converse. ©1998 Jeanne Converse.

Christmas Love. Reprinted by permission of Candy Chand. ©1999 Candy Chand.

My Appointment with Santa. Reprinted by permission of Cynthia Culp Allen and Sharon Lopez. ©1999 Cynthia Culp Allen and Sharon Lopez.

Seeing Love in the Eyes of Santa Claus. Reprinted by permission of Lorie McCrone. ©1999 Lorie McCrone.

What Goes Around Come Around. Reprinted by permission of Victor Parachin. ©1999 Victor Parachin.

Just Two Tickets to Indy. Reprinted by permission of Rick Phillips. ©1999 Rick Phillips.

The Day Mother Cried. Reprinted by permission of Gerald Moore. ©1981 Gerald Moore.

Somebody in the Corner. Reprinted by permission of Fulton Oursler Jr. ©1948 Fulton Oursler Jr.

More Inspiration to Nurture Your Spirit
Chicken Soup for the
Christian Soul

Code # 5017 Quality Paperback • $12.95

This collection will open your heart to the experience and expression of more love in your life and will remind you that you are never alone or without hope, no matter how challenging and painful your circumstances may be.

Chicken Soup for the Golden Soul

Celebrating the myriad joys of living and the wisdom that comes from having lived, this collection offers loving insights and wisdom —all centering on the prime of life. You will be sure to cherish these invaluable stories as a reminder that the soul of those young at heart is truly "golden."

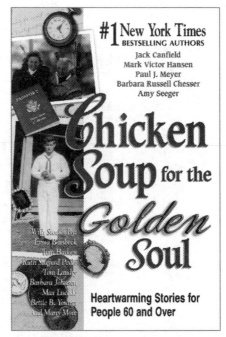

Code # 7257 Quality Paperback • $12.95

Chicken Soup for the Writer's Soul

#1 New York Times
BESTSELLING AUTHORS
Jack Canfield
Mark Victor Hansen
Bud Gardner

Chicken Soup for the Writer's Soul

101 Stories to Open the Heart and Rekindle the Spirit of Writers

Whether you're a beginning writer, seasoned pro or simply a writer a heart, the stories of purpose, passion, endurance and success contained in this volume will inform, entertain, uplift and inspire you.

In its pages, you will learn important lessons on: the importance of perseverance, the value of being yourself, the process of discovering your own voice, the need for mentors and allies, and the power of following your heartfelt dreams.

Code #7699 Quality Paperback • $12.95

What you've been waiting for...

#1 New York Times
BESTSELLING AUTHORS
Jack Canfield
Mark Victor Hansen
Kimberly Kirberger

Chicken Soup TEEN III for the Soul

More Stories of Life, Love and Learning

The third volume is here, offering you more stories on love, friendship, family, tough stuff, growing up, kindness, learning lessons and making a difference.

Chicken Soup for the Teenage Soul III

Code #7613 Quality Paperback • $12.95

Available April 2000.

Books for Life

True, heart-warming and moving stories from teens and for teens on learning to embrace life and its many challenges.

More Soup to Warm Your Heart

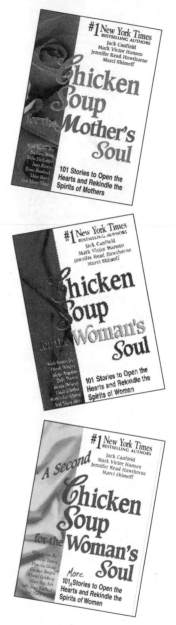

There are many ways to define a woman: daughter, mother, wife, professional, friend, student. . . . We are each special and unique, yet we share a common connection. What bonds all women are our mutual experiences of loving and learning: feeling the tenderness of love; forging lifelong friendships; pursuing a chosen career; giving birth to new life; juggling the responsibilities of job and family, and more.

These three volumes celebrate the myriad facets of a woman's life.

Chicken Soup for the Mother's Soul
Code #4606 Paperback • $12.95

Chicken Soup for the Woman's Soul
Code #4150 Paperback • $12.95

A Second Chicken Soup for the Woman's Soul
Code #6226 Paperback • $12.95